Legal Notice

This book is copyright 2016 with all rights reserved. It is illegal to copy, distribute, or create derivative works from this book in whole or in part or to contribute to the copying, distribution, or creating of derivative works of this book.

\

Acknowledgements

We thank Rick Barrett for his essay on "the Zone" from his book *Taijiquan: Through the Western Gate*; James Frazier for the excerpt from his book, *Maurice Durufle, the Man and His Music*; Professor Edward Hernandez for his essays on "Self" and the "Protestant Ethic"; Professor Jennifer Small for her essay on Argentine Tango; Barbara Gatti for her essay on the Rockettes; Richie Rosenblatt, a New York artist, for his insights for the "Artist" essay; Luca Sforza for his wonderful book jacket design.

Thanks to Devin Ronaldson for his wonderful article on myo-fascial release, and also thanks to USA Ultimate for allowing us to use some of their sentences from their web page on Ultimate Frisbee.

The following also contributed to our book and a big thanks to them: Dr. Edward Speedling, Roy Speedling, Meghan Speedling, Lauren MacDuffie, Steve Papa, Paul Candon, and Mike Keller.

Finally, thanks to Pat Moran Ronaldson who kept Tom and me nourished with her culinary delights for two years and kept us laughing.

BOOKS FROM THE GET 800 COLLECTION

28 New SAT Math Lessons to Improve Your Score in One Month
    Beginner Course
    Intermediate Course
    Advanced Course

320 SAT Math Problems arranged by Topic and Difficulty Level
New SAT Math Problems arranged by Topic and Difficulty Level
SAT Verbal Prep Book for Reading and Writing Mastery
320 SAT Math Subject Test Problems arranged by Topic and Difficulty Level
    Level 1 Test
    Level 2 Test

The 32 Most Effective SAT Math Strategies
SAT Prep Official Study Guide Math Companion
Physics Mastery for Advanced Math Students
Vocabulary Builder
320 ACT Math Problems arranged by Topic and Difficulty Level
320 GRE Math Problems arranged by Topic and Difficulty Level
320 SAT Math Problems arranged by Topic and Difficulty Level
320 AP Calculus AB Problems
320 AP Calculus BC Problems
SHSAT Verbal Prep Book to Improve Your Score in Two Months
555 Math IQ Questions for Middle School Students
555 Advanced Math Problems for Middle School Students
555 Geometry Problems for High School Students
Algebra Handbook for Gifted Middle School Students

CONNECT WITH DR. STEVE WARNER

www.facebook.com/SATPrepGet800
www.youtube.com/TheSATMathPrep
www.twitter.com/SATPrepGet800
www.linkedin.com/in/DrSteveWarner
www.pinterest.com/SATPrepGet800
plus.google.com/+SteveWarnerPhD

SAT Verbal Prep Book for Reading and Writing Mastery

Techniques and Systems for Decoding the Verbal Part of the SAT

Larry Ronaldson   Tom Speedling

Edited by Dr. Steve Warner

© 2017, All Rights Reserved
Second Edition

Table of Contents

Actions to Complete Before You Read This Book — vi

Introduction: The SAT — 7
- Reading Section — 7
- Grammar Section — 7
- Essay (Optional) — 8
- Scoring the essay — 8

Preparing for the SAT — 9
- Using this book effectively — 9
- The key to success — 9
- Check your answers properly — 9
- Take a guess whenever you cannot solve a problem — 10
- Pace yourself — 10

Reading Guide — 11
- The Steps to Success — 11
- Opening Sentences — 13

Vocabulary in Context — 23

Playing with Words — 41

Reading Practice Passages — 46
- The Blink and Think Method — 55
- Reading Test 1 — 63
- Reading Test 2 — 80
- Reading Test 3 — 97
- Reading Test 4 — 114

Grammar — 131
- Basic Definitions — 131
- Tense — 132
- Subject-Verb Agreement — 133
- Pronoun Agreement — 133
- Fragments — 134
- Run-on Sentences — 134
- Parallel Structure — 134
- Transitional Phrases — 135
- Faulty Comparisons — 135
- Mislplaced Modifiers — 135
- Dangling Participles — 135
- Diction — 136
- Idioms — 136
- Double Negative — 136
- Redundancies — 137
- Punctuation — 137
- Particular Question Types — 137

Grammar Practice Passages	**138**
Writing and Language Test 1	**139**
Writing and Language Test 2	**156**
Writing and Language Test 3	**176**
Writing and Language Test 4	**195**
Essay Writing Guide	**214**
Instructions for the Essay	**215**
How to Read the Passage	**215**
How to Write the Essay	**216**
Essentials	**218**
GO TO Words and Expressions	**219**
More Help for Writing the Opening Paragraph	**221**
Transition Words	**222**
Essay Samples	**223**
Practice Essay 1	**224**
Practice Essay 2	**230**
Practice Essay 3	**235**
Bonus Verbal Materials – Learn These and Win	**239**
Actions to Complete After You Have Read This Book	**257**
About the Authors	*258*
Books from the Get 800 Collection	*259*

ACTIONS TO COMPLETE BEFORE YOU READ THIS BOOK

1. Take a practice SAT from the Official Guide to get your preliminary SAT verbal score

2. Claim your FREE bonus

Visit the following webpage and enter your email address to receive additional material for FREE. In particular, you will receive 120 SAT math problems with full explanations.

www.thesatmathprep.com/RevSATVb2016.html

3. 'Like' my Facebook page

This page is updated regularly with SAT prep advice, tips, tricks, strategies, and practice problems. Visit the following webpage and click the 'like' button.

www.facebook.com/SATPrepGet800

INTRODUCTION
THE SAT

The SAT in its present form resembles an IQ test far less than at any time since its inception. The test consists of a reading section, a grammar section, two math sections, and an optional essay. The reading and math sections are more straightforward than they have ever been. The grammar section is now very similar to the grammar section on the ACT, although on the SAT there is less emphasis on redundancies and punctuation, and the SAT is more generous with time than the ACT. The SAT writing section is longer and much more comprehensive than the ACT. In short, the SAT is a test that strongly reflects what you were supposed to learn in the classroom. This rewards the serious student and gives less opportunity for the student who is super bright, but does not do his or her work in school.

Reading Section

The reading section consists of four single passages and one double passage. Each passage has 10-11 questions for a total of 52 questions, and you have 65 minutes to complete this section. That comes to about 75 seconds per question, but, of course, you also need to factor in the time it takes to read each passage.

The passages are drawn from Literature, History and Social Studies, Science and finally a combination of Presidential Speeches/Documents of the Founding Fathers and Global Discussions. On two of the passages (one Science passage and one History/Social Studies passage), you will need to analyze charts and graphs to answer specific questions.

There are four choices for each question, and neither the passages nor individual questions are presented in order of difficulty. This allows you to read passages first that you are the most comfortable with.

Grammar Section

The grammar section consists of four passages with a total of 44 multiple choice questions (11 questions per passage). You have 35 minutes to complete the whole section, giving you roughly 9 minutes to read each very brief passage and answer 11 questions. This might seem a bit rushed, but the ACT asks you to answer *15* questions in *even less* time, so this is actually very doable.

The passages are drawn from careers, humanities, social studies, and science. Each one is about five paragraphs long. The passages are short, about 400-450 words, and at least one of the passages contains a graph or chart on which one to three questions will be based.

As in the reading part, there are four choices for each question. The first choice is almost always NO CHANGE and the other three will give you different versions of the underlined part in the passage.

We recommend starting your grammar training early by working for 5-10 minutes a week on the grammar topic in freerice.com. It is set up perfectly to improve your score on this part of the exam, testing your knowledge of sentence structure and proper usage, and punctuation. They also ask you to correct sentences, improve expression, and pick out redundancies. Structure and language use also comes into play. This may take some adjustment, but you will soon get accustomed to it.

Essay (Optional)

The essay score does not factor into your score of 1600. It is a separate score entirely. So, while it would seem a simple decision to do the essay depending on how well you write, most of the upper echelon schools to which you will be applying will want to see an essay. Think about it. You have to be able to read a passage accurately, analyze what information from that passage you can use in your essay and then convey that information in vivid language that supports your point clearly. What college would not want to see how well you do that? Compare their reading of this essay to the college essay that you send in. Students can get help with that from their parents, teachers or Aunt Matilda. The college admissions office has no sure fire way of knowing how much of it you have written. No one is helping you to write the essay on the SAT and it is a comprehensive essay in that you must use the information of their passage to build your case. You will have to present photo ID to get into this test, so they are reasonably sure you have written it. Many people could have contributed to your common application, and your prospective college, although experienced in this sort of thing, cannot categorically say how much of it you have written. **Therefore, this essay may be a very important part of your college application process.**

Sure, the format is exactly the same from test to test, but the passages themselves will change, so you will not be able to just write something you have memorized before the test.

You have 50 minutes to write your essay. This is nice amount of time. However, you must also read a short passage upon which you will draw your information for supporting or refuting a position. You then have four pages to write your essay. The extra time will allow you to work out a solid outline, which should enable you to write a comprehensive essay. We will guide you through this process later in the book.

Scoring the essay: The rubric used to establish your score is based on reading, analysis and writing. Each of these will be scored from 1-4. You must indicate that you have actually read and grasped the passage. Simply referencing specific information from their passage is usually enough to establish that. They also want to see that you can break down someone else's argument and use that ability to create an argument of your own. For this, you will have to arrive at supportable claims based on the information in the passage and any other information that you can come up with. Finally, you have to demonstrate all of this in a clear, coherent writing style that uses solid word choices and tone, is well organized, uses good sentence variety and preferably makes the reader think. We will guide you through writing this essay later in the book.

PREPARING FOR THE SAT

There are many ways that a student can prepare for the SAT, but not all preparation is created equally. We always teach our students the methods that will give them the maximum result with the minimum effort. For 40 years, each author has spent innumerable hours finding ways to minimize the time students have to spend prepping for these standardized tests because we think they are an embarrassing waste of your time. Our book is short, but it is packed with good advice. Use it well and prosper.

The book you are now reading is self-contained. Each problem was carefully created to ensure that you are making the most effective use of your time while preparing for the SAT.

Using this book effectively

- Begin studying at least three months before the SAT.
- Do at least one full practice exam from the College Board book every two weeks. Every other week do a full math, reading, and writing exam at one sitting to develop your mental stamina.
- Choose a consistent study time and location and stick to it.
- Every time you get a question wrong, **mark it off, no matter what your mistake**.
- Don't start a practice test without sitting first for 15-20 minutes to carefully go over not only the errors you made on previous tests, but also to concretize the techniques. Have a game plan and challenge yourself to get at least 2 questions more on each test you take.

The key to success

A combination of two components will maximize your SAT score with the least amount of effort.

- Learning test taking strategies that work specifically for standardized tests.
- Taking about four practice tests before test day to make sure you are applying the strategies effectively under timed conditions.

Strategy: The more SAT specific strategies that you know the better off you will be. Throughout this book you will see many strategies being used. A lot of what we have done is to give you a mindset so that you understand how to break down choices. If you use our strategies effectively, you will never have more than two choices. However, if you do not do all of the exercises, you risk the danger of going in unprepared. This book is not the tome (large and wordy book) that most others are because every part of it is essential.

Practice: The problems given in this book, together with the problems in the practice tests from the College Board's Official Study Guide (2016 Edition), are more than enough to vastly improve your current SAT score. All you need to do is work with this book and take 7-8 practice tests over a period of three to four months and the result will far exceed your expectations.

Check your answers properly

Be careful with your bubbling. Try filling in groups of answers such as all the answers to a particular passage at one time rather than constantly going to the bubble sheet. That way it is a focused activity and you are sure you are doing it correctly.

Take a guess whenever you cannot solve a problem

There is no guessing penalty on the current version of the SAT. Whenever you do not know how to solve a problem take a guess. Ideally you should eliminate as many answer choices as possible before taking your guess, but if you have no idea whatsoever do not waste time overthinking. Simply put down an answer and move on. You should certainly mark it off and come back to it later if you have time.

Pace yourself

Do not waste your time on a question that is too hard or will take too long. After you've been working on a question for about 30 to 45 seconds you need to make a decision. If you do not know the correct answer, eliminate as many answer choices as you can and take a guess. But you still want to leave open the possibility of coming back to it later. Remember that every problem is worth the same amount. Do not sacrifice problems that you may be able to do by getting hung up on a question that is too hard for you. Just write a symbol, such as an asterisk or X, in the margin next to the number of the question you are unsure of. Then, go back to it later if you have time.

READING GUIDE

The questions are designed to discover how strong your reading ability is. Thus, they will ask for the purpose of the passage (1), words in context (2), rhetorical devices, a few content questions (4-5), attitude of the author (tone) and evidence based questions (2). Structural questions such as how different paragraphs relate to each other will also be included. You can pretty much count on these numbers, so there is a certain comfort level here.

The Steps to Success

BE PROACTIVE. Take charge of the reading section rather than let the reading passages take charge of you. Here is how to take control:

1. **Get comfortable with the order of the passages you will read.** For instance, if you are good at science, then read the science passages first. If you have a penchant for history, then read the history passages first. If you are a literature fan like I am, you may want to read the literature passage first. In other words, you do not have to read the passages in the order that they appear. Remember: you are in control.

2. **Keep track of your score in each of the reading subject areas.** For each of the three passage types (literature, social studies/history, science), complete at least six passages.. Next, average the scores for each passage type (you will have three averages). This is also another good way of determining which passages you should read first. Save the passage types you do not score well on for last. You should never feel rushed on this part of the test since you have enough time to read each passage in its entirety. But if you are a very deliberate reader, saving the passages on which you scored the lowest, for last, makes even more sense. If you do wind up running out of time, simply guess the last few answers.

3. **Look over the questions first and indicate important items with markings.** The idea here is to anticipate the answers. We recommend the following: (i) Find the two vocabulary in context questions and underline the two given vocabulary words in the passage. (ii) Bracket in the passage any other line references that are mentioned in the questions. (iii) Draw a line connecting the two sets of evidence based questions indicating that they can be dealt with simultaneously. All of this will probably take you less than 30 seconds. Time well spent. Time, you will save in answering those same questions. As you read the passage, you will be able to consider the meanings of the words in context. This way you can come up with your own meaning before you even address those questions. And as you answer the first of the evidence based questions, you will know to mark where you found that answer because you drew the line connecting the two beforehand. That line is to remind you that the evidence based question is next. In both cases, you will be saving time – considerably more than the 30 seconds spent beforehand.

4. **Always read the *italicized* blurb.** This blurb generally precedes the passage and provides very useful information about the thesis and/or the purpose of the passage. Believe it or not, you can actually answer some questions just by reading the italicized blurb alone.

5. **Read the entire passage.** Don't take shortcuts! You have the time to read the entire passage and to answer all the questions. You are given 65 minutes to read five passages and answer 52 questions.

This is plenty of time. You actually have 13 minutes for each passage. **There is no substitution for reading the entire passage.** If you have trouble reading all of the passages in the allotted time, train yourself to read faster. Use the stopwatch on your phone or a kitchen timer to push yourself. Trust us when we tell you that you **will** be able to read faster with practice.

6. **Pay particular attention to the first two and the last two sentences of the passage.** Here is where you will most often discover the thesis, purpose, and tone of the passage.

7. **Mark up the passage.** This annotation is crucial to your achieving a higher score. <u>Underline</u> important information, ⟨circle⟩ transitional words, and write notes in the margins. You may even want to write a summary sentence after reading the entire passage. This, again, is time well spent because it will make you a better reader and **save** you time on test day.

8. **Determine your own answer <u>before</u> you look at the choices.** We call this the blink and think method. All too often, students taking this exam are in a hurry – impatient. This is a mistake. The designers of the SAT want you to rush because rushing leads to wrong answers. Also, the choices for each question are deliberately chosen to mislead you. So, read the passage, examine the question, and then blink: close your eyes and come up with your own answer. Only after coming up with your own answer should you then look for that answer among the choices. Practice this technique, and soon enough it will become second nature and actually save you time.

9. **Be wary of the vocabulary in context question.** More often than not, the most obvious answer is incorrect.

10. **If you are having trouble answering the first of the paired evidence based questions, do not panic.** Simply eliminate any choices that couldn't be correct, and then use the lines in the second question to discover the answer to the preceding question. This "backward" approach works well.

These ten techniques are guaranteed to make you a more discerning reader and improve your reading comprehension scores. But you do have to **practice, practice, and practice**. Remember our mantra: **you control the test; the test does not control you.** We will be reinforcing these ten key steps later in the reading samples.

So, let's begin. A good starting point is to talk about opening sentences. Generally speaking, these are the first two sentences of the passage.

Opening Sentences

Thesis

The thesis is the main idea or contention that the author is putting forth. It is the bottom line. Although the purpose is always set forth in the opening paragraph, you will have to look to the first two and the last two sentences of the passage to determine the thesis. This is generally easier to pick up than the purpose. Once you have the thesis clearly formulated in your mind, most of the answers will flow from that. Sometimes there is no clearly stated thesis, but most often all the reader has to do is restate the central words of those first two sentences to establish clearly what the thesis is.

Tone

Tone is the writer's attitude toward his subject, his audience, or himself. It is the emotional coloring, or the emotional meaning of the work. The tone will not be an extreme emotion unless it is a fiction piece and the author is describing a character who exhibits extreme emotions. It will also seldom be a word that indicates that the author does not care, such as: indifferent, dispassionate, apathetic, stoic etc.

Types of tone: *playful, solemn; mocking, reverent; calm, excited; obsequious, condescending; bitter, angry or resigned; serious, ironic; formal, intimate: sad, upbeat. Of course, there are even more, often very subtle tones.*

Answers to tone questions will virtually never reflect indifference. If the writers have spent the energy to research and write, they generally feel something about what they are writing. Thus, the words indifferent, dispassionate, apathetic, stoic, etc. are unlikely choices. Also, authors are usually not permitted to have strong emotions. So, words like anger, ecstasy, hate, disgust, etc. are also very unlikely. However, if the author is writing about a character from his or her short story or novel, that character may certainly have a strong emotion.

Purpose

This is the question that students find the most annoying. Keep in mind that the answer to this question is almost always contained in the first two sentences of the passage. Also, even though this question is usually the first one, you do not have to answer it right away. Half the time you will be able to answer it right away. If you cannot, just cross out two or three choices, circle the number and go back to it after you finish the last question in that passage. Keep in mind that these passages contain 5 or 6 paragraphs at best. So, the likelihood of the purpose being some major undertaking is remote. If the answer could not possibly be achieved in a few paragraphs, reject it right away. Answer choices to purpose questions starting with the following words are almost always wrong: prove, establish, outline, trace, delineate.

The most common words used to describe the purpose question are:

explain, discuss, illustrate, describe, examine.

Also used are: define a concept, inform the reader, recount an event, indicate a contrast, raise concerns about.

Which of the following choices could be the purpose of the passage? These are not from any SAT. They are purely to train you. Thus, more than one answer can be correct.

Examples:

The main purpose of the passage is to:

A) delineate a number of objections to Darwin's Origin of Man
B) illustrate how scientists cracked the genome code
C) consider some of the best scientific modes of investigation
D) discuss some of the leading ideas in cancer research today

A is impossible as most of these passages are 5-6 paragraphs and we could never "delineate" a number of objections; B is also something that would take many chapters of a book; C and D are both legitimate choices because you can "consider" and "discuss" pretty much anything in 5-6 paragraphs and you are only doing so to "some" modes and "some" ideas.

The main purpose of the passage is to:

A) describe the unrealistic treatment of children in medieval art
B) outline the history of art up to the Middle Ages to reveal how different this period was
C) discuss the treatment of children in the Middle Ages and suggest what relationship this might have had upon the art of that period
D) trace the evolution of realistic representation on Western Art

A and **C** are certainly doable as you are only discussing and suggesting in C and describing in A and what you are doing in each case is not so complicated that it cannot be done in those five paragraphs. To outline the whole history of art right up to the Middle Ages would take you many chapters, and to trace the whole evolution of realistic representation in Western Art would also be time consuming

Examples: Below are fifteen opening sentence groupings. In the lines below each, try to list the thesis, purpose and tone. All three will not be there for each one, but you should be able to get at least two. It is important that you make an honest effort to write down what you think the thesis, purpose, and tone are before you look at the answers below and their explanations. The bold print indicates a solid answer and that is followed in each case by a sentence explaining how we figured out that answer.

1. American Football did not mandate the use of helmets until 1939 in colleges and 1943 in the NFL. Although serious injuries had occurred, the popularity of the sport precluded any serious consideration of stopping the sport or even making it less dangerous.

Thesis:_____

Purpose:_____

Tone:_____

Thesis: **That because football is so popular, the steps that should have been taken to curtail serious injuries were not made.** The second sentence clearly states that even though serious injuries were regularly occurring, very little was done to prevent those injuries because the sport was so very popular.

Purpose: **To examine the reasons that football executives have failed to implement the necessary safety precautions for its members.** Coming up with the purpose is very difficult at first in most cases. For the thesis, we just have to take the key words and restate them, but for the purpose we have to get a sense of where the passage is going. In this case, we see a key word "although," which sets up an immediate contrast. From that, the purpose starts to come into focus because a specific reason has been given for their lack of effort in remedying a bad situation.

Tone: Although written in a somewhat **objective, journalistic tone**, it still does smack of "shame on you, football owners." We see this in words such as **"mandate," "serious injury" and "making it less dangerous."**

2. Although A-Rod is considered one of the greatest hitters in baseball history, even many of his fans admit that his character is less than savory. Both his on and off field antics have led many to consider him a pariah and they will demand that a very large asterisk be placed next to all of his records because of his steroid and other chemical injections.

Thesis:_____

Purpose:_____

Tone:_____

Thesis: **Despite A-Rod's heroics, he is not completely deserving of being placed with Babe Ruth, Henry Aaron, and Willy Mays.** Again, "although" lets us know there is a contrast and from there it is not too difficult to state clearly for ourselves what the author's thesis is.

Purpose: **To discuss A-Rod's place in baseball history.** Although purpose and thesis are not always the same, they are often very close with the purpose emanating from the thesis.

Tone: **Derogatory, damning.** We see this in the choice of words and phrases: **"less than savory," "antics," and "pariah."**

3. William Blake, English poet and artist, thought that money should never be a consideration in the pursuit of art. Samuel Johnson, English author, thought that only a fool would attempt art except for profit. Whom striving artists tend to agree with might well determine their success.

Thesis:_____

Purpose:_____

Tone:_____

Thesis: **The motivation for producing art varies widely.** Sometimes the thesis is just very obvious as in this case.

Purpose: **To discuss the relationship between art and money.** All we have to do here is to place the word "discuss" in front of the thesis and the purpose is clear.

Tone: **Objective-Balanced.** Although there is **tension** in that the two authors disagree so much, that is not the attitude of the author of the passage.

4. Many of us truly love our pets, bestowing on them talents they do not possess. But what of happiness? Are they truly happy and, if so, how is that happiness manifest?

Thesis: _____

Purpose: _____

Tone: _____

Thesis: **None.** Since the author is merely raising a question, there is no specific thesis here. That is unfortunate for the reader in that almost half the questions revolve around a stated thesis when there is one.

Purpose: **To discuss the possibility and quality of happiness in animals.** Whenever the author raises a question, the answer to that question is pretty much going to be the purpose of the passage.

Tone: **Objective**

5. Many cultures throughout civilization have refused to consider the mystery of creation, conserving their energy for the work of this world. Although this has proven somewhat successful in a number of them, it demonstrates a reluctance to imagine the new, a failing that has undone many.

Thesis: _____

Purpose: _____

Tone: _____

Thesis: **Some civilizations crumble because of their failure to consider the mystery of creation and this shows an unwillingness to imagine new things resulting in their demise.** Again, taking advantage of the "although" clause, the contrast allows us to see exactly what it is that the author is positing (presenting as his thesis).

Purpose: **To examine the effects of some nations' unwillingness to imagine the new.** Once you have been able to state the thesis, all you have to do is figure out what the author might intend to do with that thesis. In most cases, it comes down to examine, illustrate, discuss, describe etc. Other than being able to answer the purpose question more easily, this allows you, the reader, to understand how to read each excerpt. It gives you a way into the passage.

Tone: **Critical.** We see this evidenced in the words "refused" "reluctance to imagine" and "failing."

6. The general public is generally swayed easily by anything labeled "scientific." It believes that science has the answers to pretty much everything. Why is it that they are so willing to delude themselves by bestowing on science the mantel of omnipotence and infallibility?

Thesis: _____

Purpose: _____

Tone: _____

Thesis: **Science does not deserve its reputation as having all of the answers.** It is evident here that the author does not agree that science has all the answers. We see this in the words "swayed", "labeled", "believes", "delude" and "mantel."

Purpose: **To unveil the charade that science is omnipotent and infallible.** Again, when the thesis is evident, it is not too difficult to decide what the likely purpose will be. If someone believes something strongly, he usually wants others to see his point.

Tone: **Cautionary.** The words in quotes (thesis) demonstrate this attitude.

7. Confucius, who has inspired two thousand years of Chinese culture, did so without the commandments laid down by Moses, Jesus, Mohammed or Buddha. Rather than having "priests or rabbis" deciding what people should or should not do, each family head did so and the head of state did this for the entire people.

Thesis: _____

Purpose: _____

Tone: _____

Thesis: **Confucius founded a set of beliefs that differs radically from those of most major religions.** "Did so without" and "rather" both steer us in the right direction.

Purpose: **To examine how Confucius led his followers in an entirely different way than other religious leaders.** It is not enough to know that he did this; any thinking reader also wants to know why he did this.

Tone: **Detached.** No strong attitude is evident here as the author is simply stating an observation.

8. What separates the Hindu religion from so many others is that it saw the world as very complex, overflowing with variety. Thus, it has refused to limit itself to one god or one book or for that matter one anything.

Thesis: _____

Purpose: _____

Tone: _____

Thesis: **The Hindu religion embraces many gods and many perspectives.** "Refused to limit itself" is a great guide to the thesis.

Purpose: **To examine the central differences in the Hindu religion.** Again, once we know the thesis, in most cases we want to examine if it is at all different or controversial.

Tone: **Detached.** No strong feeling is exhibited here.

9. Observing the muscular development of the babes held by the madonnas in the tapestries at the Cloisters, I wondered what that told us about the medieval view of childhood. Upon further research, I have concluded that they truly had no concept of childhood, seeing children as just younger adults.

Thesis:_____

Purpose:_____

Tone:_____

Thesis: **People in the Middle Ages had no concept of childhood.** It does not get much easier than this. Just take the words from the second sentence and restate them. So, I suppose it begs the question, "Why bother?" The simple answer is that just stating the thesis clearly in your mind allows you to see how so many of the answers are just restatements of the basic theme.

Purpose: **To examine the implications of a society that did not have a distinction for childhood.**

Tone: **Objective.** The passage does not indicate whether this insight is positive or negative. Just that it seems to be.

10. Miss Keeldar and her uncle had characters that would not harmonize–that never had harmonized. He was irritable, and she was spirited; he was despotic and she liked freedom; he was worldly, and she, perhaps, romantic.

Thesis:_____

Purpose:_____

Tone:_____

Thesis: **Two characters had widely different characters and personalities.** This should take you no more than 3-4 seconds after you read those two sentences.

Purpose: **To discuss the implications that such differences might have.** It is one thing to suggest that something is so. It is yet another to indicate what point you are trying to make. The best way to do that is to present some ideas to make your point clearer. That will be the purpose of many passages.

Tone: **Tension.** Practically every word in the opening sentences present a cause for tension.

11. All along the burnished footpaths of Greek Street, the shopkeepers are out already, the second wave of early risers. Of course, they regard themselves as the first wave. The grim procession of factory workers less than an hour ago might as well have happened in another country in another age. Welcome to the real world.

Thesis:_____

Purpose:_____

Tone:_____

Thesis: **The factory workers are non-entities as far as society in general and the shop keepers in particular look upon them.** The shop keepers are so self-absorbed that they don't even acknowledge the factory workers so this thesis almost writes itself.

Purpose: **Examine the attitudes towards lower-class factory workers.** The writer wants us to consider how the shopkeepers got to the point where they could just take the factory workers for granted.

Tone: The shopkeepers are **dismissive** of the factory workers. The fact that they don't even stop for a moment to consider the plight of workers who have to get up a full hour earlier than themselves demonstrates that for them they do not exist.

12. To my father and most of his cronies, having fought in the "big one" was essential to their definition of a man. Unless you had experienced the "blood, sweat and tears" of war, how could you even begin to see yourself as a man?

Thesis:_____

Purpose:_____

Tone:_____

Thesis: **Men in previous generations who have fought in wars believe that true manhood emanates from having served in a big war.** Both sentences reinforce this idea with phrases like "definition of a man" "how could you?" "blood, sweat and tears" and "see yourself as a man."

Purpose: **To discuss a specific definition of manhood.** Once you have established a clear thesis in your mind, just consider what the author might intend in the rest of the passage and it should come fairly easily.

Tone: **Detached.** The author never indicates strongly enough whether he agrees or disagrees with this sentiment.

13. Years ago when you observed a youngster at play and compared that to an adult at play, there was an obvious chasm. Today, the similarities are far more prevalent and that does not bode well for our future.

Thesis:_____

Purpose:_____

Tone:_____

Thesis: **It bodes poorly for us that adults and children play in a similar fashion.** When you see a strong statement in the first two sentence such as "does not bode well", you can pretty much assume that will be the thesis.

Purpose: **To discuss the repercussions of the shrinking difference between how adults and children play.** Most of the time when you have a clear thesis such as this, just consider whether the author is likely to discuss, examine, etc. and you will have a clear purpose.

Tone: **Alarm.** Any time you see such strong words as "does not bode well," there will be a certain level of alarm.

14. Our country has for many years made it too easy for other countries, but now we need to become a sanctuary of abundance in a world of need. "Spare the rod and spoil the child' applies to our treatment of other countries as well as to our rearing of children. If we don't, we will all go the way of the dodo bird.

Thesis:_____

Purpose:_____

Tone:_____

Thesis: **If our country continues to try to feed the world, we will all die. We must stop populating the world.** Even though you might disagree with the sentiments of the two sentences, you must take what is there and restate it. Here, it is evident that the author feels that sharing our wealth will lead us to ruin (the way of the dodo bird).

Purpose: **To examine a strong stand that the author wants us to take in regard to the rest of the world.** Since this is so strong a stance, you would know that the author would want to examine it very carefully.

Tone: **Categorical, absolute, definite.** The author clearly feels strongly about this as he uses strong phrases such as "spare the rod..." and "dodo bird."

* Sometimes you will strongly disagree with the author and even find what is said abhorrent. You still must follow the argument and answer the questions.

15. Just as Huck Finn's neighbors never for a moment entertained the idea that Blacks might be equal in every way to Whites, the founding fathers never considered that women should take part in government. Their thinking, their writings, embodied the central concept that men, and men only, should govern.

Thesis:_____

Purpose:_____

Tone:_____

Thesis: **The Founding Fathers did not believe that women should govern.** This is just a restatement of the key words, but it is very accurate.

Purpose: **To discuss the thinking behind the Founding Fathers' belief that only men should govern.** When an author makes such an extreme statement, we always want to look into it more deeply and that's what discussing allows us to do.

Tone: **Emphatic.** There is no hemming or hawing here. The author lets you know exactly what he feels.

Process of Elimination:

There are some other basic ways of eliminating wrong answers.

If an answer goes against everything you know that makes sense and is therefore foolish or just plain stupid, it will never be the answer to an SAT question. Try the following questions. These are not from any SAT, so more than one question could be right. Cross out any choices that you believe defy common sense.

Use Common Sense. Eliminate choices that are silly or just couldn't be.

ex.#1 The purpose of playing team sports is to:

A) learn how to work together towards a common goal
B) improve one's ability to be a team player at his or her job
C) learn to dominate other groups
D) to show off one's talents

ex.#2 According to the passage, the first thing you should do when you are having difficulty breathing is to:

A) strengthen your abdominals
B) try to respirate more
C) increase your red blood cell count
D) increase the number of your respiratory passages

Answer to #1: Choices C and D go completely against what we know to be true about why we play team sports. Thus, we can comfortably reject them.

Answer to #2: B is the answer as A and C are obviously wrong - they would never help you to breathe. D looks good at first until we realize that it would take a good while to develop a respiratory passage.

Avoid Extremes

Try to avoid extreme answers on this test. Because a test taker might be able to find a rare exception, that question would have to be thrown out. The test makers seldom use extreme choices.

If a choice is easy to dispute, then it is an unlikely answer. The following words make a choice easy to dispute. Answers with these words should be avoided: always, never, absolutely, categorically, each, all, will, totally, must, emphatically, certainly and really any word that indicates that there are no exceptions.

Gravitate towards choices that contain words that are hard to dispute such as: occasionally, some, most, sometimes, might, seldom, may, can, could be, etc.

Ex. 1 If you had a choice between A) The mayor had many supporters and B) Everyone supported the mayor, which would you choose?

She or he might be a wonderful mayor but the possibility of "everyone" supporting the mayor is remote. Thus, A is a better choice.

Ex.2 A) There are 12 million people in the Sao Paolo. B) The population of San Paolo is very large.

Here you would choose B because, unless a specific number has been cited, it is unwise to choose A on this test. All someone has to do is find a discrepancy in that number and that answer would have to be thrown out. No test maker wants to take that chance.

Identify extremes in the following questions:

With which of the following would the author be most likely to agree?

A) Scientific breakthroughs are always the result of painstaking trial and error by well-educated men and women.
B) Modern science should never consider scientific tenets prevalent before 1900.
C) Science is often advanced by accidents that curious people examine in a very determined manner.
D) Imaginative leaps in the dark can sometimes produce more scientific discoveries than those made with traditional methods.

In A, "always" makes that answer unlikely; B "never" knocks this choice out; C and D both make sense and are not extreme choices so either could be a viable answer.

Which of the following statements about modern man's connection to the computer world is supported by the passage?

A) The internet can be helpful at times.
B) If countless brilliant men and women in past centuries did not need the internet, neither does modern man.
C) Without the use of sophisticated computer and internet technology, mankind will not be able to navigate the difficulties that lie ahead.
D) Information obtained by the use of the internet is more valuable than that gained by traditional library research techniques.

B, C, and D all use phrases that indicate extremes and therefore cannot be acceptable answers. A uses the phrase "can be" and pretty much anything can be, thus this is a solid choice.

VOCABULARY IN CONTEXT

Introduction

The focus of the vocabulary in context questions on the SAT reading section is on widely used words and phrases found in texts of various subjects that high school students use in the classroom or for homework. The concentration of these questions will be on assessing the meanings or inferences of the words and phrases in the way in which they are employed. You will not be expected to study enigmatic and cryptic vocabulary just for the test, only to forget them soon after. That being said, the two vocabulary in context questions you will encounter after each reading passage will not be easy. They are designed to be demanding.

Become familiar with the following techniques and you will ace this part of the reading comprehension.

Rule 1: Always go back to the passage. Find the referenced word and try to come up with a word of your own to replace it. This is critical because so often the most obvious answer is wrong. Don't be lazy, or it will cost you. The good news is that there is always a clue in the sentence to help you.

Example: As used in line 33, the word "grasp" most nearly means

A) seize
B) grapple
C) clasp
D) understand

Now, if you were lazy and did not take the time to go back to the passage, you might assume the answer to be A, B, or C, BUT you would be wrong because the passage states, "the students were unable to grasp the teacher's meaning until he clarified the answer with several examples." See what we mean about the most obvious answer being incorrect? However, the clue word "meaning" is there to point us in the right direction. It's just a matter of being careful.

Try these:

1. The famous detective, noted for his remarkable **faculties**, was able to solve the case of the museum's missing painting in just two days.

A) branches of learning
B) group of teachers
C) mental abilities
D) facts of life

2. The presidential candidate slightly **doctored** her standard campaign speech for the collegiate audience.

A) accommodated
B) remedied
C) revived
D) misadjusted

3. My English professor questioned the accuracy and **currency** of my bibliography.

A) complexity
B) proximity
C) value
D) prevalence

4. "How dare you!" my mother howled in **consummate** frustration.

A) utter
B) acquired
C) depleted
D) fulfilled

5. Many of the students at the university would often ask the dean for advice on choosing their majors because she had a **discriminating** way of discerning the correct match.

A) imprudent
B) tentative
C) perceptive
D) biased

6. It appears that the journalist was trying to **intimate** that there was more to the story.

A) personalize
B) hint
C) familiarize
D) threaten

7. After having heard and read such vibrant descriptions of the artist's work, we were disappointed with the **pedestrian** tone of her latest painting.

A) compelling
B) traveling
C) judicious
D) dull

8. The president's advisors shared his deep **conviction** that the previous administration's economic policies were misguided.

A) guilt
B) certainty
C) mistrust
D) anxiety

9. The scientists were accused of **fabricating** the research data.

A) employing
B) manufacturing
C) constructing
D) misrepresenting

10. It is of **capital** importance to find adequate housing for the victims of the devastating storm.

A) economic value
B) proper
C) chief
D) punishable

Explanations

1. C. mental abilities. This is the best answer because such a famous detective would have to have superior mental abilities in order to solve this mystery in so short a time. We don't often read the word or use it in that context, and that's why we have to take the time to take the word back to the sentence in which it was used. Choices A and B are tempting, but incorrect as used here. Choice D is silly, as so many of the answers are. (The silly answers are easy to spot and eliminate. They also offer some comic relief; enjoy them!)

2. A. accommodated. This is the best answer because if you try to come up with your own word for "doctored" what would it be? Think about it. Would you really choose "remedied" or "revived"? I don't think so. Choice D is the opposite of what we want because the candidate wanted to adjust or accommodate her speech to suit her audience. (And I don't mean she dressed up when I mentioned "suit"!)

3. D. prevalence. Most of us would think of money when we see the word "currency," but, again, that's not the case here. The author is referencing the state of now, as in "current events." So, although you might initially think the answer to be "value," it doesn't make sense. Choices A and B wouldn't work either.

4. A. utter. This is the best answer because none of the answers fit. Remember, the process of elimination is your best friend. So, even if you did not know what the word "utter" meant, that does not mean you can't figure out the best answer. So, from the context the word "utter" most nearly means "complete." Notice how sentence punctuation (!) also helps to determine meaning.

5. C. perceptive. The word "discriminating" is probably most often used in a negative sense as in "…and she was discriminated against because of her religion." However, in this sentence, the word clearly has a positive meaning because of the words "advice" and "discerning." That's why the answer has to be C; it's the only positive choice.

6. B. hint. This is the best answer because of the phrase, "more to the story." The journalist suggested there was additional information. Like most of the other examples we have seen, the word "intimate" has several meanings. The one we are used to would be "deep" as in "Although I work with many students, I don't have the same kind of intimate relationship with them as I do with my own children." On this kind of test, the secondary definition is often the correct one. This can be troublesome, but hardly impossible.

7. D. dull. Pedestrian means dull?! Yes, it does. You certainly don't want a person walking or "traveling" here. The context clue is the word "disappointed." Ergo, we need the negative choice, and there is only one: dull. Simple, really.

8. B. certainty. We should be able to discern that choices A and D do not fit. You might be tempted to go for "mistrust," but take another look and you will see that a negative choice doesn't make sense.

9. D. misrepresenting. This is the best answer because the clue word "accused" informs us that we need a negative answer. The other choices are not negative.

10. C. chief. Again, the word "capital" has several meanings, which are seen here in some of the choices, but the one we need is "main" or "chief" because it's vital that we aid the "victims."

Rule 2: Another very important technique is to look for trigger words that can shift the meaning of the sentence. Take a typical trigger word like **but** and see how it changes the meaning of this sentence:

I had been looking forward to dinner, **but** when I saw my mom bring out a plate of liver, I lost my appetite. (Ugh! You get the idea.)

On the test, it would look like this: Anita was generally very energetic, but today she was decidedly **indolent**.

So, now we know we are looking for a word that is **opposite** the clue word "energetic." Let's look at the choices for the word "indolent."

A) sociable
B) sluggish
C) inspired
D) conspicuous

Now the answer becomes clear: B. sluggish.

Other trigger words that indicate that the meaning of the word in context will be **opposite** of the meaning of the clue word or phrase are: **yet, rather, although, though, paradoxically, ironically, despite, whereas, in contrast, while, until, far from being.**

On the other hand, words like **because** and **since** indicate that the word in context is similar to the clue word. Be alert for these words because they are like manna from heaven, gifts from the gods!

Here are some examples:

1. *Despite* the writer's complicated use of words, his overall tone was quite **lucid.**

A) credible
B) discreet
C) clear
D) complex

2. Suzanne chose to stay home by herself and finish her novel rather than partying with her friends *because* she was basically **diffident.**

A) conceited
B) outgoing
C) shy
D) friendly

3. Doctors were concerned that the new drug would create side effects, some of them predictable, *but* others completely **erratic.**

A) obsolete
B) unstable
C) unvarying
D) unchanging

4. *Unlike* most of her early poems in which Sylvia Plath's allusions to religion are subtle, in her later works, her criticisms became quite **scathing.**

A) impersonal
B) understated
C) sophisticated
D) harsh

5. *While* the principal acclaimed the latest revisions to the science textbook, our teacher positively **disparaged** them.

A) criticized
B) commended
C) articulated
D) embellished

6. *Whereas* the coaches of the rival teams were respectful of each other during the actual game, during the post-game interviews they lost no opportunity to **defame** the other's character.

A) compliment
B) condemn
C) abide
D) endorse

7. *While* he was amicable by nature, the drill sergeant had to maintain a **somber** demeanor with his new recruits.

A) serious
B) encouraging
C) friendly
D) depressive

8. The new television series was cancelled after only three episodes *since* critics gave it **vitriolic** reviews.

A) biting
B) fervent
C) profound
D) rave

9. *Although* Hemingway's literary style can be considered rather concise, his conversational manner was actually **turgid**.

A) abridged
B) dated
C) restrained
D) rambling

10. *Though* the editorial's appraisal of the mayor's tenure is the most perceptive I have ever read, it, nonetheless, contains some **equivocal** comments.

A) astute
B) discerning
C) muddled
D) discriminating

So, how did you do? Did you notice how the trigger words affect the meanings of the words in context? Practice this technique and your scores are sure to rise. Check out the correct answers.

Explanations

1. C. Clear. Now, remember the first step is to find the clue word or phrase. In this case, that would be the word "complicated." The trigger word is "despite," which tells us that the word in context is the **opposite** of complicated. So, think about this for a minute. Forget about looking at the choices. What word do you think might mean the opposite of complicated? Let's try to come up with a few: clear, simple, disentangled, obvious, distinct. Now look at the choices and see if any are similar to those in our group. Voila! There it is! (Coming up with your own answer before looking at the choices, makes you a more discerning reader.)

2. C. shy. Here the clue phrase is "by herself," so the trigger word because alerts us that "diffident" means the same thing. Well, that eliminates B and D. Choice A is not the best answer because a conceited or know-it-all person would most likely be "partying."

3. B. unstable. In this sentence, we want the opposite of "predictable." Hmm. You should be able to figure out that choices C and D mean the same thing, so they're out. "Obsolete" means out-of-date, which is not the meaning we are looking for.

4. D. harsh. Right away we notice that the sentence begins with "Unlike." Again, we are looking for opposites. (As you might have noticed, you will encounter more negative trigger words than positive ones. It doesn't matter because all the trigger words help us.) The clue word in this sentence is "subtle," which means slight or not obvious. See any choice that might work? Not sure? All right, let's back into this answer by the process of elimination. We can get rid of A, "impersonal," because we are talking about religion and that's as personal as it gets. Choice B is not the best answer because of the prefix "under." This is the opposite of what we are looking for. Now, we are left with only two choices. The worst scenario is a 50/50 chance of success. Not such bad odds, if you had to guess, and I would! But you don't have to in this case. You should be able to discern that the answer must be negative because of the clue "criticisms." "Sophisticated" is a positive word, so the only choice left is D.

5. A. criticized. This is the best answer because while the clue word "acclaimed" is positive, the trigger word "while" points us to a negative choice. That only leaves choice A.

6. _____ This is the best answer because (Why don't you try this one. See if you can supply both the answer and rationale. Look below for the answer.)

_____
_____
_____
_____

7. A. serious. In this sentence we are presented with two very different sides of the sergeant's personality – his personal and his professional demeanors. Well, the trigger word "While" clues us that we need the opposite of "amicable" (I studied French in school and know that the word **ami** means friend. Maybe, you took Spanish and remember that **ami**go also means friend.) But, for the sake of argument, let's say that you have no idea of what the word amicable means. Since the sergeant is training new recruits, shouldn't we expect him to be serious (but not depressed) about his duties? Choices B and C would not make sense.

8. _____ This is the best answer because (Come on, try another.)

_____
_____
_____
_____

9. D. rambling. This is the best answer because we are looking for the opposite of "concise" or brief. We can eliminate A and C because "abridged" and "restrained" are synonymous with concise. "Dated" means out of date or old-fashioned, so that's out.

10. C. muddled. The clue word here is "perceptive," which, of course, is positive. We need a negative choice. Notice any negative answer? Can you eliminate any positive ones? Get the idea. Only C is negative.

*6. B. condemn. This is the best answer because the clue word is "respectful," but the trigger word "Whereas" points us to a negative answer. "Compliment," "abide" and "endorse" are all positive.

*8. A. biting.** This is the best answer because of the same reasoning employed in the previous explanation. The clue words "cancelled" and "critics" are negative and the trigger word "because" informs us that we need another negative word; therefore, the answer must be A. All the other choices are positive.

Rule 3: When the word in context is preceded or followed by the word **and**, the word on the opposite side will be similar in meaning. Let's look at some examples:

1. Columbus *continually petitioned* Queen Isabella for funds to support his explorations *and* his **doggedness** paid off when she finally agreed to give him the money that led to his discovery of America.

A) magnetism
B) apathy
C) persistence
D) ferociousness

2. The scientist's *application and* **diligence** led to his success in gene research.

A) indifference
B) disregard
C) wisdom
D) industry

3. Sometimes the young queen's lack of sophistication and **urbanity** led her to make embarrassing mistakes at court.

A) simplicity
B) finesse
C) naivete
D) crudeness

4. It was **precarious** *and dangerous* to ascend the mountain during the snowstorm, but the rescuers had no option if they were to save the stranded climbers.

A) certain
B) treacherous
C) guarded
D) secure

5. The problem was so *perplexing and* **convoluted** that it took experts months to unravel it.

A) tiresome
B) poorly organized
C) irritating
D) enigmatic

6. The innocent young boy was fooled by his older brother, a particularly **disingenuous** *and deceitful* person, into doing something dishonest.

A) fraudulent
B) forthright
C) sincere
D) resolute

7. Hannah described the new movie as **vapid**, *blah and banal,* just a typical boring Hollywood film that was very predictable.

A) spicy
B) stale
C) original
D) uncommon

8. Because Australia has more venomous creatures than any other country, residents must be *wary and* **circumspect** of such dangers as they move about in rural areas.

A) indifferent
B) careless
C) vigilant
D) vicarious

9. My teacher's advice was both concise *and thoughtful,* although brief, it was **pensive**.

A) skeptical
B) compact
C) shallow
D) contemplative

10. Frampton Nuttel was a *very nervous and* **fractious** person, always pacing about in an uneasy manner.

A) restive
B) patient
C) reclusive
D) ravenous

Explanations

1. C. persistence. This is the best answer because the clue phrase "continually petitioned" combined with the word "and" should lead you to the answer. None of the other choices fit. "Magnetism" suggests charisma – nah! "Apathy" – absolutely not; we want the opposite meaning. Choice D is much too extreme.

2. What do you think? (Don't forget to write down your reasons for the answer.)
_____
_____
_____
_____

3. B. finesse. This is the best answer because we need a word similar to "sophistication." Choice A is obviously out because it is contrary to the meaning we are looking for. The same can be said for choices C and D.

4. B. treacherous. We know we need a word something like dangerous. Let's look at the other possibilities.: certain, guarded and secure. These are all synonyms of "safe," and, therefore, can be eliminated.

5. D. enigmatic. Here the clue is "perplexing," (and, also, the fact that it took experts months to unravel the problem.) The answer is a tough vocabulary word, but if you apply the process of elimination, finding the correct answer is easy.

6. Here is another one for you to try.
_____
_____
_____
_____

7. B. stale. Well, maybe the clue word "banal" is difficult, but we all should know the meaning of "blah"! Lol. Choices A and C are not what we are looking for. Don't be fooled by the prefix "un" in choice D. "Uncommon" means original, which is incorrect.

8. C. vigilant. If you are vigilant, you are on guard. A vigil is a watch, observance or lookout, which makes sense with the venomous creatures about. Choices A and B clearly have nothing to do with being alert. Choice D is an SAT vocabulary word, but one you should know from your readings in high school.

9. D. contemplative. This is the best answer because it fits well with the clue word "thoughtful." When you contemplate something, you are thinking about it. Choices B and C are not even close, and choice A, "skeptical" is a "doubtful" answer. (Sorry, I couldn't resist that one. If you didn't get the joke, look up the word. Sometimes, those who laugh last, laugh best.)

10. A. restive. The word nervous is the clue. That being understood, choice B, "patient" can be eliminated. "Ravenous" means voracious or really hungry, so that's not working. A recluse is a hermit, so wanting to be by yourself in not the meaning we are looking for.

*2. D. industry. This is the best answer because of the clue word "application."

If you apply yourself, you are working, and industry, as we all know, means business, activity, production or application. You might be tempted to choose "wisdom," but it does not "work" here.

*6. A. fraudulent. If you weren't aware the prefix "dis" indicates a negative word. The clue words "disingenuous" and "dishonest" are both negative. Choices B, C, and D are all positive. Also, we should realize that fraud is a crime and, therefore, dishonest.

Rule 4: When you have a word in context followed by a comma, semi-colon or colon, the word or phrase following that punctuation mark will be a synonym for the word in context. Even if there are a few words between the blank and the punctuation, the same rule applies. Let's see how this technique works.

This new book on Ernest Hemingway centers on his **camaraderie,** on his social life rather than his novels.

A) ambition
B) gregariousness
C) separation
D) aloofness

As always, the first step is to find the clue word or phrase. In this case, it's easy because it comes immediately after the comma. So, we need a word that means "social life." Not sure of the answer? Don't forget that the process of elimination is your best friend. We should be able to eliminate choices C and D because they would be contrary to the concept of sociability. Choice A, "ambition," which means desire or drive, does not fit the meaning of the sentence. It's fun to use mnemonics to help remember the meanings of SAT vocabulary words. For example, my mnemonic for the word **gregarious** is my Greek friend Greg Arious. I have a snap shot of him at a party surrounded by all his friends. He's holding a gyro in one hand and a soda in the other and he's sporting the biggest grin. So, I always remember that gregarious means social. Working with vocabulary is a lot of fun.

Here are some more examples of this very effective technique:

1. The diva was notorious for her **peevish** attitude; she easily became whiny if her every whim was not immediately realized.

A) scrupulous
B) irresponsible
C) patient
D) testy

2. The restaurant draws a **motley** clientele: a heterogeneous mix of people can be found there.

A) disparate
B) ebullient
C) uniform
D) compatible

33

3. The teacher admonished her students to avoid **plagiarism**, or presenting other people's words and ideas as if they were their own.

A) coherence
B) augmentation
C) editorializing
D) piracy

4. Even after many attempts to placate him, Dwayne remained **contentious**, quarreling with everyone about the project.

A) cooperative
B) cantankerous
C) somber
D) affable

5. It was an **enigmatic** problem, one that is difficult to understand and hard to analyze.

A) colloquial
B) lucid
C) explicit
D) unfathomable

6. This new book on Cicero, the first century lawyer, focuses mainly on his **rhetoric**, the use of language to persuade.

A) strategy
B) metaphor
C) eloquence
D) reticence

7. Idi Amin, once King of Uganda, was so convinced of his own power that he often acted without **compunction**; he felt no guilt about killing hundreds of his own people.

A) remorse
B) indifference
C) disdain
D) antipathy

8. Eli Manning, the New York Giants quarterback, seems **unflappable** even in the most chaotic situations, unconcerned and difficult to rile.

A) nonchalant
B) disconcerted
C) lackluster
D) agitated

9. Wolfgang Amadeus was a true **prodigy**; his ability at a very early age to compose symphonies and play a number of instruments made him stand out.

A) zealot
B) maverick
C) libertarian
D) whiz

10. The emissary was very **obsequious**, complimenting everyone just to get something out of them.

A) assertive
B) ingratiating
C) brazen
D) tenacious

Explanations

1. D. testy. Couple the words diva, notorious and whiny and you should have little trouble picking out the correct answer. You know that the sentence demands a negative choice, so A and C are out. "Irresponsible" or thoughtless is negative, but not in the way the sentence suggests.

2. A. disparate. Well, you might not recognize the meaning of the word "motley," but the clue "heterogeneous" is a word that all high school juniors and seniors should know. Choices C and D are synonymous, so you can't choose either. "Ebullient" means exuberant. That only leaves choice A. What's a good definition or synonym for "disparate"? *Having trouble – look below.

3. D. piracy. This is the best answer because it is the only choice that makes sense. "Coherence" contains the root **here (to stick)**, as in adhere, as in, 'The stamp would not **adhere** to the envelope." So, sticking together is not the answer. "Augmentation" means "adding to," so, that's out. Editorials are the opinions of the editors of papers or magazines, and not the meaning we need here. **Piracy** or copying is the only answer that fits. Arrr, is that clear matey?

4. B. cantankerous. "Quarreling," which follows the comma, is the clue word in this sentence. I don't want to argue with you, but clearly, we need a negative choice. That being said, choices A and D are eliminated. "Somber" is negative, I grant you, but the sentence doesn't suggest that Dwayne was gloomy or serious.

5. (Why don't you try the next two.)
_____
_____
_____
_____
_____

6.
_____
_____
_____
_____
_____

7. A. remorse. The word "guilt" is the major player in this sentence. Can you discern the choice that has the similar meaning? Can you eliminate any that do not? We need a positive word. Remember it says, "**without** compunction." Therefore, choices B, C, and D are all incorrect.

8. A. nonchalant. In this sentence, **unflappable** means "unconcerned and difficult to rile." Choices B and D are synonymous, which eliminates both. (Thank you!) As an ardent Giant fan, I hope no one chose C. Eli Manning, who led his team to two Super Bowl victories, does not lack luster!

9. D. whiz. "Ability" is the clue that propels us to the finish line. A "whiz" is a very intelligent person. Gosh, any greenhorn knows that! A "zealot" is a fanatic; a maverick is a rebel, and a libertarian is someone who believes in equal rights for all. (Again, this question is fair because all of the word choices are not esoteric. They are words that we come across in our high school reading.)

10. B. ingratiating. This is the best answer because of the phrase, "complimenting everyone just to get something out of them." Groveling and submissive people such as these are hardly "assertive" or "brazen." Whenever I see the word tenacious, it reminds me of tentacles, which won't let go. This idea of never giving up is not what we are looking for in this instance.

* Disparate means diverse or dissimilar.

* 5. D. unfathomable. This is the best answer because the phrase "one that is difficult to understand" is synonymous with the word in context, **enigmatic**. Notice that choices B and C mean the same thing, so we can get rid of both. Now you are left with only two possible answers – those are great odds. Again, at this point in our educations, most, if not all, students should know the meaning of these two words. Possibly, the prefix **un** in front of fathomable might confuse the unwary test taker, but not you!

* 6. C. eloquence. Persuasive language is the clue for the meaning of **rhetoric**. "Strategy" suggests thinking or planning, not language. A "metaphor" is an unlikely comparison, such as, "This book is the Rosetta Stone for unlocking the secrets of the new SAT." Choice D, which means shy or reserved is definitely not what the author intended. Eloquence has to do with speaking well, and that is why it is the best answer.

Rule 5: Try to determine if the word in context is positive or negative. We have mentioned this rationale in some of the previous explanations, but let's focus on this technique for a while, just to hone our skills. This is an effective approach that you can probably use in 50% of the vocabulary in context questions. Let's see how this works.

Sound pollution, a growing **peril** to marine life and especially whales, is now a major concern among marine biologists.

A) resolution
B) confirmation
C) complement
D) liability

The clue words "pollution" and "concern" immediately indicate that the answer we are looking for is definitely negative. Choices A and B are clearly positive. "Resolution" means a decision or a settlement – those are good things. The same is true for "confirmation," which means acceptance or approval. So, both are inappropriate answers. The word "complement" means enhancement or enrichment, and, besides not making sense here, is also positive. See how this works? It's really a great way to solve the words in context questions.

If the sentence reads: I was pleased and **gratified** to accept the award. The word in context has to be in the same neighborhood as **pleased**. Let's look at the possible answers.

A) despondent
B) discontent
C) euphoric
D) querulous

Do you see a choice that goes along with **pleased**? You know the answer must be positive. Remember this: the Latin prefixes **de** and **dis** almost always indicate a negative meaning. So, choices A and B are eliminated. Here is something else to remember: harsh sounding words are usually negative as well. Say the word "querulous" out loud. Can you hear the harsh "k" sound? It's negative, and it's out. The answer has to be C. You don't even have to know that the word euphoric means happy. By the process of elimination, it has to be correct.

On the other hand, what if the sentence read: I was **wretched** when I received the rejection notice from my publisher. Now, we can ascertain that the answer is negative because of the clue word "rejection." Let's look for the suitable choice.

A) crestfallen
B) elated
C) proud
D) fired up

Here, again, the answer is clear because B, C, and D are all positive. The answer must be "crestfallen." Not sure what "crestfallen" means? Who cares! It has to be the right choice. This is a wonderful technique.

Try these:

1. Derek Jeter was often characterized as one of the most **lithe** baseball players on the Yankees because of his flexibility and grace on the field.

A) fickle
B) supple
C) disingenuous
D) unyielding

2. The students characterized their teacher as **cantankerous** because she had an irascible disposition.

A) grumpy
B) genial
C) amiable
D) civil

3. In the story, "Beauty and the Beast," Beauty is at first **appalled** by the Beast, but she is gradually won over by his unconditional love.

A) reassured
B) comforted
C) disconcerted
D) encouraged

4. What started out as a playful competition between the boys, soon turned **contentious**.

A) cordial
B) ambivalent
C) bellicose
D) cooperative

5. We were all inspired with Meg's **resolute** attitude in dealing with adversity.

A) pessimistic
B) timid
C) meek
D) uncompromising

6. The contestant's brave smile **belied** the turmoil he was feeling as he awaited the judge's decision.

A) contradicted
B) endorsed
C) concurred
D) attested

7. Eager to **debunk** the myth that women are the weaker sex, Riley spent years gathering anecdotal evidence to demonstrate women's emotional and physical powers.

A) affirm
B) deflate
C) prove
D) corroborate

8. The researcher was further **empowered** by the attention her work received from the scientific community and by the opportunities that were suddenly open to her.

A) invigorated
B) disheartened
C) debilitated
D) sapped

9. Many doctors have discovered, to their surprise, that even antibiotics can have **deleterious** effects when used in excess.

A) significant
B) injurious
C) therapeutic
D) subtle

10. Socrates is said to have been endowed with an inborn **sagacity**, an ability to understand universal truths.

A) imagination
B) inability
C) wisdom
D) creativity

Answers

1. B supple. This is the best answer because all of the other choices are negative.

Listen to the pronunciation of "fickle." Hear that harsh "k" sound. The meaning is negative, so eliminate it. Choices C and D have negative prefixes, so they are also out. Can you see the effectiveness of this approach? You can't always use it, but when you can, it's great.

2. A. grumpy. The use of sound, again, is the way we can determine that the word in context is negative. Can you eliminate any positive answers? Yes, yes and yes. Wow!

3. C. disconcerted. This answer, too, has to be negative because Beauty is at **first** (feeling unhappy and upset) **appalled**, but later won over by love. When you look at the answers, your choice is an easy one.

4. C. bellicose. We need a contrary answer once more. Choices A and D are immediately eliminated. "Ambivalent" contains the Latin prefix **ambi** meaning both or on both sides. (He is an unusually skillful pitcher because he is ambidexterous.) We don't want both, we just want one – the negative meaning.

5. D. uncompromising. Finally, we need a positive answer. Don't let the **un** fool you. "Uncompromising" means determined or steadfast. All the other answers are negative, so you would have picked the correct answer in any case.

6. A. contradicted. This is the best answer because we know we need a contrasting word with the clue "smile." Choice B is obviously incorrect. Maybe you're not 100% certain about "attested" or "concurred," but look at choice A. You have to know that this word is definitely negative.

7. B deflate. Can you guess the rationale here? That's right – it's the same as most of the explanations above. The prefix de almost always signals a negative meaning, and that is the case in this sentence. And all of the other choices are… Say it. Positive!

8. A. invigorated. This is the best answer because the word **empowered** and the fact that opportunities were "open" to her point to a positive choice.

9. B. injurious. Key clues here are the words "surprise" and "excess." Couple that with the negative prefix **de** in the word **deleterious** and that's that. ("Subtle" means faint or indirect, so it doesn't fit.)

10. C. wisdom. This one is a bit tougher than the last few, but hardly impossible considering that we need a positive word that means understanding. Would you choose a different answer? Why?

Congratulations! Your practice with the above exercises on the Vocabulary in Context question should guarantee an improvement in your overall score.

* Make sure you check out the Bonus Verbal Materials on Page 170 to enhance your ability to work with words in context and to prepare you for college reading.

Note: You should have noticed that there were several positive words beginning with a harsh "k" sound (such as comforted, cordial, cooperative, and concurred). Of course there will be some exceptions, but most often the odds will be greatly in your favor. The guide for positive and negative prefixes (found in the Bonus Verbal Materials just mentioned) should certainly supersede this rule.

PLAYING WITH WORDS

There is no substitute for a strong vocabulary. It allows you to understand people better, to read and attend college lectures more effectively, to take tests more successfully and to impress those around you. In the few months that you have to prepare for the SAT, you can enhance your vocabulary only to a certain point. Therefore, you are going to have to find ways of figuring out words that you do not know. So, make a strong effort to get comfortable with the following techniques that will enable you to narrow choices.

SOUND system

This first technique is very helpful, but it is not something that you can use right away unless you have an excellent musical ear, which unfortunately most of us do not. By practicing this, you add a new weapon in your arsenal to beat the SAT.

All words in English have a dominant vowel that the voice naturally falls on or emphasizes as we pronounce it. If that vowel is long, the word will most often be negative. If short, it will be positive unless it is followed or surrounded by negative consonants such as G, R, Q, K, C, CH. Also, anytime the letter S, a very smooth consonant, is followed by Q, K or C, it will result in a harsh sound, making the word negative. Think of skunk, scram, scurrilous, scuttle. The smooth consonants are L, S, M, N, F (PH) and V.

If holding your jaw as you pronounce the word, you have to stretch your mouth a good deal, or you can actually hear the letter pronounced as you would if you were saying the alphabet, then it is a long vowel and the word will likely be negative. *Remember that we are dealing with only the vowel that the voice falls on. Thus, "willowy" will be positive even though we can hear the o, which is a long vowel. Our voice falls on the "i" and thus the short vowel followed by two letter l's will be positive. Try the following words, which describe someone who is less than average weight. If the person described is thin to an unhealthy level, then the word is negative. If to a healthy or beautiful level, then positive.

    Slender   Slim   Bony   Scrawny   Svelte   Emaciated   Gaunt   Sylph   Lissome

Notice that slender is accented on the first e, a vowel that is short and surrounded by soft consonants such as s, l, n. Thus, the word is positive. Same with slim. A short vowel surrounded by s, l and m, all soft.

You can hear the o in bony, so this is negative. Scrawny has the harsh sc sound, an r and the long aw, vowel sound and is thus negative.

Svelte has a short e surrounded by an s and l and is positive.

Emaciated sounds very smooth as far as consonants, but vowels are always more important. Since we hear our voice emphasize the first a and it is long, the word is negative.

Gaunt has the harsh G and the long au sound, and so it's negative.

Sylph has the short y and is surrounded by s, l and ph and so it's positive.

Lissome has a short i and is surrounded by s, l and m and so it's positive.

Practice on the following words, which mean either brief and to the point (positive) or long-winded (negative).

1. Pithy   2. Concise   3. Verbose   4. Maunder   5. Garrulous   6. Prolix   7. Prate   8. Terse

9. Glib   10. Loquacious   11. Logorrhea   12. Blatherskite   13. Laconic   14. Jabber

Answers:

1. Pos	6. Neg	11. Neg
2. Pos*	7. Neg	12. Neg.
3. Neg	8. Pos	13. Pos
4. Neg	9. Pos	14. Neg
5. Neg	10. Neg	

* Yes, there is one exception here in "concise." The accent is on the second vowel "i," which is long and the word is positive, so this is not a perfect system. After you get good at it, you will be right 98% of the time, which is very good, indeed.

Another way to do this is simply to ask yourself if you would feel complimented or insulted if someone called you that word (adjective).

So, using all of our techniques, which of the following are positive adjectives?

- A) salutary
- B) malignant
- C) florid
- D) felicitous
- E) cognizant
- F) mellifluous
- G) eccentric
- H) acrimonious
- I) skeptical
- J) benign
- K) dulcet
- L) repugnant

Salutary you can get from your Italian "salud," something Italians say to each other when eating or drinking something wonderful. It means "to your health" and therefore if something is "salutary", it is good for your health.

Malignant and florid you can get from your languages also. We know that bene means good and mal is bad. Thus, a benign tumor will not kill you, but a malignant one has a good chance of doing so.

Felicitous, cognizant, and mellifluous come from Spanish. We remember the song Feliz Navidad or might say this to each other in class. From florid we notice the word flor, flower, and thus language that is florid is flowery or ornate. From the first person singular of conocer (to know) we remember cognosco and it is not much of a jump to realize that if we are cognizant of something we know it or are aware of it. We are literally acquainted with it.

Eccentric, acrimonious and skeptical all sound harsh and are therefore negative.

Eccentric means that we are outside the center and therefore not part of the group and therefore unknown or odd as far as others are concerned.

Acr means harsh or bitter or sharp and thus if we have acrimony for someone, we are bitter towards them.

Skeptical starts with the ugly Sk sound and means doubtful.

Dulcet from your Spanish- sweet, agreeable, candy. Thus, dulcet sounds would be sweet or soothing sounds.

Pug is not a very nice sound, so repugnant will be negative. It means abhorrent or horrid to the senses.

Finally, mellifluous sounds very mellow. It literally means flu - flowing in a very smooth way.

For **verbs,** just put your word in the smallest possible sentence that makes sense.

BUNGLE. She bungled it. Ask yourself if that action seems negative or positive. The "g" sound should tip you off that it is negative. Basically, she messed up.

ENCROACH. You can hear the "O" sound so it is long and you also have the C and R before it and the CH after it. This word does not have a chance of being positive. Those of you who watch football know that if a defensive player comes across the line before the ball is hiked, his team receives a 5 yard penalty for "encroachment."

He has gone into an area he is not allowed to be.

CRINGE. She cringed. Even though the vowel is short, the combination of the C and R before it and the G after it lets you know it will be negative. Long accented vowels are virtually always negative, but short vowels can be negative too if they are surrounded by a very harsh consonant. Cringe means to be embarrassed or to pull back quickly in a humble way.

Are you a careful thinker?

A great deal of this test is to determine not how much you know, but how carefully you can think. So much of this test comes down to just being very careful. If you are, you will get every one of these questions correct. I have had numerous fifth graders get them all right and yet many of the top students in the New York area have struggled with this test, missing as many as 4 questions. That should never have happened and would not have had they forced themselves to be boringly careful. Good luck!

Careful Thinking Test

1. How many eighths are there in 16/2?

A) 8
B) 1
C) 64
D) 6
E) 32

2. In a different language, "bod pu" means "white tub", "tag pu mag" means "little white swan", and "mag wub" means "little pig." What is the word for "swan" in that language?

A) bod
B) pu
C) mag
D) tag
E) wub

3. 40 is to 60 as 20 is to which of the following?

A) 30
B) 120
C) 10
D) 50
E) 90

4. If you are facing west and turn to your right and then make a 180 degree turn and then turn right, in which direction are you facing?

A) east
B) west
C) north
D) south
E) northwest

5. Write the three letters that should appear next in the series.

   D C B I H G N M L S R Q ___ ___ ___

6. There are four equal sized boxes and inside of each box there are two smaller boxes and inside each of the smaller boxes there are 3 even smaller boxes. How many boxes are there altogether?

A) 27
B) 33
C) 21
D) 36
E) 44

5 6 8 11 15 20 26 33 45

7. One number in the sequence above is incorrect. What should that number be?

A) 45
B) 41
C) 39
D) 44
E) 40

8. A journey always involves

A) planning
B) a destination
C) distance
D) a human being
E) a map

9. Cross out the letter before the letter in the word PREDATE, which is in the same position in the word as it is in the alphabet. Answer: _____

Why did we do this test?

Sometimes when something seems very easy we don't bring our A game to it. Because these questions are mostly so easy that a number of fifth graders missed only one, we don't focus as much as we should and we pay the price by missing questions that we should be able to do in our sleep.

Explanations

1. **C.** We all know that there are 8 one eighths in every number and that 16 divided by 2 is 8. **Rule: Focus completely on every question.**

2. **D.** This is a perfect example of the rule given in the first explanation. If we had taken the time just to write what each nonsense word meant on the side of the paper, we could have done this question very easily. The answer is TAG. **Rule: Proceed in an orderly fashion.**

3. **A.** This is just an analogy question. Since 40 is 2/3 of 60, 20 must be 2/3 of 30.

4. **B.** Question #4 is also very easy. We could have drawn a simple compass on the page and just navigated it or used the room we are in and just turned mentally in it to realize that we were still facing WEST. **Rule: Try to simplify things. Getting too complicated will wear you out and result in some bad answers.**

5. **X W V.** #5 does demand some patience, but that is what this test often takes. So many of us get worked up on a test and start to work too fast. **Rule: It is better to get all of the questions we do right and leave a few out than to rush and get nervous and then miss many questions.** The pattern reverses the order of three letters in the alphabet then skips the next two. The answer is : X W V

6. **D.** #6 demands that we don't waste time. We could just as easily work with one box and then multiply by 4 at the end as fill up all sorts of boxes and start counting them. So, **Rule: Don't waste time.** We will see this often when you are asked to read 10-20 lines from the passage when all you really have to do is to read one sentence or often one word. If you have just read 2-3 sentences in the previous question and then are sent to the next sentence following those sentences and the word is Yet, But or However, you don't have to read further because the answer will just be the opposite of what you have just read. Thus you have saved yourself from reading perhaps 15 lines.

7. **B.** #7 is a great question and is at the heart of why most students miss critical reading questions. Had you paid attention to the question that asks "What should that number be?" you would have realized that the question does not ask you which number is wrong, but what the number should have been. The answer is: B- 41. **Rule: Make sure you understand exactly what the question is asking. If you do this carefully before you back and read the 3 sentences in the passage, you will seldom miss a critical reading question.**

8. **C.** #8 is often missed because students don't keep in mind that in an answer choice, every word counts. You could have 5 words that are exactly the same as the words you thought should be in an answer, but if there is a word that does belong in the answer, that is sufficient to make it an unacceptable choice. Since we have the word "always" in the question, it knocks out all of the choices except distance. **Rule: Every word counts in both the question and the choices.**

9. **E. Rule: Make sure you understand the question.** Yes, some of the questions are convoluted, but if you stay with and break it down and understand exactly what the question is asking, you can get it. Students are so happy to realize that d is the fourth letter in the alphabet and the fourth letter in the word that they forget that the question asks you to choose the letter "before" that letter, which is "e."

READING PRACTICE PASSAGES

The reading passages that follow will give you the chance to practice the techniques you have just learned and allow you the opportunity to hone those skills.

Remember what we said about the importance of marking up the passages. This is crucial to your doing well on this part of the test. Underline important information, circle transitional words, and write notes in the margins. We have provided three examples on the next few pages of how this might be done.

One last point, and this is very important. Always check your answers in the practice tests and the additional sample questions provided in this book. Carefully study the explanations for any you answered incorrectly. You don't want to make the same mistake twice. Don't be lazy; take the time to go over your answers.

The following passage is adapted from a Recent NASA report on the advisability of using laser technology in dealing with NEOs.

Astronomical telescopes and deep space radar systems have observed the existence of at least 2000 Near Earth Objects (NEO), such as asteroids and comets, which potentially could destroy most
5 life on Earth. An asteroid with a diameter of 0.2 km would strike the Earth with a power rivaling the strength of a multiple warhead attack with the most powerful hydrogen bombs. This strike would throw up a cloud of dust rivaling the most powerful
10 volcanic explosion, which would seriously affect climate on the scale of two to three years. A strike by a larger asteroid, say 1 km (especially in the ocean), would create a gigantic tsunami that would flood and obliterate coastal regions. More
15 significantly, it would eject a massive dust cloud that would alter our biosphere to the point that life as we know it would within cease to exist with no chance of recovery in the near term.

The consensus in the astronomical and
20 astrophysics community was that most of the known NEOs do not pose a near term threat, and therefore that these objects do not present any danger to the Earth and its biosphere in the foreseeable future. However, the recent collision of
25 the comet Iauki with Jupiter and the discovery of an uncatalogued asteroid, which passed near Earth without any advanced warning, have increased concerns.

Several schemes have since been discussed for
30 dealing with NEO on collision courses with the earth. These include blowing them up with nuclear weapons or landing on them and using small, shaped nuclear detonations to steer the asteroid into a passing orbit. However, fragmentation may not be
35 a solution because the center of mass of the resulting cloud of debris would continue on the original collision trajectory. Also, we presently do not have the lift capability to land and place nuclear devices on asteroids without extremely long lead
40 times. The research and development of a nuclear deflection system would cost billions and would still require sufficient warning of an impact to be implemented.

A better system would he one that is on station
45 and could be used routinely to shape asteroid orbits over long periods of time so that they do not pose a potential threat. Phased Array Laser Systems (PALS) could be developed and orbited. Space-based laser constellations (SBL) are presently under
50 development and will be tested during the next decade.

Coupling PALS with powerful telescopes, such as those being developed under the Next Generation Space Telescope (NGST) project, would provide
55 long-term warning for implementation of an overall NEO avoidance system.

1. The primary purpose of the passage is to

    A) dramatize the danger of possible NEO collisions.
    B) highlight the tremendous cost of dealing with NEOs.
    C) propose solutions to the NEO problem.
    D) demonstrate the effectiveness of laser technology.

2. All of the following were discussed as ways of dealing with NEOs EXCEPT

    A) destroying them with nuclear devices.
    B) the employment of lasers.
    C) creating a nuclear deflection system.
    D) using astronauts and space vehicles to steer NEOs out of harm's way.

3. According to the chart, "Close" applies to all of the following EXCEPT

    A) distance.
    B) velocity.
    C) approach.
    D) recent.

Object Name	Close Approach Date	CA Distance* (AU)	CA Distance* (LD)	Estimated Diameter**	H (mag)	Relative Velocity (km/s)
(2016 VZ3)	2016-Nov-13	0.0971	37.8	120 m - 260 m	21.8	20.64
(2016 VX1)	2016-Nov-13	0.0134	5.2	25 m - 55 m	25.2	17.04
(2016 VQ4)	2016-Nov-14	0.0716	27.9	21 m - 47 m	25.5	6.43
(2016 UB107)	2016-Nov-14	0.0215	8.4	26 m - 57 m	25.1	4.90
(2016 VP2)	2016-Nov-14	0.0653	25.4	48 m - 110 m	23.7	15.34
(2015 XC352)	2016-Nov-14	0.1474	57.4	19 m - 43 m	25.7	3.63
(2016 UC57)	2016-Nov-15	0.1052	40.9	48 m - 110 m	23.7	5.16
(2016 VE4)	2016-Nov-15	0.0135	5.2	14 m - 31 m	26.4	7.30
(2016 LC9)	2016-Nov-15	0.1299	50.5	11 m - 24 m	27.0	4.61
96590 (1998 XB)	2016-Nov-15	0.1198	46.6	880 m	16.2	11.02

RECENT CLOSE APPROACHES TO EARTH
1 AU = ~150 million kilometers
1 LD = Lunar Distance = ~384,000 kilometers

* Close Approach (CA) Distance is the distance between the Earth center and asteroid center.
** Diameter estimates based on the object's absolute magnitude.

Explanations

1. **C. propose solutions to the NEO problem.** This is the best answer because increased concerns about NEOs have generated several "schemes" to eliminate their threat including the best of them: lasers.

2. **D. using astronauts and space vehicles to steer NEOs out of harm's way.** This is the best answer because all of the other choices are clearly mentioned as possibilities. "Steering" is mentioned, but with "shaped nuclear devices" only.

3. **B. velocity.** This is the best answer because "Close" can clearly be seen to be used with all of the other choices.

The following excerpt is from Edgar Allan Poe's short story, "The Cask of Amontillado."

THE thousand injuries of Fortunato I had borne as I best could; but when he ventured upon insult, I vowed revenge. You, who so well know the nature of my soul, will not suppose, however, that I gave
5 utterance to a threat. At length I would be avenged; this was a point definitively settled—but the very definitiveness with which it was resolved, precluded the idea of risk. I must not only punish, but punish with impunity. A wrong is unredressed
10 when retribution overtakes its redresser. It is equally unredressed when the avenger fails to make himself felt as such to him who has done the wrong.

It must be understood that neither by word nor deed had I given Fortunato cause to doubt my good
15 will. I continued, as was my wont, to smile in his face, and he did not perceive that my smile now was at the thought of his immolation.

He had a weak point—this Fortunato—although in other regards he was a man to be respected and
20 even feared. He prided himself on his connoisseurship in wine. Few Italians have the true virtuoso spirit. For the most part their enthusiasm is adopted to suit the time and opportunity—to practice imposture upon the British and Austrian
25 millionaires. In painting and gemmary, Fortunato, like his countrymen, was a quack—but in the matter of old wines he was sincere. In this respect I did not differ from him materially: I was skillful in the Italian vintages myself, and bought largely
30 whenever I could.

It was about dusk, one evening during the supreme madness of the carnival season, that I encountered my friend. He accosted me with excessive warmth, for he had been drinking much.
35 The man wore motley. He had on a tightfitting parti-striped dress, and his head was surmounted by the conical cap and bells. I was so pleased to see him, that I thought I should never have done wringing his hand.

40 I said to him: "My dear Fortunato, you are luckily met. How remarkably well you are looking to-day! But I have received a pipe of what passes for Amontillado, and I have my doubts."

"How?" said he. "Amontillado? A pipe?
45 Impossible! And in the middle of the carnival!"

"I have my doubts," I replied; "and I was silly enough to pay the full Amontillado price without consulting you in the matter. You were not to be found, and I was fearful of losing a bargain."

50 "Amontillado!"
"I have my doubts."
"Amontillado!"
"And I must satisfy them."
"Amontillado!"
55 "As you are engaged, I am on my way to Luchesi. If anyone has a critical turn, it is he. He will tell me——"

"Luchesi cannot tell Amontillado from Sherry."

"And yet some fools will have it that his taste is
60 a match for your own."

"Come, let us go."
"Whither?"
"To your vaults."
"My friend, no; I will not impose upon your
65 good nature. I perceive you have an engagement. Luchesi——"

"I have no engagement;—come."

"My friend, no. It is not the engagement, but the severe cold with which I perceive you are afflicted.
70 The vaults are insufferably damp. They are encrusted with nitre."

"Let us go, nevertheless. The cold is merely nothing. Amontillado! You have been imposed upon. And as for Luchesi, he cannot distinguish
75 Sherry from Amontillado."

Thus speaking, Fortunato possessed himself of my arm. Putting on a mask of black silk, and drawing a roquelaire closely about my person, I suffered him to hurry me to my palazzo.
80 There were no attendants at home; they had absconded to make merry in honor of the time. I had told them that I should not return until the morning, and had given them explicit orders not to stir from the house. These orders were sufficient, I
85 well knew, to insure their immediate disappearance, one and all, as soon as my back was turned. I took from their sconces two flambeaux, and giving one to Fortunato, bowed him through several suites of rooms to the archway that led into the vaults. I
90 passed down a long and winding staircase, requesting him to be cautious as he followed. We came at length to the foot of the descent, and stood together on the damp ground of the catacombs of the Montresors.

1. The main idea of the first paragraph is to

   A) establish the tone of the passage.
   B) emphasize the long-standing feud between the antagonists.
   C) explain Poe's concept of revenge.
   D) introduce the protagonist.

2. As used in line 17, "immolation" most nearly means

   A) success.
   B) immortality.
   C) demise.
   D) recognition.

3. It can reasonably be inferred from the passage that during the carnival season

   A) people drank to excess.
   B) people dressed in costume.
   C) people rarely stayed at home.
   D) friends visited friends.

4. Which choice provides the best evidence for the answer to the previous question?

   A) Lines 33-34 ("He accosted … much")
   B) Lines 35-37 ("The man … bells")
   C) Lines 55-56 ("As you … he")
   D) Lines 80-81 ("There were … time")

5. All of the following are true of the narrator EXCEPT

   A) He is genuinely concerned about his friend's health.
   B) He is a wine connoisseur.
   C) He was overjoyed at meeting Fortunato at this time.
   D) He was not surprised that his servants were not at home.

6. As used in line 56, "critical" most nearly means which of the following?

   A) serious.
   B) significant.
   C) dismissive.
   D) discriminating.

7. The narrator would agree with which of the following statements?

   A) All's well that ends well.
   B) The end justifies the means.
   C) Revenge is a dish best served cold.
   D) Keep your friends close and your enemies even closer.

8. Which choice provides the best answer to the previous question?

   A) Lines 3-6 ("You, who … settled")
   B) Lines 8-9 ("I must … impunity")
   C) Lines 76-79 ("Thus speaking … palazzo")
   D) Lines 91-94 ("We came … Montresors")

9. The primary purpose of the third paragraph (lines 18-30) is to

   A) offer a reason for the narrator's melancholy.
   B) insinuate how the narrator planned to lure Fortunato.
   C) demonstrate the necessity for the narrator's caution.
   D) illustrate the narrator's respect for Fortunato.

Explanations

1. **C. explain Poe's concept of revenge.** This is the best answer because the narrator informs us in the first three sentences that Fortunato has somehow "insulted" him and he "vowed revenge." He then explains his ideas of what revenge entails. While there is some truth in all of the other choices, none of them captures the central idea.

2. **C. demise.** This is the best choice, as Montresor clearly wishes Fortunato great harm because of the insult. All the other choices are positive, and we definitely do not want a positive word here. (Just a reminder: words that begin with the prefix "DE" are usually negative. In this case, demise means death.)

3. **B. people dressed in costume.** This is a safe bet because both characters are dressed in costume. Fortunato is wearing a clown costume, while Montresor wears "a mask of black silk." There is no evidence to support any of the other answers. Although Fortunato appears drunk, Montresor is not.

4. **B. Lines 35-37 ("The man ... bells").** These lines are appropriate because they describe Fortunato's costume.

5. **A. He is genuinely concerned about his friend's health.** This is the best answer because, as we previously mentioned, Montresor seeks to avenge Fortunato's insult; he could care less about Fortunato's well-being. Montresor may appear to care, but it is a ruse. Choice B is true. Montresor mentions that he "was skillful in the Italian vintages." C is also true: he is happy to have an opportunity to kill Fortunato! D is true as well: Montresor admits he "insures their immediate disappearance."

6. **D. discriminating.** This is the synonym we are looking for because the meaning in this context is "demonstrating good taste." Montresor supposedly needs to verify if the wine he purchased is indeed Amontillado. That's why he is allegedly seeking Luchesi's advice.

7. **C. Revenge is a dish best served cold.** This is the best answer because the entire passage is about how Montresor wants to avenge the insult. He says so in the very first sentence. He also specifically states, "At **length** I would be avenged." The other choices miss the point.

8. **A. Lines 3-6 ("You, who ... settled").** This is the best answer for the same reasons mentioned above.

9. **B. insinuate how the narrator planned to lure Fortunato.** This is correct because Montresor sets up Fortunato with the Amontillado. He knows Fortunato will want to verify that the wine is what Montresor paid for because he fancies himself an expert – much more so than Luchesi. Choice A is incorrect because no reason is mentioned. C is also wrong because there is nothing cautious about the narrator. As for choice D, I think we all can tell that Montresor has no respect for his "friend."

The following is adapted from a speech delivered by John F Kennedy at his inauguration in Washington on January 20, 1961.

The world is very different now. For man holds in his mortal hands the power to abolish all forms of human poverty and all forms of human life. And yet the same revolutionary beliefs for which our
5 forebears fought are still at issue around the globe.

We dare not forget today that we are the heirs of that first revolution. Let the word go forth from this time and place, to friend and foe alike, that the torch has been passed to a new generation of Americans.
10 Let every nation know, whether it wishes us well or ill, that we shall pay any price, bear any burden, meet any hardship, support any friend, oppose any foe, to assure the survival and the success of liberty.

This much we pledge - and more. To those old
15 allies whose cultural and spiritual origins we share, we pledge the loyalty of faithful friends. United, there is little we cannot do in a host of cooperative ventures. Divided, there is little we can do - for we dare not meet a powerful challenge at odds and split
20 asunder.

To those new states whom we welcome to the ranks of the free, we pledge our word that one form of colonial control shall not have passed away merely to be replaced by a far more iron tyranny.
25 We shall always hope to find them strongly supporting their own freedom - and to remember that, in the past, those who foolishly sought power by riding the back of the tiger ended up inside.

To those nations who would make themselves
30 our adversary, we offer not a pledge but a request: that both sides begin anew the quest for peace, before the dark powers of destruction unleashed by science engulf all humanity in planned or accidental self-destruction. We dare not tempt them with
35 weakness. For only when our arms are sufficient beyond doubt can we be certain beyond doubt that they will never be employed.

But neither can two great and powerful groups of nations take comfort from our present course -
40 both sides overburdened by the cost of modern weapons, both rightly alarmed by the steady spread of the deadly atom, yet both racing to alter that uncertain balance of terror that stays the hand of mankind's final war.

45 So, let us begin anew - remembering on both sides that civility is not a sign of weakness, and sincerity is always subject to proof. Let us never negotiate out of fear, but let us never fear to negotiate.

50 Let both sides explore what problems unite us instead of belaboring those problems which divide us. Let both sides, for the first time, formulate serious and precise proposals for the inspection and control of arms, and bring the absolute power to
55 destroy other nations under the absolute control of all nations. Let both sides seek to invoke the wonders of science instead of its terrors.

Together let us explore the stars, conquer the deserts, eradicate disease, tap the ocean depths, and
60 encourage the arts and commerce.

In your hands, my fellow citizens, more than mine, will rest the final success or failure of our course. Since this country was founded, each generation of Americans has been summoned to
65 give testimony to its national loyalty. Now the trumpet summons us again - not as a call to bear arms, though arms we need; not as a call to battle, though embattled we are; but a call to bear the burden of a long twilight struggle, year in and year
70 out, "rejoicing in hope, patient in tribulation", a struggle against the common enemies of man: tyranny, poverty, disease, and war itself.

Can we forge against these enemies a grand and global alliance, north and south, east and west, that
75 can assure a more fruitful life for all mankind? Will you join in that historic effort?

In the long history of the world, only a few generations have been granted the role of defending freedom in its hour of maximum danger. I do not
80 shrink from this responsibility - I welcome it.

I do not believe that any of us would exchange places with any other people or any other generation. The energy, the faith, the devotion which we bring to this endeavor will light our
85 country and all who serve it. And the glow from that fire can truly light the world.

And so my fellow Americans, ask not what your country can do for you; ask what you can do for your country. My fellow citizens of the world, ask
90 not what America will do for you, but what, together, we can do for the freedom of man.

1. The tone of this passage can best be described as

   A) informative.
   B) despondent.
   C) resolute.
   D) fervent.

2. The purpose of the first two paragraphs is to

   A) invoke the spirit of the American Revolution.
   B) highlight how much the world has changed.
   C) send a message of peace.
   D) cite the U.S. resolve to eliminate poverty.

3. As used in line 59, "eradicate" most nearly

   A) look carefully.
   B) challenge.
   C) immunize.
   D) exterminate.

4. Which choice provides the best evidence for the answer to the previous question?

   A) Line 1 ("The world … now")
   B) Lines 1-3 ("For man … life")
   C) Lines 3-7 ("And yet … revolution")
   D) Lines 7-9 ("Let the … Americans")

5. President Kennedy uses the rhetorical device in paragraph four in order to

   A) make a promise.
   B) issue a warning.
   C) Express hope.
   D) Invite new allies.

6. As used in line 84, "endeavor" most nearly means which of the following?

   A) enterprise.
   B) time.
   C) generation.
   D) trial.

7. According to the passage, with which of the following statements, would President Kennedy most likely agree?

   A) Give peace a chance.
   B) It's better to be safe than sorry.
   C) He who strikes first, strikes last.
   D) It takes a village.

8. Which choice provides the best evidence to support the answer to the previous question?

   A) Lines 10-13 ("Let every … liberty")
   B) Lines 21-24 ("To those …tyranny")
   C) Lines 34-37 ("We dare … employed")
   D) Lines 87-91 ("And so … man")

9. It can reasonably be inferred that President Kennedy believes that

   A) the world is too dangerous.
   B) science is the key to peace.
   C) freedom is worth fighting for.
   D) weakness leads to tyranny.

Explanations

1. **C. resolute.** This is the best answer because throughout his speech President Kennedy sounds steadfast and determined, which are synonyms of resolute. "Informative" really doesn't work; it's not that kind of speech. Kennedy here is talking about his plans for the future. "Despondent," hopeless, is a negative word. It doesn't fit because the President meant to set a positive tone. One could make an argument for "fervent:" there is some passion in this speech. But there is much more firmness.

2. **A. invoke the spirt of the American Revolution.** This is the best answer because the President references the American Revolution in *both* the first and second paragraphs. Although Kennedy mentions that the "world is very different now," this is not the purpose of the first two paragraphs. Choice C, "peace," is not mentioned in those paragraphs. "Poverty" is also mentioned, but not stressed.

3. **D. exterminate.** This is the only answer that makes sense. What else would you want to do with disease?

4. **C. Lines 3-7 ("And yet ... revolution").** These are the lines in which the American Revolution are referenced twice. The other lines do not apply.

5. **B. issue a warning.** This is the correct answer because by saying that "those who foolishly sought power by riding the back of the tiger ended up inside," the President is cautioning those new states to refrain from abusing power. The other choices do not refer to a metaphor about the tiger.

6. **A. enterprise.** The key to solving this question is to check and see what the word in context refers back to in the preceding paragraph: the role of defending freedom. Once we establish this, the answer is clear.

7. **D. It takes a village.** This is the best answer because throughout his speech, Kennedy constantly uses the terms **we, us, together, etc.** From the first paragraph in which the President uses the universal term, *man*, to the last, where he calls on *my fellow citizen of the world*, Kennedy is asking for everyone (in the global village) to become involved. Choice A is too narrow; the other sentiments are not expressed in the passage.

8. **D. Lines 87-91 ("And so ... man").** These lines are appropriate for the reasons stated above. Again, the other lines do not apply.

9. **C. freedom is worth fighting for.** This is the best answer because Kennedy clearly says so in the second, twelfth, thirteenth, and final paragraphs. Enough said!

The Blink and Think Method

"Blink and Think" is a method that we developed and used effectively during our tenure with Sullivan Tutorials for many years. If you are in the New York City area, they can be reached at SullivanTutorials@gmail.com.

As we mentioned previously, it is always best when answering a reading comprehension question to come up with your own answer before looking at the choices. Students are often in too much of a hurry, racing to finish reading the passage, thereby overlooking important information. Then, they quickly scan the question and rush to look at the choices. This is a mistake. What you should do is read and savor the passage by marking it up, then look at the first question, close your eyes and think of your own answer without looking at the choices (Thus, the phrase, "blink and think"). Only then should you consider the given choices. Most of the time you will see the answer you came up with among these choices. You should do this for every question. If you take the time to do this, you will increase your reading prowess and achieve consistently higher scores. This may seem time consuming at first, but with just a little practice the process will become second nature.

There are some very compelling reasons why this method is so effective. The first is that the designers of the SAT, and tests like it, deliberately choose answer choices in such a way as to draw you away from the correct answer. That's right: the choices are purposely misleading. Well, after all, it is a test. Even so, that doesn't mean we have to fall into these traps.

Another reason that this technique works so well is that thinking of your own answers first is how your brain operates every single day of your life. When your mom asks, "Do you need anything from the mall?" you think about what you might want and give her an answer. "Video games." Your mom does not say, "Do you need anything from the mall?" A. underwear, B. socks, C. sensible shoes, D. none of the above. When your buddy asks, "Who's the best quarterback in the NFL?" you take a few minutes to consider and come up with a name. Your buddy does not say, "Who's the best quarterback in the NFL?" A. Geno Smith, B. Jay Cutler, C. Mark Sanchez, D. Tim Tebow. You get the idea. Thinking of your own answer first is the natural way of reasoning. (And, yes, we were kidding about those quarterbacks being the best.)

So, this is how the system works. You start with a sample test, but before you take it, white out or block out the choices to each question, but be sure to keep a copy of the original test. As you read the passage, mark it up the way we suggested, and, in addition, write the main idea of each paragraph in the margin. Now, when you read the questions, you'll be forced to write in your own answers in the spaces where the choices were. After you've finished, compare your answers with the original choices in the copy, which you have saved, and see how close you were to the actual answers. You should be pleasantly surprised at how well you have done.

We have employed this technique with hundreds of students over the years with great success. Now, we want to share this method with you. Try it with these next two sample tests and see how well you do. We have conveniently provided you with the questions without choices first, followed by the same questions with answer choices on the following page.

Argentine Tango as an Emotional Language. This article is by Dr. Jennifer Small who is a renowned Tango Dancer.

Argentine Tango is a conversation between two individuals via the body and an emotional connection joined by the music. Its language has been influenced by many other cultures throughout its history. Because
5 of this the Argentine tango can be considered an international language that everyone can experience and understand regardless of where they are from or what spoken language they speak. No matter where you come from you can understand and respect tango.
10 Because it is more like a language it is very different than other partner dances such as waltz, foxtrot, rumba and cha cha. The main differences between Argentine Tango and the American and International Standard ballroom dances are related to the way in which the
15 various movements of the dance are combined, the musicality, how the partners hold each other and the emotional connection and synchronicity of two minds and bodies.

Argentine Tangos' true essence is the embrace. The
20 embrace can be thought of as the pure concept of the couple with opposing energies that move in the same direction. The tango embrace is different than those of other dances since it does not have a single "correct" body position that must be maintained at all times. The
25 couple explores new possibilities of movement and expression by choosing to modify their physical position by changing from close embrace where partners are connected by the chest to a more open embrace that can be elastic and transitional where the
30 chests do not touch. Followers have some control over the embrace and can choose the position that is most comfortable and allows for the best connection physically and emotionally.

Unlike American and International Standard dances
35 there is no true Argentine Tango syllabus. There is no "Argentine Tango Basic." If you feel lost, forget what you wanted to do, or were derailed by other dancers there is no default motion to go back to. For Argentine Tango dancers they simply pause, breathe, and begin again
40 doing whatever feels natural to the music at the time. Dancers learn movements and are encouraged to mix-and-match the movements to develop their own patterns and figures. This concept is another fundamental component of tango: the exploration of improvisation,
45 the creativity in sharing the stage between leader and follower. The leader comes up with a pattern to match his or her interpretation of the music and the follower interprets what is felt from the lead. It is like a conversation between two bodies and two minds.

50 Another by-product of the lack of basic steps or syllabus is that the musicality is completely up to the interpretation of the lead and, at certain times, the follower. When watching a group of dancers at a Milonga, an Argentine Tango dance party, no two
55 couples will be moving at the same speed or doing the same, exact pattern. Each leader interprets the music in his own way in the moment. A follower could dance the same, exact song with ten different leads and each dance would be a completely different interpretation of the
60 music. Thus, Argentine Tango dancers strive to not only learn steps and figures, but to find the inner desire and motivation to merge the interpretation of the music with the movement of two bodies moving synergistically.

1. The purpose of this passage is to

_____

2. The style of the passage is primarily

_____

3. As used in line 37, "derailed" most nearly means

_____

4. According to the passage, Argentine Tango, unlike other dances,

_____

5. Which choice best provides evidence for the previous question?

_____

6. The goal of the dancers while dancing tango is to

_____

7. As used in line 63, "synergistically " most nearly means

_____

8. The tone of the passage is

_____

9. In the third paragraph (lines 34-49), the author claims that "Argentine Tango Basic" is

_____

10. The author most likely makes reference to the Milonga in line 54 to clarify that

_____

1. The purpose of this passage is to

   A) demonstrate how tango is superior to other dances such as foxtrot, waltz, rumba, etc.
   B) demonstrate how tango is a communication between two minds and bodies.
   C) delineate the various types of embrace used when dancing.
   D) emphasize the importance of all dancers performing in a synchronized way.

2. The style of the passage is primarily

   A) informative.
   B) persuasive.
   C) creative.
   D) literary.

3. As used in line 37, "derailed" most nearly means

   A) intimidated by.
   B) intrigued by.
   C) thrown off by.
   D) trained by.

4. According to the passage, Argentine Tango, unlike other dances,

   A) does not follow a particular syllabus and is virtually never the same even with the same dancers.
   B) requires tremendous athletic ability.
   C) is learned best by constant repetition.
   D) does not require music.

5. Which choice best provides evidence for the previous question?

   A) Lines 1-3 ("Argentine Tango ... music")
   B) Lines 12-18 ("The main ... bodies")
   C) Lines 19-22 ("Argentine Tangos' ... direction")
   D) Lines 50-53 ("Another by-product ... follower")

6. The goal of the dancers while dancing tango is to

   A) find a way to merge the interpretation of the music with the movement of the dancers.
   B) compete at a level they have not been able to accomplish previously.
   C) create new dance steps never seen before.
   D) achieve perfect timing.

7. As used in line 63, "synergistically" most nearly means

   A) in perfect harmony.
   B) in a creative, innovative and productive manner.
   C) in perfect, military timing.
   D) with Rockette precision.

8. The tone of the passage is

   A) exhilarated.
   B) apprecitive.
   C) didactic.
   D) whimsical.

9. In the third paragraph (lines 34-49), the author claims that "Argentine Tango Basic" is

   A) a dance syllabus.
   B) a physical and emotional connection.
   C) easily learned.
   D) not required.

10. The author most likely makes reference to the Milonga in line 54 to clarify that

    A) each couple should have only one leader.
    B) Argentine Tango is like a party.
    C) Argentine Tango is an interpretive dance.
    D) Argentine Tango dancers will always be moving at the same speed.

Explanations

1. **B. demonstrate how tango is a communication between two minds and bodies.** It never says that tango is superior so A is out; not C because there is no breakdown of different kinds of embrace; D is no good because the essay points out that Tango does not emphasize synchronized dancing.

2. **A. informative.** This is because it consistently gives information and makes distinction; not B because it never tries to persuade the reader to take up tango; not C because it does not use rhetorical devices to make its points; not D because it does not use a literary style.

3. **C. thrown off by.** A and D are never mentioned and C, intrigued by, does not fit.

4. **A. does not follow a particular syllabus and is virtually never the same even with the same dancers.** This is clearly the answer here as athletic ability and constant repetition are not mentioned (B and C). D cannot be the answer as music is mentioned several times.

5. **D. Lines 50-53 ("Another by-product … follower").** This is our answer as it clearly mentions the lack of syllabus and the emphasis on interpretation, which makes each dance different; none of the other excerpts support this idea.

6. **A. find a way to merge the interpretation of the music with the movement of the dancers.** This is the answer because this idea is mentioned a number of times. B is out because the essay does not mention competition; C is not good because it never talks about this goal; D is no good because perfect timing is not emphasized.

7. **B. in a creative, innovative and productive manner.** This is our answer because it mentions all of these qualities of good tango; C and D are pretty much opposite of what tango is striving for; A is good, but not specific enough.

8. **B. appreciative.** This is our answer because it is positive about tango at every turn; A, exhilarated, is too extreme; C, didactic, means to teach and there is no mention of that; D, whimsical, relates to one's fancy and that idea is not developed

9. **D. not required.** This is the correct choice because the author mentions that there is no syllabus for this dance; it's a matter of improvisation. For the reason just mentioned, choice A is out. Although choices B and C are important elements of Argentine Tango, they are not mentioned in the third paragraph.

10. **C. Argentine Tango is an interpretive dance.** This is the correct choice because the author mentions that during this dance each leader interprets in his own way. Choice A is incorrect because while each couple does have a leader, that is not why the Milonga is referenced. Choice B is silly. The writer states that during this dance, "no two couples will be dancing at the same speed..."

The following essay describes an unusual action taken by a young CEO.

Revolutions can be bold, bloody, time consuming and often very costly to human lives. However, a recent one in Seattle seems only to be bold. Dan Price, who owns his private company, had been reading the works of Daniel Kahneman, a Nobel prize winning psychologist, who found that emotional well-being — defined as "the emotional quality of an individual's everyday experience, the frequency and intensity of experiences of joy, stress, sadness, anger, and affection that make one's life pleasant or unpleasant" — rises with income, but only to a point. And that point turns out to be about $75,000 a year. Making above that amount does not necessarily bring happiness, but making below that amount adds a great amount of stress to people's lives as they are constantly focusing on just scraping by instead of enjoying life.

Price decided to take his annual salary of about one million dollars and reduce it to $70,000 so that he could assure that the minimum salary in his company would now be $70,000. The median salary at the time was about $48,000. This meant that even the most menial worker in his company, such as clerks, customer service reps and salesmen, would make a very decent wage. Many workers actually saw a 48% increase in their annual salary.

Amazingly, Price was able to do this without curtailing the services he provided customers or raising prices. This is truly a bold initiative and one that may well spark a revolution in certain areas of the country and throughout the business world. Most workers do not look forward to going to work each day and one of the reasons is often that they do not feel their work is appreciated by the owners. If this initiative by Price catches on, many hypothesize that we will see far more effective workers in those companies because of the respect that workers not only have for themselves, but because the decreased levels of stress will allow them to be more productive.

Back in the days of the first financial magnates such as Andrew Carnegie, J. Pierpoint Morgan, and John. D. Rockefeller, there was a common consensus that owners should not make more than 20 times what their employees made. Today, many companies have a 300-1 ratio and some of our wealthiest citizens like Warren Buffett and Bill Gates have railed against this trend.

One leading expert on social media said patronizingly "His mind-set will hurt everyone in the end. He's young. He has a good intent, but wrong method." Other leaders said "The sad thing is that Mr. Price probably thinks happy workers are productive workers. However, there's just no evidence that this is true. So he'll improve happiness, only in the short term, and will not improve productivity. Which doesn't **bode** well for his long-term viability as a firm." Of course, this is just a sampling of so many economic and social thinkers who feel Price's bold move will doom his company in the long run. Many of these experts of course have vested interest in big business and may feel threatened by the possibility of this revolution spreading across the country.

Price is not the only "naive" person making such a move. Jim Senegal, the founder of Costco, reduced his salary to $350,000 making up the difference from what he had been paid by stock options in his own company. His workers get paid $17 per hour, which is considerably more than the minimum wage across the country. Senegal feels that making 200 times more than those workers who make you rich is "just wrong." Both he and Price still consider themselves capitalists and appear to espouse the capitalist system, which is something that some thinkers are starting to challenge as a viable way of proceeding. They feel that it is simply not designed with the welfare of the worker in mind.

The tough question that all of this begs is "What leverage do workers have to encourage owners to pursue this option?" It would appear that they have next to nothing as the job market is tight and employers can just get other people to do the work. However, if companies begin to pay their employees equitably and those companies start to demonstrate greater profits, perhaps that will be all the leverage they will need. Within weeks of Price's bold move, he had 3,500 applications for a job with his company and more companies eager to do business with him. That is certainly a vote of confidence for this quiet revolutionary.

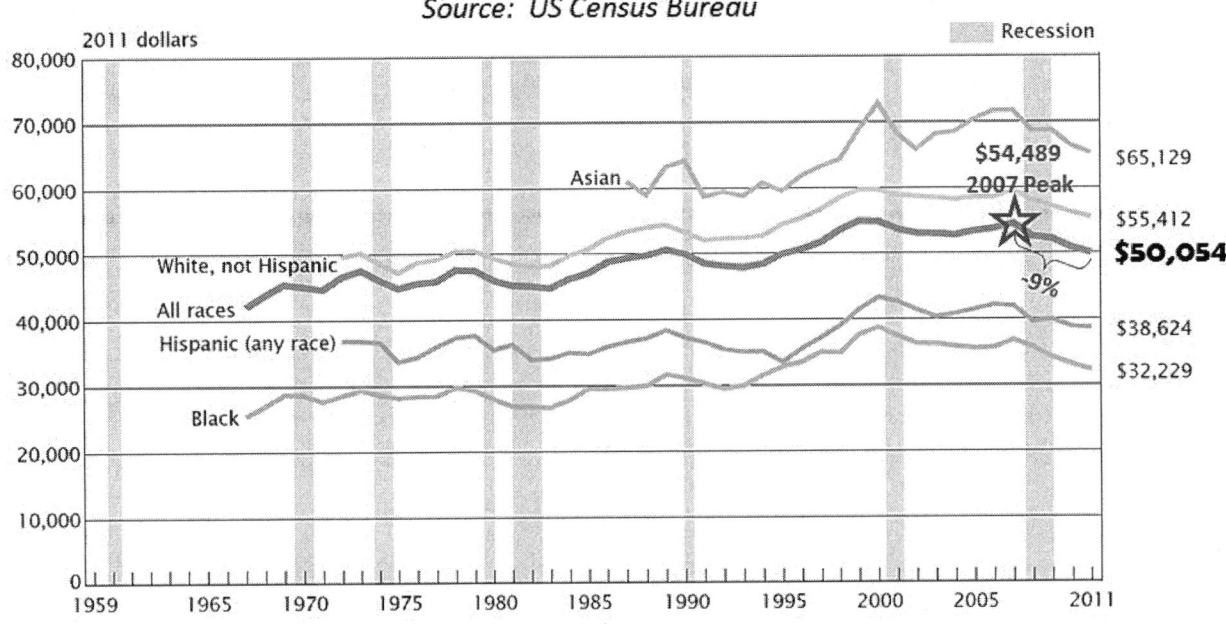

Median US Household Income
Source: US Census Bureau

1. What is the author's main purpose in writing this passage?

2. The attitude of the author towards this bold step by Price is

3. Which choice provides the best evidence for the answer to the previous question?

4. The author most likely quotes leading experts on social media in the fifth paragraph (lines 46-59) so as to

5. It can be reasonably inferred that Price's motivation for his initiative was

6. Which choice provides the best evidence for the answer to the previous question?

7. As used in line 21, "menial" most nearly means

8. As used in line 27, "curtailing" most nearly means

9. All of the the are apt synonyms for "magnates" in line 39 EXCEPT

10. Why does the writer put the word "naive" is quotation marks in line 60?

11. According to the chart, the median U.S. household income of all races

60

1. What is the author's main purpose in writing this passage?

   A) to explain how the business world works
   B) to expose the reader to a new idea that has just been implemented
   C) to discuss the success of a great businessman
   D) to demonstrate how revolutions succeed

2. The attitude of the author towards this bold step by Price is

   A) utter admiration.
   B) mild enthusiasm.
   C) skepticism.
   D) amazement.

3. Which choice provides the best evidence for the answer to the previous question?

   A) Lines 12-16 ("Making above…life")
   B) Lines 26-30 ("Amazingly, Price…world")
   C) Lines 33-38 ("If this…productive")
   D) Lines 66-67 ("Senegal feels…wrong")

4. The author most likely quotes leading experts on social media in the fifth paragraph (lines 46-59) so as to

   A) further tout Price's initiative.
   B) emphasize that money does not buy happiness.
   C) present opposing viewpoints.
   D) suggest that happy workers are productive workers.

5. It can be reasonably inferred that Price's motivation for his initiative was

   A) an attempt to enrich his company.
   B) a need for celebrity.
   C) a desire to have less stress for his workers.
   D) to try to imitate Gates and Buffett.

6. Which choice provides the best evidence for the answer to the previous question?

   A) Lines 3-12 ("Dan Price…year")
   B) Lines 17-25 ("Price decided…salary")
   C) Lines 30-33 ("Most workers…owners")
   D) Lines 43-45 ("Today, many…trend")

7. As used in line 21, "menial" most nearly means

   A) viscious.
   B) lowly.
   C) common.
   D) respected.

8. As used in line 27, "curtailing" most nearly means

   A) cutting back.
   B) incorporating.
   C) hampering.
   D) changing.

9. All of the following are apt synonyms for "magnates" in line 39 EXCEPT

   A) moguls.
   B) bigwigs.
   C) industrialists.
   D) businessmen.

10. Why does the writer put the word "naive" is quotation marks in line 60?

    A) He thinks Price is such a young, innocent person that he does not see what a mistake he is making
    B) He is using the term to be condescending or dismissive of Price.
    C) He does not agree with this assessment of Price by critics.
    D) He does not agree with what Price has done.

11. According to the chart, the median U.S. household income of all races

    A) is on the rise.
    B) reached its peak in the 1900's.
    C) is less than $75,000.
    D) is double that of the Black and Hispanic incomes.

Explanations

1. **B. To expose the reader to a new idea that has just been implemented.** This is because virtually every paragraph discusses this bold revolution that Price has initiated. A is not good because it is far too general; C because it is not discussing his success and never states or even insinuates that he is "great;" D is again far too general.

2. **B. mild enthusiasm.** This is because he uses words and phrases like "amazingly," "truly bold move" and "quiet revolutionary," which, though not over the top in praise, certainly put Price in a positive light. A and D do not work because as you remember extreme attitudes or tones are unlikely from any of our authors, but could be if it were an excerpt from a novel or short story where a character is speaking or acting. C is no good because at no point does the writer show skepticism even though he does mention the critics' viewpoints.

3. **B. Lines 26-30 ("Amazingly, Price ... world").** The previous explanation takes care of this one.

4. **C. present opposing viewpoints.** This is the best choice because the quotes are clearly critical. Choice A is incorrect because the word "tout" means praise, which is definitely not the case here. Choice B is incorrect because higher wages will bring happiness to a lot of workers. Choice D is not the answer because the critic says so directly.

5. **C. a desire to have less stress of his workers.** This is mentioned a few times in the opening paragraphs. None of the other choices are specifically mentioned or insinuated.

6. **A. Lines 3-12 ("Dan Price ...year").** This is the best answer because these lines illustrate what gave Price the idea for his initiative. Choices B, C, and D are easy to eliminate.

7. **B. lowly.** We get this one by reading the words following the comma. Remember that this is one of our best techniques for understanding words in context. Once we see that these workers are clerks, reps and salesmen rather than CEOs or executives, this is a pretty easy get. We might be tempted to go with "common," but that word does not necessarily mean lowly.

8. **C. feasibility.** A, B, and D are all tempting as they are all positive words, but none of them indicate the practicality or workableness of the move.

9. **D. businessman.** Even if you do not know all of these words, this answer should suggest itself to you as a businessman is not necessarily a "bigwig" since many just make subsistence wages.

10. **C. He does not agree with this assessment of Price by critics.** Since Senegal has done something similar to that of Price, the author does not share the negative assessment of Price as naive that the critics seem to share.

11. **C. is less than $75,000.** This is the best answer because according to the chart at its highest level, the stated income was only $54,489. All of the other choices are incorrect.

Reading Test 1

65 MINUTES, 52 QUESTIONS

DIRECTIONS

Each passage or pair of passages below is followed by a number of questions. After reading each passage or pair, choose the best answer to each question based on what is stated or implied in the passage or passages and in any accompanying graphics (such as a table or graph).

Questions 1 - 10 are based on the following passage.

This passage is an excerpt from the book Taijiiquan through the Western Gate by Tai Chi master, Rick Barrett

My friend, Read, reached into his toolbox and picked up a drill bit called a speed-bore. He pointed to a broom leaning against the wall 15 feet away. In a flash, his make-shift knife was firmly in the broomstick.
5 Throwing a tiny blade 15 feet away into an object only slightly larger than the knife itself seems so improbable. Read had to perform myriad calculations in less than a second, taking into account his current body position, arm strength, size and weight of the bit, distance from
10 the target, force and velocity required, number of spins, trajectory, etc. Any athlete knows that the thinking mind is only a hindrance at such times. Such computations are not done by the reasoning mind.
  Athletes speak reverently of being "in the Zone." It is
15 a magical state where everything is working well together. Effortlessly. Every cell seems to cooperate at such a high level that the body almost disappears. The state may be transitory and unpredictable, but while you are visiting, putts drop, crosscourt volleys find the lines,
20 and a ninety-mile-an-hour fastball hangs so long you can count the seams. A basketball player in the Zone always wants the ball with the game on the line. When asked what they are thinking during such performances, all the great ones say they have no thoughts. Others say
25 respectfully, "He was unconscious!"
  Peak performance is not just a result of natural ability and lots of training. Many amazing athletes never meet expectations. There are other qualities that coaches look for, intangibles that allow even a moderately gifted
30 athlete to perform at championship level. There is something special about them that cannot be described in ordinary language.
  The Zone is not restricted to million-dollar professionals and world-class athletes. We ordinary folks
35 can have glimpses of it as well. It requires being familiar enough with a particular activity and comfortable enough with the physical demands of performance to allow concerns about those things to disappear. This may happen a lot more often than we are aware. Familiarity
40 and ease in our mundane activities resonate with the exalted Zone experience, but may be dismissed because we take these things for granted.
  I may be so comfortable driving a certain route in my car that I engage in a lively conversation and do not even
45 think about the actions of driving until I magically appear at my destination. Time and space alter significantly. There may be no perception of time at all. I trust my game so much that little or no thought is required. This might explain the 120 words a minute
50 typist or the violinist playing Paganini or even a physicist being able to come up with a theory that changes our world.
  For most athletes, the ability to play in the Zone wanes with age, but for one group, Taijiquan masters and
55 a number of their disciples, it is present even at advanced age.
  Morehei Ueshiba, the founder of the Japanese martial art aikido, was a slight man in his seventies when he deftly flipped hundred-pound sacks of rice with a long
60 spear in a demonstration for the emperor. Yang Chien-Hou, a great Tai Chi master, defeated nine opponents at

once when almost eighty. These martial artists display an effortless competence similar to what we see in athletes in the Zone. This ability does not come from size, speed
65 and strength because at their age, they no longer have these.

Imagine if we could be in the Zone in virtually everything we do. We could live a life devoid of stress and achieve levels of competence unheard of. Prince
70 Hamlet tells his best friend, Horatio, that there are "more things in heaven and earth than are thought of in your philosophy." Perhaps Taiji and the Zone are two cogent examples of that.

1. It can be reasonably inferred that being "in the zone" is achieved by:

   A) being at one with the thing you are doing.
   B) paying close attention to detail.
   C) being intensely aware of your surroundings.
   D) knowing your subject very well.

2. Which choice provides the best evidence for the answer to the previous question?

   A) Lines 11-12 ("Any athlete ... times")
   B) Lines 14-17 ("It is ... disappears")
   C) Lines 26-28 ("Peak performance ... expectations")
   D) Lines 39-43 ("Familiarity ... granted")

3. The author uses the anecdote about Read in order to illustrate:

   A) the element of chance.
   B) the art of knife throwing.
   C) the physics of being in the zone.
   D) the complexity of the brain.

4. Which choice provides the best evidence for the answer to the previous question?

   A) Lines 7-11 ("Read had...trajectory, etc.")
   B) Lines 14-16 ("Athletes speak ... together")
   C) Lines 33-38 ("The Zone .... disappear")
   D) Lines 39-42 ("Familiarity and ... granted")

5. The literary device used in the final paragraph, lines 70-73 is:

   A) personification.
   B) irony.
   C) metaphor-simile.
   D) hyperbole.

6. As used in line 40, "mundane" most nearly means

   A) everyday.
   B) extraordinary.
   C) professional.
   D) favorite.

7. The purpose of the passage is to:

   A) describe some amazing feats by athletes.
   B) educate the reader about an elevated level of unconscious effort.
   C) demonstrate specific steps to getting in the Zone.
   D) indicate why many of us never achieve a high level of expertise.

8. The tone of the passage is

   A) provocative.
   B) poignant.
   C) practical.
   D) upbeat.

9. The author mentions the elderly martial artists to make which point?

   A) You are never too old to learn.
   B) You can learn a lot from old people.
   C) The exception does not make the rule.
   D) One does not need speed, strength and power to be effective.

10. As used in line 54, "wanes" most nearly means

    A) emboldens.
    B) incorporates.
    C) lessens.
    D) succumbs.

Questions 11 - 20 are based on the following passage and supplementary material.

This passage focuses on Title IX, the amendment that changed women's sports and women forever.

One of the great achievements of the women's movement was the enactment of Title IX of the Education Amendments of 1972. The law states: "No person in the United States shall, on the basis of sex, be
5 excluded from participation in, be denied the benefits of, or be subjected to discrimination under any education program or activity receiving Federal financial assistance." Although it is best known for transforming the sports world, this "education" law also includes
10 access to higher education, standardized testing, and education for parenting and pregnant students and an avenue for dealing with sexual harassment.

Just over forty years ago, a woman's sport was square dancing, and home economics was her
15 major. Few advanced to higher education, and sports or academic scholarships were rare. If women played sports, they were considered mean, unfeminine and often labeled as lesbian.

Back then, girls played sports, but they played to
20 empty arenas and gymnasiums. Often even their family members did not come to watch. Cheerleaders received more attention than top college athletes, who often had to promise not to promote themselves and had to have car washes, bake sales and the like just to get money for
25 travel and equipment.

There were, of course, great women athletes and in some sports, golf and tennis, for instance, they did receive attention and even got paid, but certainly not at the level that men were paid. Perhaps one of the
30 strongest indications of the impressive change that Title IX has brought is that female tennis players at majors have been paid the same prize money as their male counterparts for a number of years now. Female basketball players, however, are paid, but not even close
35 to the salary of any of the men. In fact, today, the estimated median salary of men — half the players make more than that — is $2.5 million. The league minimum is $473,604. The cap for an 11 member women's team is $878,000. Even prorated for the 34-game season, it's less
40 than the median NBA salary of one player.

Fifty years ago, Pele, the great Brazilian soccer player, was paid $2 million a year while the top paid baseball player, Willie Mays, received $125,000. Since he was paid almost seventeen times what the next highest
45 paid athlete in the world was being paid, and he played soccer, the most popular sport in the world, he was arguably the most well-known person in the world. Today, Mia Hamm, the most prolific women's scorer in history is almost as well-known even though her highest

salary ever was only $85,000 a year. Despite this financial discrepancy, she epitomizes what Title IX has meant to so many female athletes.

Although the emphasis is on sports, it is no surprise that Title IX has empowered women in almost every field of business, military, education and politics. Many college presidents, business CEOS, doctors, and politicians are now women and two of them, Hillary Clinton and Elizabeth Warren are now being considered for the Presidency.

Just as the ability to play sports gave men confidence for so many years, it has allowed women to see themselves in an entirely new light. Of course, it has not been an utterly smooth win for women as there is still inequity, and lawsuits are continuously brought up to counter this law, but so far it has had a very positive effect for both women and men. Men now have partners who are more fully realized as human beings because society has finally allowed them to develop to their fullest potential. They are involved with a person who can complement them on so many different levels.

Today, young people have become inured to seeing female athletes such as Serena Williams, Rhonda Rousey, Danica Patrick, Lindsey Vonn, Becky Hammon, and Hope Solo on television, magazines and billboards. Women are playing virtually every sport, even boxing, wrestling, and rugby, sports that traditionally were played only by men. Had Title IX not been passed and implemented, few of us would know any of these wonderful athletes.

Of course, the Women's Suffrage Movement and the nineteenth amendment are ultimately responsible for the many positive changes made for women since 1920, but Title IX remains one of the great changes for women in the late twentieth century. It has necessitated a great deal of adjustment on the part of men, but those who truly appreciate women will be thankful for how it has transformed their lives and in so doing has enhanced the lives of men as well.

11. The purpose of the passage is to:

A) delineate all the rulings of Title IX.
B) prove that Title IX has had only positive effects.
C) discuss the many benefits of Title IX since its inception.
D) explain why men agreed to this new ruling.

12. As used in line 48, the word "prolific" most nearly means:

A) amazing.
B) productive.
C) artistic.
D) sneaky.

High School Participation			
Year	1971-1972	2005-2006	Percent Increase
Female	294,015	2,953,355	904%
Male	3,666,917	4,206,549	15%

—National Federation of State High School Associations, 2006

Collegiate Participation			
Year	1971-1972	2004-2005	Percent Increase
Female	29,977	166,728	456%
Male	170,384	222,838	31%

—NCAA Sports Sponsorship and Participation Report, 1981-82—2004-05

13. Which of the following does the author NOT use to present his case?

    A) Statistics
    B) A reference to a political figure
    C) Allusions to literature
    D) Examples from sports

14. Which of the following does the author see as the most impressive change Title IX has brought for professional women's sports?

    E) that they now play rugby
    F) that some female athletes are well-known
    G) that women tennis players get paid the same as men in major events
    H) that women are in better shape

15. What does the author see as the ultimate advantage that Title IX has brought to women and society?

    A) Women are allowed to be doctors and CEOS.
    B) Women can make money from commercials.
    C) Women can compete on an equal level with men and have earned the respect they deserve.
    D) It has enriched society by giving it women who are more fully realized as individuals.

16. Which choice provides the best evidence for the answer to the previous question?

    A) Lines 13-18 ("Just over ... lesbian")
    B) Lines 29-35 ("Perhaps one ... men")
    C) Lines 48-52 ("Today, Mia ... athletes")
    D) Lines 60-70 ("Just as ... levels")

17. As used in line 71 "inured" most closely means?

    A) anxious at
    B) accustomed to
    C) aware of
    D) inspired by

18. The tone of the essay is:

    A) enthusiastic.
    B) objective.
    C) ironic.
    D) combative.

19. What explicit meaning may correctly be drawn from the data in the table?

    A) Male participation in high school and collegiate sports has remained static since Title IX.
    B) Female participation in collegiate sports has increased more than 500%.
    C) Female participation has shown the greatest increase in high school.
    D) The decline in male participation can be directly attributed to the increase in female participation.

20. Based on information in the both the passage and the table, which statement is true.

    A) Men's participation in high school and college sports is at risk.
    B) Title IX has benefited both men and women.
    C) Title IX has empowered women in every field of business, military, education, and politics.
    D) Title IX is the greatest achievement in the women's movement.

Questions 21 - 30 are based on the following passage

The following passage is excerpted from a short story published in 1926. The story revolves around a hard working washerwoman and her unemployed, insecure husband.

It was eleven o'clock of a Spring night in Florida. It was Sunday. Any other night, Delia Jones would have been in bed for two hours by this time. But she was a wash-woman, and Monday morning meant a great deal
5 to her. So she collected the soiled clothes on Saturday when she returned the clean things. Sunday night after church, she sorted them and put the white things to soak. It saved her almost a half-day's start. A great hamper in the bedroom held the clothes that she brought home. It
10 was so much neater than a number of bundles lying around.

She squatted in the kitchen floor beside the great pile of clothes, sorting them into small heaps according to color, and humming a song in a mournful key, but
15 wondering through it all where Sykes, her husband, had gone with her horse and buckboard.

Just then something long, round, limp and black fell upon her shoulders and slithered to the floor beside her. A great terror took hold of her. It softened her knees and
20 dried her mouth so that it was a full minute before she could cry out or move. Then she saw that it was the big bull whip her husband liked to carry when he drove.

She lifted her eyes to the door and saw him standing there bent over with laughter at her fright. She screamed
25 at him.

"Sykes, what you throw dat whip on me like dat? You know it would skeer me—looks just like a snake, an' you knows how skeered Ah is of snakes."

"Course Ah knowed it! That's how come Ah done it."
30 He slapped his leg with his hand and almost rolled on the ground in his mirth. "If you such a big fool dat you got to have a fit over a earthworm or a string, Ah don't keer how bad Ah skeer you."

"You aint got no business doing it. Gawd knows it's a
35 sin. Someday Ah'm goin' tuh drop dead from some of yo' foolishness. 'Nother thing, where you been wid mah rig? Ah feeds dat pony. He aint fuh you to be drivin' wid no bull whip."

"You sho is one aggravatin' nigger woman!" he
40 declared and stepped into the room. She resumed her work and did not answer him at once. "Ah done tole you time and again to keep them white folks' clothes outa dis house."

He picked up the whip and glared down at her. Delia
45 went on with her work. She went out into the yard and returned with a galvanized tub and set it on the washbench. She saw that Sykes had kicked all of the clothes together again, and now stood in her way truculently, his whole manner hoping, praying, for an
50 argument. But she walked calmly around him and commenced to re-sort the things.

"Next time, Ah'm gointer kick 'em outdoors," he threatened as he struck a match along the leg of his corduroy breeches.
55 Delia never looked up from her work, and her thin, stooped shoulders sagged further.

"Ah aint for no fuss t'night Sykes. Ah just come from taking sacrament at the church house."

He snorted scornfully. "Yeah, you just come from de
60 church house on a Sunday night, but heah you is gone to work on them clothes. You ain't nothing but a hypocrite. One of them amen-corner Christians—sing, whoop, and shout, then come home and wash white folks' clothes on the Sabbath."
65 He stepped roughly upon the whitest pile of things, kicking them helter-skelter as he crossed the room. His wife gave a little scream of dismay, and quickly gathered them together again.

"Sykes, you quit grindin' dirt into these clothes! How
70 can Ah git through by Sat'day if Ah don't start on Sunday?"

"Ah don't keer if you never git through. Anyhow, Ah done promised Gawd and a couple of other men, Ah aint gointer have it in mah house. Don't gimme no lip neither,
75 else Ah'll throw 'em out and put mah fist up side yo' head to boot."

Delia's habitual meekness seemed to slip from her shoulders like a blown scarf. She was on her feet; her poor little body, her bare knuckled hands bravely defying
80 the strapping hulk before her.

"Looka heah, Sykes, you done gone too fur. Ah been married to you fur fifteen years, and Ah been takin' in washin' for fifteen years. Sweat, sweat, sweat! Work and sweat, cry and sweat, pray and sweat!"
85 "What's that got to do with me?" he asked brutally.

"What's it got to do with you, Sykes? Mah tub of suds is filled yo' belly with vittles more times than yo' hands is filled it. Mah sweat is done paid for this house and Ah reckon Ah kin keep on sweatin' in it."
90 She seized the iron skillet from the stove and struck a defensive pose, which act surprised him greatly, coming from her. It cowed him and he did not strike her as he usually did.

21. The purpose of the passage is to

    A) emphasize the harsh reality of being a wash woman.
    B) demonstrate the literary effectiveness of dialect.
    C) show the severity of an abusive relationship.
    D) indicate racial tensions in a relationship.

22. It can be inferred from the use of the word "mournful" in the second paragraph that

    A) Delia worries about the whereabouts of her husband.
    B) Delia has a difficult life.
    C) Delia is concerned about her pony and carriage.
    D) Delia is a religious woman.

23. The incident with the "bull whip" demonstrates

    A) Delia's inordinate fear of snakes.
    B) Sykes' distorted sense of humor.
    C) Sykes' callous disrespect of his wife's feelings.
    D) the necessity of certain tools needed for driving a pony and carriage.

24. Which choice provides the best evidence for the answer to the previous question?

    A) Lines 17-21 ("Just then … move")
    B) Lines 21-22 ("Then she … drove")
    C) Lines 29-33 ("Course Ah … you")
    D) Lines 36-38 (" 'Nother thing … whip")

25. The main rhetorical effect of lines 55-56 (Delia … further") illustrates

    A) Delia's work ethic.
    B) Delia's resolve to remain calm.
    C) the weight of Delia's suffering.
    D) Delia's poor posture.

26. Sykes thinks his wife only pretends to be pious because she

    A) is religious.
    B) washes white people's clothes.
    C) sings, whoops and shouts on Sunday.
    D) works on the Sabbath.

27. Which choice provides the best evidence for the answer to the previous question?

    A) Lines 39-43 ("You sho … house")
    B) Lines 44-51 ("He picked … things")
    C) Lines 59-64 ("He snorted … Sabbath")
    D) Lines 72-74 ("Ah don't … house")

28. Lines 65 and 66 ("He stepped … room") symbolically suggest Sykes'

    A) utter aversion of Delia.
    B) dislike of his wife's work.
    C) frustration with religion.
    D) hatred of white people.

29. The phrase "to boot" as used in line 76 most probably means

    A) to foot.
    B) with force.
    C) for certain.
    D) also.

30. The word "cowed" as used in the final paragraph most likely means

    A) calmed.
    B) amused.
    C) stunned.
    D) intimidated.

Questions 31 - 41 are based on the following passage and supplementary material.

<u>Myo-fascial Release:</u> *This essay is from a blog from a well-known alternative therapist, Devin Ronaldson.*

I practice Myofascial release, specifically the John Barnes Method. It's a unique, profound, and transformative style of hands on therapy. It's an "advanced" form of bodywork, requiring patience,
5 sensitivity, and a combination of firmness and gentleness.
 To understand myofascial release, you have to understand what exactly fascia is. Fascia connects and surrounds every cell of the body. It wraps around every
10 muscle fiber, muscle, tendon, bone, and organ. Fascia is the tissue that holds everything together. Without it, our bodies would not be able to stand. Contrary to what most people think, our bones don't actually hold us up. If you took away the muscles and fascia, the bones would fall to
15 the floor in a pile. The pull from the fascia connected to the bones is what holds us upright, similar to the mast of a ship, which needs cables on each side to keep it from falling.
 When you work directly with the fascia, big changes
20 happen. Pain goes away. The body is brought into alignment. A sense of freedom and motion return to the body. One might seek this work for a variety of reasons: chronic pain, lack of range of motion, poor posture, painful scars, etc.
25 Fascia plays by its own rules. The job of fascia is to hold everything together; if it's not engaged the right way, it doesn't lengthen. The general rule is that fascia starts to release after two minutes of traction. That's when the release STARTS, but a full release can take
30 significantly longer. When is the last time you held a stretch for more than a couple minutes? Even advanced yogis rarely hold a stretch for more than five or ten minutes. By holding a limb or individual muscle in traction for a prolonged time, the very structure of the
35 body softens and lengthens. How each person perceives the work varies. I've worked on people who have "passed out" during the session, entering a state somewhere between waking and sleep. Then, there have been times (often with older injuries) when most of the session is
40 spent hovering right below the pain tolerance.
 From my end, it gets a little weird sometimes. There is a "taffy pull" feeling when fascia is gradually elongating. Oddly, what I feel and see doesn't match up. For example: I'm pulling on an arm. There is a feeling
45 that the arm lengthened 6 inches over the course of a couple of minutes. I feel it, the person whose arm is being pulled feels it, but not much has visually happened. When learning, we were advised not to look directly at what we were doing, because dissonance between what
50 is felt and what is seen can be confusing.
 Fascia doesn't respond to many types of work. Myofascial release is specifically good for conditions that have not responded to therapy. You have pain; maybe you've had it for a long time. You iced it, nothing.
55 You went to the PT, got some massage, got acupuncture and herbs– nothing. You stretched the tightness, strengthened the weakness, and tried to find the emotional root of the pain. Nothing. If that's the case, then the problem lies in your fascia.
60 The structure of the body really is quite finicky. Don't engage it enough; it doesn't lengthen. Pull it too much, and the body pulls back. To get anything done, you have to stay in the sweet spot, for a long time. The challenge is that the sweet spot is always changing, and the
65 myofascial therapist has to make micro-adjustments to keep up. As the slack is taken up, the effect of the pull can be quite distant from where the hands are. I have experienced pulling someone's arm above his head, and his telling me he feels it in his knee. The area the pain
70 manifests is often not the source of the problem. By engaging the fascia and locating the trigger point, it becomes possible to track and release restrictions on the fly even if it leads far away from the area of the pain.
 Which is good. It means that it's possible to figure out
75 the problem with one's hands, by listening, by using intuition. If you tell a doctor that your foot hurts, the search for the cause of the pain will generally start and finish in your foot. A myofascial therapist engaging your foot into gentle traction can trace the pattern of
80 restriction to where it originates, possibly quite far from the foot. The greater the sensitivity of the therapist, the better his ability to find and release restrictions. And since there is no ceiling on how sensitive a person can be, the potential for healing is limitless.
85 Since fascia is the foundation of our structure, of our movement and our posture, it is a good place to look for answers to our problems. Fascia is always adapting to the stresses we put on it. Faulty posture or injuries cause it to shift, which in turn makes the new posture seem
90 permanent. The fascia will hold us in whatever position makes sense at the time. During an injury, scar tissue is necessary to hold things together. The goal of myofascial release is to show the body that the old pattern isn't useful anymore.

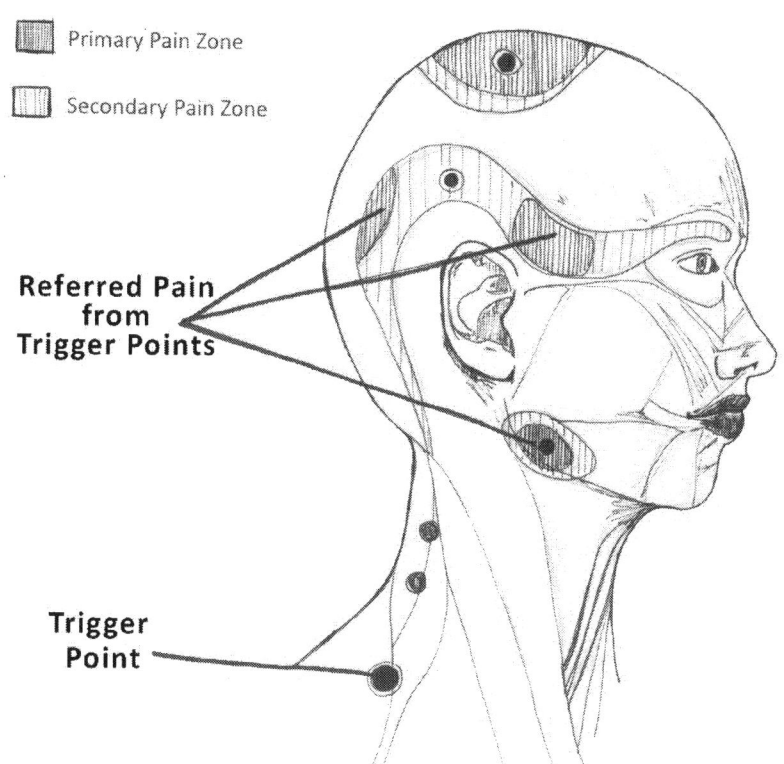

31. The purpose of the passage is to:

    A) to define the term myofascial.
    B) to indicate how myofascial release is superior to all other treatments.
    C) to give the reader insight into how myofascial release works.
    (D) to explain the medical factors of myofascial release.

32. Why does the author mention "the mast of a ship" in lines 16-17?

    A) to explain how the different parts of the body are connected.
    B) to offer a theory of alignment.
    C) to illustrate the relationship of bones and muscles to fascia.
    D) to provide background information on human anatomy.

33. In line 49, "dissonance" most nearly means

    A) similarity.
    B) dysfunction.
    C) disparity.
    D) disorder.

34. It can reasonably be inferred from the passage that a myofascial release

    A) is a subtle, complicated process.
    B) can be learned through an on-line course.
    C) is a course taken in medical school.
    D) is performed by consistent, regimented steps.

35. Which choice provides the best evidence for the answer to the previous question?

    A) Lines 19-22 ("When you ... body")
    B) Lines 25-27 ("Fascia plays ... lengthen")
    C) Lines 35-40 ("How each ... tolerance")
    D) Lines 60-73 ("The structure ... pain")

36. According to the passage, fascia is

    A) muscle.
    B) an organ.
    C) the tissue that surrounds virtually every part of the body.
    D) a combination of ligaments, muscles and cartilage.

37. Which choice provides the best evidence for the answer to the previous question?

    A) Lines 1-6 ("I practice ... gentleness")
    B) Lines 8-10 ("Fascia connects ... organ")
    C) Lines 25-27 ("Fascia plays ... lengthen")
    D) Lines 85-92 ("Since fascia ... together")

38. The main rhetorical effect of lines 48-50 is to

    A) demonstrate how far the arm can stretch.
    B) stress the importance of visual recognition.
    C) suggest that the fascia doesn't always respond to stimulus.
    D) illustrate the inconsistency between sight and touch.

39. As used in line 60, "finicky" most nearly means

    A) flexible.
    B) affable.
    C) demanding.
    D) permissive.

40. The author would probably agree with all of the following EXCEPT:

    A) doctors seldom look outside the immediate area of complaint for the source of the problem.
    B) fascia is the foundation of our structure, movement and posture.
    C) people react differently to myofascial treatments.
    D) myofascial release should be used only as a last resort after other treatments have failed.

41. The relationship between lines 69-73 ("The area ... pain") and the figure serves to

    A) summarize the basic tenets of myofascial release.
    B) demonstrate the concept of fascia restrictions.
    C) reinforce the idea that the area of pain is not necessarily the source.
    D) provide examples of micro-adjustments during myofascial release.

Questions 42 - 52 are based on the following passages.

Compare and contrast the first essay written by a modern philosopher, with the following excerpt from Jonathan Swift's Gulliver's Travels, written in 1726.

Passage 1

Today, there is tremendous debate as to who a parent is, and who should be in charge of raising the child. What with in vitro fertilization and anonymous donors on the physical end and blended families, single parents,
5 grandparents and same sex parents raising children on the social end, it has become far from clear what defines a parent. Plato posited that children should be reared by the state as it was too important a job to leave up to individuals. He also felt it fairer that all children receive
10 equal education and treatment in general. He said the rich and powerful would not want to do this, but it was their responsibility to do so. He saw women and men as equals intellectually and therefore saw no reason that both women and men could not raise children for the
15 state. So, even then society had begun to question what a parent's role is in raising children even if fortunately, they did not actually carry out the wishes of their leading philosopher. Today, in most cultures, we believe it is not only the obligation, but the right of a parent to raise his
20 or her own children. So often though, the "parent' is a grandparent, step-mom or dad, uncle or aunt or gay couple. Among the rich, it is often a "nanny" because both parents are professionals or in many cases not disposed towards the daily chores of raising children.
25 Thus far, social scientists have not been able to determine who the "best" parent would be, but Plato's strange ideal has not made any serious breakthrough in our thinking.

Passage 2

"For since the conjunction of male and female is
30 founded upon the great law of nature, the Lilliputians will have it that men and women are joined together by the motives of concupiscence, for which reason they will never allow that a child is under obligation to a father for begetting him, or from his mother for bringing him into
35 the world, since their thoughts in these encounters were otherwise employed. Thus, they feel that parents are the last of all others to be trusted with the education of their own children. Therefore, they have in every town public nurseries, where all parents are obliged to send their
40 infants of both sexes to be reared and educated when they come to the age of twenty moons. They have certain professors well skilled in preparing children for such a condition of life that well befits the rank of their parents and their own capacities and inclinations ...... Their
45 parents are suffered to see them only twice a year; the visit is not to last above an hour. They are allowed to kiss the child at meeting and parting, but a professor, who always stands by on these occasions, will not suffer them to whisper or use any fondling expressions, or bring any
50 presents of toys, sweetmeats and the like."

42. Which statement is addressed in both passages

   A) That men and women are equally good at child rearing
   B) That it is unclear who a parent is in many cases
   C) That it is uncertain who the best parents are
   D) That birth parents are not necessarily the best ones to raise their own children

43. What is the difference in tone of the two passages?

   A) categorical … explanatory
   B) informational … dogmatic
   C) judgmental …speculative
   D) historical … authoritative

44. As used in line 7, "posited" most nearly means

   A) put forth
   B) denied
   C) demanded
   D) objected

45. What is the attitude of the author of Passage 1 towards the effectiveness of Plato's ideas on raising children?

   A) dubious
   B) supportive
   C) shocked
   D) indifferent

46. Which choice provides the best evidence for the answer to the previous question?

    A) Lines 7-9 ("Plato posited … individuals")
    B) Lines 10-12 ("He said … so")
    C) Lines 12-15 ("He saw … state")
    D) Lines 15-18 ("So, even … philosopher")

47. The author of passage 1 would most likely agree with which of the following?

    A) The rich are not kindly disposed towards raising their children.
    B) Modern society has blurred the lines of parenting.
    C) Plato insisted that children should be treated as adults.
    D) Today, parents are the last ones to be trusted with their children's upbringing.

48. Which choice provides the best evidence for the answer to the previous question?

    A) Lines 1-7 ("Today, there … parent")
    B) Lines 7-15 ("Plato posited … state")
    C) Lines 18-20 ("Today, in … children")
    D) Lines 22-24 ("Among the … children")

49. Which of the following most nearly means "concupiscence" in line 32 of the second essay?

    A) desire
    B) morality
    C) love of children
    D) civic pride

50. The main rhetorical effect of lines 29-36 is to

    A) emphasize the moral obligations of a mother and father.
    B) point out the obligation of children to their parents.
    C) suggest that men and women are not thinking about children when mating.
    D) encourage parents to have jobs before they think of raising children.

51. The word suffer(ed) as used in lines 45 and 48 most nearly means

    A) tolerate pain
    B) punish
    C) permit
    D) prohibit

52. The most obvious contrast in the two passages is:

    A) editorial… literary
    B) philosophical… journalistic
    C) satirical… expository
    D) sociological…persuasive

Explanations

1. **A. being at one with the thing you are doing.** This is the answer because it is reinforced throughout the passage. B and C are really the opposite since the passage points out that both are counterproductive. D certainly seems helpful, but it is never developed in the passage.

2. **B. Lines 14-17 ("It is … disappears").** This is the answer because it is "a magical state where everything is working together." How else could we achieve this? A acknowledges a barrier to getting into the zone, but does not show how to get into it; C mentions things that help to get one ready for the zone, but does not deal with the essential aspect; D does not indicate how one can get into the zone.

3. **C. the physics of being in the zone.** Everything in this passage and particularly in paragraph 4 deals with how being in the zone is accomplished. A, chance, is not considered and B is too specific; D is not developed at all.

4. **A. Lines 7-11 ("Read had...trajectory, etc.").** A is the answer as it details specific physical actions. None of the others even begin to do this and thus do not support the answer.

5. **D. hyperbole.** This is our answer because he compares it to all the things "in heaven and earth" and that's pretty much everything. Hyperbole, which we remember from our charts in math is an exaggerated curve and in literature is any gross exaggeration. A must be an example of a concept being given human characteristics and that is not present here; there is no irony or metaphor present

6. **A. everyday.** We want a word that means daily or regular. Everyday fits the bill. B is the opposite meaning of what we want; C indicates someone getting paid for something and there is no indication of that here; D, favorite, has nothing to do with our answer.

7. **B. educate the reader about an elevated level of unconscious effort.** At almost every turn the author is attempting to define for us and educate us about an "elevated level of unconscious effort." A is incorrect because even though he does cite some amazing athletic feats, those are just examples to make his point; C specific steps are never mentioned; D although we might be able to infer why many of us never achieve getting into the zone, it is never specifically dealt with in the passage.

8. **D. upbeat.** In every paragraph we sense a high level of excitement. This author not only knows what he is talking about, but is very upbeat about the phenomenon; A is incorrect because at no moment is he attempting to provoke the reader; B poignant means deeply felt in that it brings out strong emotions in us and almost brings us to tears. There is none of that here at all; C is not acceptable because there are no practical steps towards achieving this zone.

9. **D. One does not need speed, strength and power to be effective.** The author constantly makes the point that even those lacking these traits can still get into the zone; A, B, and C are time honored adages, but they have nothing to do with what the author is developing in this passage.

10. **C. lessens.** We all know that this ability must lessen with age in most people. He has made the point that those who have developed this ability through many years of practice do not see it diminish all that much, but for most athletes there certainly is a lessening of this ability; A, embolden means to make stronger and bolder and that is the opposite of what we want here; B, incorporate means to embody and that is not what is asked for; D, succumb, means to give into but we could not replace "wane" with this and get the meaning we intend.

11. **C. discuss the many benefits of Title IX since its inception.** Virtually every paragraph extols the benefits of Title IX. A and B are not acceptable because of the words all and only. Remember that these exclusive words make that answer very improbable. D is not good as the passage never goes into any reasons that men had for or against this ruling

12. **B. productive.** This is our answer as she has produced the most goals in history. C, sneaky, and D, artistic, certainly do not work; A, amazing, looks good, but is not specific enough.

13. **C. Allusions to literature.** We see one reference to a political figure, many stats and plenty of examples from sports.

14. **C. that women tennis players get paid the same as men.** This is certainly an incredible situation given the huge discrepancy in basketball salaries.

15. **D. It has enriched society by giving it women who are more fully realized as individuals.** This theme is repeated throughout the last three paragraphs of the essay.

16. **D. Lines 60-70 ("Just as ... levels").** This paragraph spells out the many reasons Title IX has enhanced women's lives.

17. **B. accustomed to.** This is clearly best here. Sometimes it is actually helpful to take any word that you think might possibly work and read it in place of the original word. That should be enough to clinch it for you. Try not to look at the choices until you have come up with a word or your own. Then, take your chosen word back to the sentence and read it in context to make sure it works.

18. **A. enthusiastic.** Although it is certainly objective, there is a strong level of enthusiasm for Title IX throughout this passage.

19. **C. Female participation has shown the greatest increase in high school.** This is the best answer because it can be substantiated from the table. Choices A and B are not accurate, and there is no evidence to support choice D.

20. **B. Title IX has benefited both men and women.** This is the best answer because the table clearly shows an increase in male participation. Also, the author emphasizes this idea in the last sentence of the passage.

21. **C. show the severity of an abusive relationship.** Let's look at the evidence: the callous practical joke, the brutal things Sykes says to Delia, his threats and the clear implication in the last line of how Sykes has hit his wife many times in the past. All are examples of a long-standing, abusive relationship.

22. **B. Delia has a difficult life.** After reading the explanation for the answer to question one, need I say more?

23. **C. Sykes' callous disrespect of his wife's feelings.** This is the best answer because of the awful way this brute treats his wife from the beginning to the end of the passage. While it is true that Delia has a phobia for snakes and that Sykes does have a perverse sense of humor, the best answer is C. Choice D doesn't really figure into the mix.

24. **C. Lines 29-33 ("Course Ah … you").** This is the best answer because in these lines Sykes states that he really doesn't care how much his insensitive joke frightens his wife. The other quotes don't address Sykes' callous attitude as clearly.

25. **C. the weight of Delia's suffering.** Having to put up with a bully for a husband and loads of wash, Delia suffers her way through life. This can be seen and almost "felt" when her "shoulders sagged." The other choices are obviously inappropriate, although choice D gave me a laugh.

26. **D. works on the Sabbath.** A hypocrite is someone who pretends to be pious without really being so. Since the fourth commandment states that no work should be done on the Sabbath, Sykes refers to his wife as a hypocrite because she washes clothes on Sunday. (Ironically, the money Delia receives for her work pays for the house Sykes lives in and the food he eats.) Choice A is not the best answer because of the word "pretends." You might be tempted to pick choice B, but because it doesn't include the phrase "on the Sabbath," it is incorrect. The singing whooping and shouting are all part of the Sunday service, so that answer is out.

27. **C. Lines 59-64 ("He snorted … Sabbath").** This is the best answer because in these lines Sykes labels his wife a "hypocrite." This is so clearly what the reader is looking for that there is really no reason to explain any further.

28. **D. hatred of white people.** Sykes has already made his feelings about white people known to the reader on lines 41-43 when he says, "Ah done tole you time and time again to keep them white folks' clothes outa dis house." So, when he steps on the "whitest" clothes, he is making a racial statement to be sure. All of the other answers are true, but the symbolism isn't there.

29. **D. also.** We should be able to figure this out from the context of the sentence: "… Ah'll throw 'em out (the clothes) **and** put my fist upside yo' head to boot (also). Notice the emphasis on the conjunction "and." The other choices don't make sense.

30. **D. intimidated.** When Delia picked up the iron skillet (frying pan) as if to hit her husband, Sykes was understandably surprised and frightened. He must have been; he didn't hit her as he usually did, right? "Calmed" is not the right word here. He certainly was not amused! He might have been "stunned," but because Delia is brandishing the skillet, "intimidated" is better.

31. **C. to give the reader insight into how myofascial release works.** This is the best answer because from the very first sentence of the passage to the last, the author is explaining the process of myofascial release. Choice A is too narrow, while choice B is to extreme. Choice D is incorrect because "medical factors" were not discussed. (Remember that the process of elimination can be your best friend on all parts of this test including and especially the reading comprehension questions.)

32. **C. to illustrate the relationship of bones and muscles to fascia.** This is the best answer because this relationship is clearly shown in lines 10-18. Choice A is too specific; it leaves too much unsaid about the release process. The same can be said for choice B. Choice D is incorrect because the reader is not presented with very much background information on human anatomy.

33. **C. disparity.** This is the best answer because "dissonance" as used here means "difference," which is the same as "disparity." Choice A "similarity" is the opposite meaning of what we need. Choice B "disfunction" and choice D "disorder" are synonymous with impairment, which is not the sense of what the author means.

34. **A. is a subtle, complicated process.** This is the best answer because the reader should be able to discern just this from reading paragraph eight. Choices B and C were never mentioned. The word "regimented" eliminates choice D as an answer.

35. **D. Lines 60-73 ("The structure ... pain").** We have already mentioned that the answer can be found in those lines. The other choices are inappropriate.

36. **C. the tissue that surrounds virtually every part of the body.** This idea is clearly expressed in paragraph two when the author states, "Fascia connects and surrounds every cell of the body." It can't get any clearer than that. Thank you! No need to clarify any further.

37. **B. Lines 8-10 ("Fascia connects ... organ").** This is the best answer because of the same reasons mentioned above.

38. **D. illustrate the inconsistency between sight and touch.** This is the best answer because of the word "dissonance," which suggests the inconsistency. Although stretching is part of the release process, we don't necessarily want to see how far the arm stretches. Ouch! So, choice A is thankfully out. The context of the paragraph clearly eliminates choice B. Choice C is never mentioned.

39. **C. demanding.** This is the best answer because the author makes the point that the body sometimes seems hard to please for the therapist, and "demanding" implies that meaning. Choices A, B, and D are all positive words, which are not needed here.

40. **D. myofascial release should be used only as a last resort after other treatments have failed.** This is the best answer for a couple of reasons. First, it's too absolute. (Answers that are too extreme are usually wrong.) Also, the practice of myofascial release is a potentially potent therapy that should be used any time, not just as a last resort. Choice A is incorrect because the author states in lines 77-79, "If you tell a doctor that your foot hurts, the search for the cause of pain will generally start and finish in your foot." Choice B is wrong because the author mentions this in the second paragraph. Remember the "mast." Lines 35 and 36 eliminate choice C.

41. **C. reinforce the idea that the area of pain is not necessarily the source.** This is the best answer because it says so in the referenced lines and also is reinforced in the diagram. In the figure, the trigger point is below the area of the pain.

42. D. That birth parents are not necessarily the best ones to raise their own children. This is the best answer because this issue is brought up in both Passage 1 with Plato and in Passage 2 with the Lilliputians. Check it out. Choices A, B, and C are mentioned in Passage 1, but not in Passage 2.

43. B. informational ... dogmatic. This is the best answer because both words are appropriate. Certainly, Passage 1 is instructive, while Passage 2 is absolute. As for choice A, one might be able to argue that Passage 1 is "categorical," or clearly expressed, however, the second word, "explanatory," doesn't fit. Both words in choice C are inapt. Although Plato is mentioned in Passage 1, the passage is not really "historical." So, choice D is out.

44. A. put forth. This is the best answer because Plato assumed or thought it was reasonable to think "that children should be reared by the state," which is what "put forth" means. Plato did not deny, demand or object to this.

45. A. dubious. This is the best answer because the author states that society **"fortunately"** did **not** "carry out the wishes of their leading philosopher" (Plato). Choice B is too positive, while choice C is too strong. The answer "indifferent" is almost always incorrect. Why would an author be indifferent about what he or she is writing about?

46. D. Lines 15-18 ("So, even ... philosopher"). These are the lines stated above in the answer to question 45. All of the other choices are inappropriate.

47. B. Modern society has blurred the lines of parenting. This is the best choice because this is the main idea that is stated in the first or topic sentence of the passage. The other answers miss the point.

48. A. Lines 1-7 ("Today, there ... parent"). This is the best answer because of the reason stated above. Obviously, the other choices are inappropriate.

49. A. desire. This is the best choice because of context. It is the only answer that makes any sense. Take another look, if you are still puzzled. Ahh!

50. C. suggest that men and women are not thinking about children when mating. As in so many reading passages, many of the questions are related. This is a case in point. The "desire" mentioned in the explanation above is exactly what the author is alluding to when he states, "since their thoughts in these encounters were otherwise employed." Choice A contains the word "moral," which discounts it as an answer. Since the author is speaking about the obligations of the parents, not the other way around, choice B is out. Choice D is silly.

51. C. permit. This is the best answer because in both cases the meaning of the word is positive. It's true. Plug in "permit" and see how it fits. All of the other choices are negative, and, therefore, incorrect.

52. A. editorial ... literary. This is the best choice because both words successfully capture the tone of the two passages. Passage 1 is informational and opinionated, while the literary work *Gulliver's Travels* is referenced in Passage 2. In choice B, the word "journalistic" makes it incorrect. In choice C, both words are inapt; the word "persuasive" in choice D is not the meaning the author suggests.

Reading Test 2

65 MINUTES, 52 QUESTIONS

DIRECTIONS

Each passage or pair of passages below is followed by a number of questions. After reading each passage or pair, choose the best answer to each question based on what is stated or implied in the passage or passages and in any accompanying graphics (such as a table or graph).

Questions 1 - 11 are based on the following passage.

This passage is taken from a short story published in 1922 about a father meeting his seventy-year-old son.

   Mr. Button's eyes followed her pointing finger, and this is what he saw. Wrapped in a voluminous white blanket, and partly crammed into one of the cribs, there sat an old man apparently about seventy years of age. His
5 sparse hair was almost white, and from his chin dripped a long smoke-colored beard, which waved absurdly back and forth, fanned by the breeze coming in at the window. He looked up at Mr. Button with dim, faded eyes in which lurked a puzzled question.
10   "Am I mad?" thundered Mr. Button, his terror resolving into rage. "Is this some ghastly hospital joke?"
   "It doesn't seem like a joke to us," replied the nurse severely. "And I don't know whether you're mad or not—but that is most certainly your child."
15   The cool perspiration redoubled on Mr. Button's forehead. He closed his eyes, and then, opening them, looked again. There was no mistake—he was gazing at a man of threescore and ten—a baby of threescore and ten, a baby whose feet hung over the sides of the crib in
20 which it was reposing.
   The old man looked placidly from one to the other for a moment, and then suddenly spoke in a cracked and ancient voice. "Are you my father?" he demanded.
   Mr. Button and the nurse started violently.
25   "Because if you are," went on the old man querulously, "I wish you'd get me out of this place—or, at least, get them to put a comfortable rocker in here."

   "Where in God's name did you come from? Who are you?" burst out Mr. Button frantically.
30   "I can't tell you exactly who I am," replied the querulous whine, "because I've only been born a few hours—but my last name is certainly Button."
   "You lie! You're an impostor!"
   The old man turned wearily to the nurse. "Nice way to
35 welcome a new-born child," he complained in a weak voice. "Tell him he's wrong, why don't you?"
   "You're wrong. Mr. Button," said the nurse severely. "This is your child, and you'll have to make the best of it. We're going to ask you to take him home with you as
40 soon as possible—sometime to-day."
   "Home?" repeated Mr. Button incredulously.
   "Yes, we can't have him here. We really can't, you know?"
   "I'm right glad of it," whined the old man. "This is a
45 fine place to keep a youngster of quiet tastes. With all this yelling and howling, I haven't been able to get a wink of sleep. I asked for something to eat"—here his voice rose to a shrill note of protest—"and they brought me a bottle of milk!"
50   Mr. Button sank down upon a chair near his son and concealed his face in his hands. "My heavens!" he murmured, in an ecstasy of horror. "What will people say? What must I do?"
   "You'll have to take him home," insisted the nurse—
55 "immediately!"
   A grotesque picture formed itself with dreadful clarity before the eyes of the tortured man—a picture of himself walking through the crowded streets of the city with this appalling apparition stalking by his side. "I can't. I can't,"
60 he moaned.

1. In line 9, "lurked" most nearly means

   A) stalked.
   B) merged with.
   C) waited hidden.
   D) relished eagerly.

2. Mr. Button's initial reaction upon seeing his son was

   A) fear.
   B) curiosity.
   C) anxiety.
   D) anger.

3. The first paragraph focuses primarily on

   A) Mr. Button's reaction.
   B) a description of the nursery.
   C) the white, sterile atmosphere.
   D) a description of the "baby."

4. The word that best describes the old man in lines 15-20 is

   A) sleeping.
   B) annoyed.
   C) uncomfortable.
   D) curious.

5. It can reasonably be inferred from the passage that both the nurse and Mr. Button are startled when they

   A) first see his son.
   B) hear the old man speak.
   C) initially realize that the old man is Mr. Button's son.
   D) comprehend the incongruity of the situation.

6. Which choice provides the best evidence for the answer to the previous question?

   A) Lines 1-9 ("Mr. Button's eyes … question")
   B) Lines 10-14 ("Am I … child")
   C) Lines 21-24 ("The old …violently")
   D) Lines 37-43 ("You're wrong … know")

7. As used in line 26, "querulously" most nearly means

   A) questioningly.
   B) complainingly.
   C) affably.
   D) forlornly.

8. Mr. Button's questions on lines 28-29 indicate his

   A) nervousness.
   B) incredulity.
   C) scorn.
   D) impatience.

9. The old man's tone in lines 34-35 is

   A) confused.
   B) surly.
   C) sarcastic.
   D) ambivalent

10. Which of the following best describes the relationship between Mr. Button and his son?

    A) Mr. Button is incredulous while his son is unhappy.
    B) The son is tired while Mr. Button is excited.
    C) Both Mr. Button and his son are curious about their situation.
    D) Mr. Button is horrified while his son is indifferent.

11. Which choice provides the best evidence for the answer to the previous question?

    A) Lines 10-11 ("Am I ... joke")
    B) Lines 15-20 ("The cool ... reposing")
    C) Lines 28-31 ("Where in ... you")
    D) Lines 44-52 (I'm right ... horror")

Questions 12 - 21 are based on the following passage and supplementary material.

In March of 2013, Mayor Michael R. Bloomberg commemorated 10 years of NYC311, the nation's largest and most comprehensive government information and services center. NYC311 is available 24 hours a day, 7 days a week in nearly 180 languages and now serves more than 60,000 customers filing 7,700 daily requests via phone, online and text message. Since its launch, it has received more than 158 million calls and has been a clearinghouse for all things New York City government, providing information on more than 4,000 topics, routing details to the appropriate City agencies and providing customers with service request numbers for use in tracking the progress of their inquiry. In doing so, it has helped increase the accessibility and responsiveness of City agencies, allowing them to better focus on the key public services they provide. In addition, it has served as a paradigm for non-emergency government service delivery operations, hosting hundreds of delegations from dozens of countries and many major cities in the United States while they designed their own 311 operations.

Before Mayor Bloomberg established the 311 call center, the city relied on approximately 35 agency help lines as well as the Mayor's Action Center to handle complaints and questions from residents and visitors. If you were living in New York City in 2002 and woke up to a freezing apartment, or if you could not drive to work because someone had parked across your driveway, or if your neighbor's dog had been barking for hours and you wanted to report it, what would you do? You could pick up the phone book only to find some 16 pages of listings for city agencies. That's right - 16 pages! Back in 2001, when Bloomberg was a mayoral candidate, he, himself, ran into the same problem. As the story goes, he was walking with his aides when he spied a leaking fire hydrant. When he asked the members of his group what agency would one contact to remedy the problem, one of his aides told him the responsible agency was the DEP. Bloomberg was surprised because he had taken it for granted that it would be the fire department. It seemed the logical choice. How would one know which agency to call, he wondered. On returning to his office he picked up the phone book and was faced with the same 16 pages of city agencies. That's when he got the idea of having one central number to call for all non - emergency government service, which he made part of his campaign platform. Today, this procedure is much easier and streamlined. Virtually all of these agency call lines and the action center have now been folded into 311. Since its inception in March 2003, the number of calls received each year has grown significantly from 1.2 million in year 2003 to 22.8 million in 2012.

Among the top ten inquires received in 2012 were noise complaints, requests for bus or subway information, and parking violation ticket assistance. Certain types of calls are seasonal. In the summer months there are more calls made about where senior citizens can go to escape the heat and the Summer Youth Employment Program. In the winter months the number of complaints about lack of heat or hot water is higher. Not surprisingly, quality of life complaints such as blocked driveways are year - round phenomena.

You can imagine that there would be some strange calls as well. Paul J. Cosgrove, the commissioner of the Department of Information Technology and Telecommunications has been quoted saying, "You know, when you receive 40,000 calls a day, you're bound to get a few questions that don't always align with any service the City of New York provides. We've received calls from people wondering who won 'American Idol,' or what the daily lottery numbers were. We've had people ask us why pets can't be claimed on income tax returns and how many planets there are. My personal favorite is the call we received by someone asking how to boil a chicken."

To date, NYC311 has received more than 158 million total calls since inception, 85 percent of which were answered in 30 seconds or less. The average speed of answer for all calls has been 22 seconds, with the average 311 call lasting 218 seconds or 3.6 minutes.

Rank/Service Group	# of Calls	% of all 311 Calls
1 Noise Complaint	2,595,494	1.68
2 Heat Complaint - Inadequate Heat	2,065,835	1.34
3 Bus and Subway Information	1,999,063	1.30
4 Landlord Maintenance Complaint	1,689,908	1.10
5 Find a Police Precinct or Police Service Area	1,269,275	0.82
6 Plan Examiner Appointment	1,158,577	0.75
7 Refuse/Freon Removal Scheduling	1,120,398	0.73
8 Garbage or Recycling Collection Inquiry	1,111,157	0.72
9 Parking Violation - Ticket Assistance	1,042,381	0.68
10 Service Request Status	1,019,390	0.66

Visits to 311Online, launched in 2009, total nearly 7 million and more than 300,000 text sessions have been supported since 2011.

More people have used NYC311 in the last 10 years than attended every single home game of every New York pro sports team – and the U.S. Open – during those 10 years put together.

12. The passage most strongly suggests that the most significant factor about the NYC311 number is

    A) the huge number of calls serviced.
    B) the large amount of useful information provided.
    C) the extraordinary number of resolved complaints.
    D) the simplicity of the system.

13. Which choice provides the best evidence for the answer to the previous question?

    A) Lines 1-7 ("In March ... message")
    B) Lines 7-13 ("Since its ... inquiry")
    C) Lines 47-49 ("Today, this ... 311")
    D) Lines 84-87 ("More people ... together")

14. As used in line 17, "paradigm" most nearly means

    A) system.
    B) model.
    C) precedent.
    D) portal.

15. It can reasonably be inferred from the passage that before the establishment of NYC311 that

    A) there was no method of dealing with non-emergency calls.
    B) very few calls were made to city agencies.
    C) people used the 911 number for non-emergency requests.
    D) contacting the correct city agency presented a problem to callers.

16. Which choice provides the best evidence for the answer to the previous question?

    A) Lines 4-7 ("NYC311 is ... message")
    B) Lines 25-32 ("If you ... pages!")
    C) Lines 50-52 ("Since its ... 2012")
    D) Lines 76-80 ("To date ... minutes")

17. The anecdote about mayoral candidate Bloomberg (lines 32-47) serves to

    A) illustrate the need for one central number for all non-emergency calls.
    B) call attention to the problem of faulty fire hydrants.
    C) suggest that Bloomberg was the first person to come up with the idea of NYC311.
    D) provide an explanation for why Bloomberg made the establishment of NYC311 an essential component of his campaign platform.

18. As used in line 48, "streamlined" most nearly means

    A) maintained.
    B) convoluted.
    C) simplified.
    D) resistant.

19. All of the following would be appropriate reasons to call 311 EXCEPT

    A) alternate side parking.
    B) Potholes.
    C) movie times.
    D) graffiti.

20. The tone of the passage can best be described as

    A) humorous.
    B) historical.
    C) anecdotal.
    D) informative.

21. It can reasonably be inferred from the chart that

    A) the majority of calls are complaints of one kind or another.
    B) a large number of people use public transportation.
    C) the smallest percentage of calls are information requests.
    D) some calls are refused.

Questions 22 - 31 are based on the following passage.

In this passage taken from a 2012 book by Jim Frazier titled, Maurice Duruflé: The Man and His Music, the author reflects on a famous French composer and his most popular composition.

One of the most popular musical compositions of the twenty-first century is the *Requiem* composed by the French organist Maurice Duruflé. Written for choir, soloists, orchestra and organ, the work was designed to
5 be performed at Roman Catholic funerals. But the most remarkable feature of the work is that it was commissioned by the Nazi government during the Second World War. In the late 1930s, before the war began, grave economic conditions in France had become
10 a serious concern of the government. In an effort to ameliorate the situation, the government began awarding commissions to composers in 1938, providing them the incentive to work. It was a radical notion to institute such a program in response to the worsening economy.
15 After invading France in 1940 the Nazis established their headquarters in the town of Vichy, in central France, and continued the program of commissions established by the former French government, eventually awarding a total of eighty-one commissions throughout
20 the war to composers needing financial incentive to produce new works. Because the Vichy government took music seriously for its propaganda value, it generally restricted its awards to composers who upheld the conservative, anti-modernist, and pro-Catholic
25 sentiments of the regime.
Because of his adherence to these values, Maurice Duruflé was commissioned in 1941 to write a symphonic poem for 10,000 francs. The monetary award for the commission was not intended to be generous, but was
30 large enough to free Duruflé to devote his time to the composition for as long as needed, roughly six to twelve months.
But it took Duruflé six years to complete his work, far longer than was anticipated by the authorities. The war
35 had ended by then, and a new French government had replaced the Vichy regime. In 1948 Duruflé was paid 30,000 francs, instead of the contracted 10,000 francs, for writing what proved to be the greatest composition of his career, and one of the greatest choral works of the
40 twentieth century.
No one knows how Duruflé may have justified writing a requiem instead of a symphonic poem. A symphonic poem is an orchestral work having non-musical themes that are either poetic, literary, pictorial,
45 or realistic, but not, as a rule, religious. It usually consists of a single movement, in contrast to a multi-movement symphony. A nine-movement choral work with religious purposes, like Duruflé's *Requiem*, simply does not fit the description of a symphonic poem.
50 Whether the German authorities even cared could well be doubted. And if the fee Duruflé received for the commission was modest, the royalties from the *Requiem* eventually proved considerable.
For about sixty years after the war the commission
55 was a well-kept secret, no doubt because some people in France would have considered it "proof" that Duruflé was a collaborator with the Germans. It wasn't until about 2001 that a handful of music historians in France and North America learned the truth of the commission,
60 and in 2002 it became public knowledge.
Though Duruflé's loyalties were never really in doubt, many people in France denied the truth of the commission, including some of Duruflé's family members, colleagues, friends, and devotees. But there is
65 no evidence suggesting that, after the war, the commissions were construed as awards for collaborating with Vichy. It cannot be inferred that by accepting his commission Duruflé was a sympathizer with the Vichy regime. Like countless others in occupied France, he was
70 simply trying to make an honest living under desperate economic and political circumstances.
The *Requiem* had its premiere on French radio in 1947 and its popularity among choral ensembles in North America and France has grown over the years, despite its
75 unique and controversial origins.

22. The main idea of the passage is to

    A) demonstrate how music transcends time.
    B) explain the differences between a symphonic poem and a requiem.
    C) explain the reasons the Vichy government awarded incentives to composers.
    D) illustrate how both the motives of a composer and subject of his composition were considered questionable.

23. As used in line 11, "ameliorate" most nearly means

    A) amend.
    B) worsen.
    C) tolerate.
    D) abide.

24. All of the following are themes found in a symphonic poem EXCEPT

    A) poetry.
    B) funerals.
    C) pictures.
    D) literature.

25. A requiem, on the other hand, includes all of these elements EXCEPT

    A) choir.
    B) single movement.
    C) religion.
    D) soloists.

26. According to the passage, the most extraordinary characteristic of the *Requiem* is that

    A) it took six years to complete.
    B) it has a religious theme.
    C) it was commissioned by the Nazi government.
    D) it is considered the greatest choral work of the 20th century.

27. Which choice provides the best evidence for the answer to the previous question?

    A) Lines 5-8 ("But the … War")
    B) Lines 33-34 (But it … authorities")
    C) Lines 41-53 ("No one … considerable")
    D) Lines 72-75 ("The *Requiem* … origins")

28. The author suggests that Duruflé's commission was a well-kept secret for some 60 years because

    A) of the desperate economic and political circumstances.
    B) even though Duruflé's commission was meager, later royalties proved substantial.
    C) Duruflé might have been seen as corroborating with the new French government.
    D) Duruflé may have been looked upon as sympathetic to the Vichy regime.

29. Which choice provides the best evidence for the answer to the previous question?

    A) Lines 8-10 ("In the … government")
    B) Lines 26-28 ("Because of … francs")
    C) Lines 57-60 ("It wasn't … knowledge")
    D) Lines 64-71 ("But there …circumstances")

30. As used in line 26, "adherence" most nearly means

    A) faithlessness.
    B) aversion.
    C) devotion.
    D) adoption.

31. The Nazi government continued to support the French government's policy of sponsoring composers mainly

    A) in response to a worsening economy.
    B) for propaganda value.
    C) to provide financial incentives for artists.
    D) in an attempt to ameliorate an already troublesome situation.

Questions 22 - 31 are based on the following passages.

The passages below discuss the perception of nineteenth century women. They are taken from a speech, which was an appeal for equal treatment of the sexes in the courts.

Passage 1

At Athens, an ancient apologue tells us, on the completion of the temple of Minerva, a statue of the goddess was wanted to occupy the crowning point of the edifice. Two of the greatest artists produced what each
5 deemed his masterpiece. One of these figures was the size of life, admirably designed, exquisitely finished, softly rounded, and beautifully refined. The other was of Amazonian stature, and so boldly chiseled that it looked more like masonry than sculpture. The eyes of all were
10 attracted by the first, and turned away in contempt from the second. That, therefore, was adopted, and the other rejected, almost with resentment, as though an insult had been offered to a discerning public. The favored statue was accordingly borne in triumph to the place for which
15 it was designed, in the presence of applauding thousands, but as it receded from their upturned eyes, all, all at once agaze upon it, the thunders of applause unaccountably died away- a general misgiving ran through every bosom-the mob themselves stood like statues, as silent
20 and as petrified, for as it slowly went up, and up the soft expression of those chiseled features, the delicate curves and outlines of the limbs and figure, became gradually fainter and fainter, and when at last it reached the place for which it was intended, it was a shapeless ball,
25 enveloped in mist. Of course, the idol of the hour was now clamored down as rationally as it had been cried up, and its dishonored rival, with no good will and no good looks on the part of the chagrined populace, was reared in its stead. As it ascended, the sharp angles faded away,
30 the rough points became smooth, the features full of expression, the whole figure radiant with majesty and beauty. The rude hewn mass, that before had scarcely appeared to bear even the human form, assumed at once the divinity that it represented, being so perfectly
35 proportioned to the dimensions of the building, and to the elevation on which it stood, that is seemed as though Pallas herself had alighted upon the pinnacle of the temple in person, to receive the homage of her worshippers.

Passage 2

40 The woman of the nineteenth century is the shapeless ball in the lofty position, which she was designed fully and nobly to fill. The place is not too high, too large, too sacred for woman, but the type that you have chosen is far too small for it. The woman we declare unto you is
45 the rude, misshapen, unpolished object of the successful artist. From your standpoint, you are absorbed with the defects alone. The true artist sees the harmony between the object and its destination. Man, the sculptor, has carved out his ideal, and applauding thousands welcome
50 his success. He has made a woman that from his low stand point looks fair and beautiful, a being without rights, or hopes, or fears but in him- neither noble, virtuous, nor independent. Where do we see, in Church or State, in school –house or at the fireside, the much
55 talked of moral power of woman? Like those Athenians, we have bowed down and worshiped in woman, beauty, grace, the exquisite proportions, the soft and beautifully rounded outline, her delicacy, her refinement, and silent helplessness- all well when she is viewed simply as an
60 object of sight, never to rise one foot from the dust from which she sprung. But if she is to be raised up to adorn a temple, or represent a divinity- if she is to fill the niche of wife and counselor to true and noble men, if she is to be the mother, the educator of a race of heroes or
65 martyrs, of a Napoleon, or a Jesus- then must the type of womanhood be on a larger scale than that yet carved by man.

32. The literary form of Passage 1 can best be described as a(n)

    A) anecdote.
    B) parable.
    C) allusion.
    D) paradox.

33. According to the author of passage 1 the two statues differed in all of the following ways EXCEPT

    A) size.
    B) shape.
    C) popularity.
    D) color.

34. In line 13, "discerning" most nearly means

    A) intelligent.
    B) insulted.
    C) curious.
    D) attractive.

35. It can be reasonably inferred that the mob mentioned on line 19

    A) were captivated at the sight of the statue.
    B) were suddenly disturbed by what they were seeing.
    C) felt affronted.
    D) became afraid.

36. The author of Passage 1 would probably agree that the "Amazonian" statue

    A) continued to embarrass the populace.
    B) was beautifully transformed by proportion and height.
    C) was angrily pulled down as fast as it had been raised.
    D) resembled a shapeless ball.

37. Which choice provides the best evidence for the answer to the previous question?

    A) Lines 9-10 ("The eyes … contempt")
    B) Lines 13-25 ("The favored … mist")
    C) Lines 25-29 ("Of course … stead")
    D) Lines 32-34 ("The rude … represented")

38. The narrator compares the woman of the nineteenth century to

    A) the delicately carved statue.
    B) a martyr.
    C) the Amazonian figure.
    D) a successful artist.

39. Which choice provides the best evidence for the answer to the previous question?

    A) Lines 40-42 ("The woman … fill")
    B) Lines 44-46 ("The woman … artist")
    C) Lines 47-53 ("The true … independent")
    D) Lines 61-67 ("But if … man")

40. The relationship between the two passages is best described as which of the following?

    A) Passage 1 criticizes the existence of a certain viewpoint whereas Passage 2 suggests that this viewpoint has merit.
    B) Passage 1 presents a mythical tale while Passage 2 provides a more modern application.
    C) Passage 1 describes what the two statues represent whereas Passage 2 disagrees with those interpretations.
    D) Passage 1 emphasizes the beauty of women while Passage 2 stresses the wisdom of women.

41. As used in line 62, "niche" most nearly means

    A) obligation.
    B) function.
    C) style.
    D) celebrity.

42. In both passages, the narrator seems to prefer

    A) "admirable design."
    B) Greek influences.
    C) "the rude, misshapen, unpolished object."
    D) grace and beauty.

Questions 43 - 52 are based on the following passage and supplementary material.

Transcript of President Barack Obama's speech at Georgetown University announcing his new climate change policy.

On Christmas Eve, 1968, the astronauts of Apollo 8 did a live broadcast from lunar orbit. And later that night, they took a photo that would change the way we see and think about our world.
⁵ It was an image of Earth—beautiful; breathtaking; a glowing marble of blue oceans, and green forests, and brown mountains brushed with white clouds, rising over the surface of the moon...
Even the astronauts were amazed. "It makes you ¹⁰ realize," Lovell would say, "just what you have back there on Earth."
And around the same time we began exploring space, scientists were studying changes taking place in the Earth's atmosphere. Now, scientists had known since the ¹⁵ 1800s that greenhouse gases like carbon dioxide trap heat, and that burning fossil fuels release those gases into the air. That wasn't news. But in the late 1950s, the National Weather Service began measuring the levels of carbon dioxide in our atmosphere, with the worry that ²⁰ rising levels might someday disrupt the fragile balance that makes our planet so hospitable. And what they've found, year after year, is that the levels of carbon pollution in our atmosphere have increased dramatically.
That science, accumulated and reviewed over decades, ²⁵ tells us that our planet is changing in ways that will have profound impacts on all of humankind.
The 12 warmest years in recorded history have all come in the last 15 years. Last year, temperatures in some areas of the ocean reached record highs, and ice in ³⁰ the Arctic shrank to its smallest size on record—faster than most models had predicted it would. These are facts.
Now, we know that no single weather event is caused solely by climate change. Droughts and fires and floods, they go back to ancient times. But we also know that in a ³⁵ world that's warmer than it used to be, all weather events are affected by a warming planet. The fact that sea level in New York, in New York Harbor, are now a foot higher than a century ago—that didn't cause Hurricane Sandy, but it certainly contributed to the destruction that ⁴⁰ left large parts of our mightiest city dark and underwater.
The potential impacts go beyond rising sea levels. Here at home, 2012 was the warmest year in our history. Midwest farms were parched by the worst drought since the Dust Bowl, and then drenched by the wettest spring ⁴⁵ on record. Western wildfires scorched an area larger than the state of Maryland. Just last week, a heat wave in Alaska shot temperatures into the 90s.
And we know that the costs of these events can be measured in lost lives and lost livelihoods, lost homes, ⁵⁰ lost businesses, hundreds of billions of dollars in emergency services and disaster relief. In fact, those who are already feeling the effects of climate change don't have time to deny it—they're busy dealing with it. Firefighters are braving longer wildfire seasons, and ⁵⁵ states and federal governments have to figure out how to budget for that. I had to sit on a meeting with the Department of Interior and Agriculture and some of the rest of my team just to figure out how we're going to pay for more and more expensive fire seasons.
⁶⁰ Farmers see crops wilted one year, washed away the next; and the higher food prices get passed on to you, the American consumer. Mountain communities worry about what smaller snow packs will mean for tourism—and then, families at the bottom of the mountains wonder ⁶⁵ what it will mean for their drinking water. Americans across the country are already paying the price of inaction in insurance premiums, state and local taxes, and the costs of rebuilding and disaster relief.
So the question is not whether we need to act. The ⁷⁰ overwhelming judgment of science—of chemistry and physics and millions of measurements—has put all that to rest. Ninety-seven percent of scientists, including, by the way, some who originally disputed the data, have now put that to rest. They've acknowledged the planet is ⁷⁵ warming and human activity is contributing to it.
So the question now is whether we will have the courage to act before it's too late. And how we answer will have a profound impact on the world that we leave behind not just to you, but to your children and to your ⁸⁰ grandchildren.
As a President, as a father, and as an American, I'm here to say we need to act.

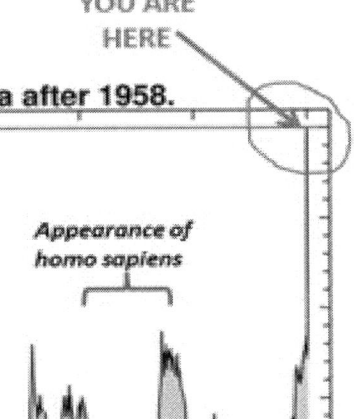

43. The passage primarily focuses on which of the following aspects of climate-change?

    A) The tremendous cost involved
    B) The preponderance of scientific evidence
    C) The disturbing news of rising levels of carbon dioxide
    D) The serious threat it imposes to the future of humanity

44. Which choice provides the best evidence for the answer to the previous question?

    A) Lines 17-23 ("But in ... dramatically")
    B) Lines 24-31 ("That science ... facts")
    C) Lines 48-51 ("And we ... relief")
    D) Lines 76-80 ("So the ... grandchildren")

45. Obama's tone is best described as

    A) desperate.
    B) cynical.
    C) concerned.
    D) informative.

46. As used in line 7, "brushed" most nearly means

    A) skimmed.
    B) painted.
    C) swept.
    D) covered.

47. The main rhetorical effect of lines 5-11 is to

   A) emphasize the fragility of our planet.
   B) provide a view of earth never seen before.
   C) highlight how our perspective of earth was changed.
   D) convey the majesty of our planet.

48. It can reasonably be inferred from the passage that

   A) the effects of climate change can be altered.
   B) most scientists disagree with the President's assessment.
   C) hurricane Sandy was a direct result of global warming.
   D) the last 12 years have been the warmest in history.

49. Which choice provides the best evidence for the answer to the previous question?

   A) Lines 24-28 ("That science … years")
   B) Lines 34-40 ("But we … underwater")
   C) Lines 69-72 ("The overwhelming … rest")
   D) Lines 76-80 ("So the … grandchildren")

50. As used in line 72, the phrase "to rest" most nearly means

   A) sleep or quiet relaxation.
   B) cessation of work, exertion or activity.
   C) what is left over or remaining.
   D) condition of being resolved.

51. The President refers to Hurricane Sandy (lines 38 and 39) primarily in order to

   A) highlight the storm's destructive impact.
   B) illustrate an example of nature's wrath.
   C) support the idea that severe weather is influenced by global warming.
   D) suggest that weather events such as hurricanes, droughts, floods, and fires go back to ancient times.

52. Which one of the following claims is supported by both the passage and the graph?

   A) 2012 was the warmest year in human history.
   B) Human activity has contributed to the rising levels of carbon pollution in our atmosphere.
   C) Carbon dioxide levels caused Hurricane Sandy.
   D) Carbon dioxide levels have been measured and studied for several decades.

Explanations

1. **C. waited hidden.** This is your best choice. Obviously, the old man has as many questions, as does his dad. None of the other choices make sense.

2. **A. fear.** This is the best answer because it says so on lines 10-11: "…his terror resolving into rage." Anger, yes, but first the terror or fear. Choices B and C are not strong enough.

3. **D. a description of the "baby."** Let's back into this answer using the process of elimination. A is out because we don't see Mr. Button's reaction until the second paragraph. Choice B is easy to eliminate because there is no evidence to support it. As for choice C, while the word "white" is mentioned twice, it doesn't apply to the sterile atmosphere, only to the color of the blanket and the beard.

4. **C. uncomfortable.** This is an interesting question because it is so typically "SATish." Although the reader is directed to lines 15-20, he or she must also look for clues that may come before and after those lines; sometimes, more lines than you would think. So, in addition to the description in those lines of the old man's feet hanging over the sides of the crib, the word "crammed" was used in line 3. Later in lines 26-27 we hear the old man say, "I wish … you get them to put a comfortable rocker here." Now you should be able to discern why C is the best answer.

5. **B. hear the old man speak.** This is the best answer because both Mr. Button and the nurse clearly did not expect to hear this "baby" speak because when he does, they both "start violently." Choice A is out because they first see the old man at different times. Choices C and D are really the same, aren't they? So, it couldn't be one because it could then be the other.

6. **C. Lines 21-24 ("The old … violently").** We have seen this to be best answer in the rationale to the previous question.

7. **B. complainingly.** This is the best answer because the old man is, as we have already determined, clearly uncomfortable.

8. **B. incredulity.** Here, again, the student is asked to discern the best answer from several good ones. While Mr. Button is certainly A nervous and C scornful, he is much more disbelieving. Wouldn't you be under the circumstances?

9. **C. sarcastic.** Just listen to the old man's reaction, in line 33, when his own father rejects him shouting, "You lie! You're an imposter!," the old man says to the nurse, "Nice way to welcome a new-born child." Now that humor is soo dry, it actually drips with sarcasm. Lol.

10. **A. Mr. Button is incredulous while his son is unhappy.** We have seen this answer to be true in some of the previous questions and rationales. Choices B and C are too weak, while in choice D you might argue that Mr. Button is horrified, but his son is hardly indifferent.

11. **C. Lines 28-31 ("Where in… you").** This is the best answer because it captures Mr. Button's incredulity when he shouts, "Who are you?" and his son's unhappiness when he querulously "whines."

12. **D. the simplicity of the system.** This is the best answer because before the advent of NYC311, trying to find the right agency to call in reference to a complaint or information was problematic to say the least. 16 PAGES! Choices A and B are true according to the passage and the chart, but the most significant factor is the simplicity of using just one central number for all non-emergency calls. Choice C is probably accurate as well, but misses the point for the same reason.

13. **C. Lines 47-49 ("Today, this ... 311").** This is the best answer because in these lines it clearly states that now the procedure for making non-emergency calls is easier and streamlined. The other line choices do not apply.

14. **B. model.** If you look back at the passage at how the word is used in context you will see that "hundreds of delegations from dozens of countries and many major cities" came to New York City to learn how to set up a similar system for themselves. Isn't that how a model is used? NYC311 is indeed a "system," but that's not how the word "paradigm" is employed here. There really was no precedent for NYC311, that's what makes it so effective and unique. I suppose the number is a sort of figurative doorway of sorts, but that's a stretch. (Apologies to all those Sci-fi and fantasy fans out there.)

15. **D. contacting the correct city agency presented a problem to callers.** This is the best answer because of those infamous 16 pages. Choice A is incorrect because there indeed was a method of dealing with non-emergency calls, but it was cumbersome. Choices B and C might be true, but were never mentioned.

16. **B. Lines 25-32 ("If you ... pages!").** This is the best answer because it refers to the problem of so many pages of government agencies. The other line choices are inappropriate.

17. **A. illustrate the need for one central number for all non-emergency calls.** This is the best answer because this is the main idea of the anecdote as well as the entire passage. At this juncture that should be clear. Choice B is silly. Choice C may be true, but who knows? Choice D is too extreme because of the word "essential."

18. **C. simplified.** This is the best answer because the word "streamlined" means trimmed: reduced to essentials or lacking anything extra. The reader should definitely understand the word to be positive, so choices B and D are out. Choice A doesn't make sense in this context.

19. **C. movie times.** Don't forget we are looking for a wrong answer choice, and inquiring about the starting time of your favorite film is rather trivial and inapt. All of the other answers are valid reasons to call NYC311.

20. **D. informative.** This is the best answer because this passage is simply chocked full of good information about this number system. While there are some funny moments (Boiling chicken?); those are few. The same can be said for B and C as well. Elements of both are present, but not present enough.

21. **B. a large number of people use public transportation.** This is the best answer because 1,999,063 is a lot of people! Choice A is incorrect. The majority of calls are not complaints. Count the numbers. C is also incorrect. As a matter of fact, it is the largest percentage. While some calls are about refuse, no calls are refused as I recall.

22. **D. illustrate how both the motives of a composer and the subject of his compositions were considered questionable.** This is the best answer because it does mention in the passage that some might have questioned the composer's loyalties. As for the work itself, the excessive length of time it took to complete and reason he chose to write a requiem instead of a symphonic poem, make it questionable. Choice A is not the best answer because although music does indeed transcend time, this idea is not evident in the passage. Choices B and C are mentioned, however, it should be clear that this passage is specifically about Duruflé and his *Requiem*.

23. **A. amend.** The idea of awarding commissions was to financially support composers and in this way improve their monetary situation in a suffering economy. Choice B is wrong because, although the awards might have been construed as radical, they were clearly meant to help. Choices C and D are synonymous, so it can't be either.

24. **B. funerals.** This is an easy one. The author gives us the definition of a symphonic poem in lines 43-46. Just use the process of elimination.

25. **B. single movement.** This is the best answer because it says so in lines 46-48.

26. **C. it was commissioned by the Nazi government.** It says so in the third sentence of the first paragraph. Choice A is incorrect because although it took Duruflé six years rather than the one, consider the quality of his work. While religion is a characteristic of the *Requiem*, it's not an extraordinary one. Choice D is too extreme.

27. **A. Lines 5-8 ("But the ... War").** This is the best answer because it is clearly stated in these lines. Check it out. No need for further explanation.

28. **D. Duruflé may have been looked upon as sympathetic to the Vichy regime.** Be careful here. You might want to choose C, but this answer contains the phrase, "the new French government." There would be nothing wrong with that; it was the possibility of corroborating with the Vichy or Nazi regime that might have been an issue, and that is why D is the correct answer. Choices A and B really don't apply.

29. **D. Lines 64-71 ("But there ... circumstances").** The best answers to these questions are not difficult. You do have to read the lines given and that can be time consuming and tedious, but the upside is that these questions are easy, as is this one. Look and see.

30. **C. devotion.** Well, we should be able to figure out that we need a positive word because Durufle did, indeed, receive the commission. That eliminates choices A and B. Choice D just doesn't fit.

31. **B. for propaganda value.** Here, we are faced with a choice of really just two, B or C. The Nazi government was providing financial incentives for the composers, but it was only a means to an end – propaganda.

32. **B. parable.** This is the best answer because this type of short, simple story contains a moral; it teaches a lesson. An anecdote is just an entertaining story. An allusion is a literary reference and a paradox is a contradiction, both of which do not apply here.

33. **D. color.** Remember that the word **EXCEPT** tells us that we are looking for an incorrect answer. That being said, notice that choice A wouldn't work because the one sculpture was the "size of life," while the other was "Amazonian," or larger than life. Shape is not the best answer because the first statue was "exquisitely finished" and the latter looked more like "masonry." If you look back to lines 9-11, you will see why popularity is incorrect. So, the statues differed in size, shape and popularity, but not color.

34. **A. intelligent.** This is the best answer because the general consensus of the public was that their intelligence had been questioned. "I mean, really, do you think anyone with a brain would choose that 'rude hewn mass' over the beautiful and delicately carved sculpture?" You might be tempted to choose "insulted," but it was their intelligence that had been insulted. Also, wouldn't it be redundant to say "… as though an insult had been offered to an 'insulted' public." So, again, **intelligent** is the best choice.

35. **B. were suddenly disturbed by what they were seeing.** This is the best answer because the phrase "general misgiving" on line 18 supports this choice. Choice A is not the best answer because the word "captivated" suggests a positive attraction, which is not the case here. "Affronted" means insulted and we have ruled that out in the explanation of the previous question. Some students might choose answer D because the word "petrified" can mean afraid, but in this case the word means to become stiff like a statue.

36. **B. was beautifully transformed by proportion and height.** This is the best answer because this is an important part of the lesson of the story. Choice A is incorrect because of the word "continued." Choice C is wrong because it was the other way around. The first statue was pulled down. The same can be said for choice D. The "shapeless ball" refers to the first statue.

37. **D. Lines 32-34 ("The rude … represented").** This is the best answer because the "rude hewn mass" is the "Amazonian" figure that has become beautifully transformed. The other choices are inappropriate.

38. **A. the delicately carved statue.** This is the best answer because the narrator says so in the first and second sentences of Passage 2. If man sees woman as "too small" then it follows that he underestimates her because he sees her only for her exquisite, statuesque beauty. Woman is subservient because she is not appreciated for her nobility, virtue or independence. Choice B and D are incorrect because the martyrs and artists, in this case, would be men. Answer C is opposite of what is intended.

39. **A. Lines 40-42 ("The woman … fill").** By this time you should have figured out that the "shapeless ball" refers to the first statue; the one that the author is comparing to 19c women. The other choices don't apply to this comparison.

40. **B. Passage 1 presents a mythical tale, while Passage 2 provides a more modern application.** This is the best answer because a myth is traditionally an ancient and fictitious tale, which is true of Passage 1; on the other hand, Passage 2 is referring to 19c women, which is long removed from ancient Greece. Choice A is contradictory and, therefore, eliminated. In choice C the author doesn't exactly "describe" what the statues represent, and if he did, Passage 2 would **not** disagree with them. Passage 1 does not stress the beauty of women, so choice D is out.

41. **B. function.** Here you might want to substitute a word of your own for "niche." The word "role" comes to mind and would work well here. Isn't "role" a synonym for "function." The only other choice that comes close would be "obligation," but a woman would not necessarily be required to fill those functions, although she may want to do so.

42. **C. "the rude, misshapen, unpolished object."** This is the best answer because it is explicitly stated in both passages. At this juncture, you should be aware that this is so, simply from having answered the previous questions. The other choices are not true of both passages.

43. **D. The serious threat it imposes to the future of humanity.** This is the best answer because this really is the reason for the President's initiative on climate-change. At the conclusion of his speech he highlights his worry about the damaging effects of climate-change not only as President, but also as a father, i.e. he's worried for future generations. All of the other answer choices are true, but they are not the main idea.

44. **D. Lines 76-80 ("So the ... grandchildren").** This is the best answer because it is in these lines that Obama expresses his concerns about how our actions now on climate-change will impact future generations, and this is the central message of his speech. The other quotes address related issues, but, again not the main one.

45. **C. concerned.** While one might make an argument for D "informative," the better answer is the President's fear, worries or concern about the future of our planet. Choice A "desperate" is too strong and B "cynical" is almost the opposite of his tone.

46. **A. skimmed.** All of us I would venture have seen this picture of the planet earth as it appears from space: the beautiful blue of the ocean, the green and brown of North and South America, the wisps of white clouds. Can you see it? Focus on those wisps of white. They appear to be **lightly brushed** or **skimmed** on the surface. Choice B is too broad for this picture; it suggests **covering,** which is not the meaning. For the same reason choice D is out. Choice C "swept" means more like to move swiftly and steadily, and, again, this is not what the author meant.

47. **C. highlight how our perspective of earth was changed.** This is the best answer because the passage says so. Thank you! I love questions like this one where the answer is directly stated as it is here on lines 3 and 4, "... a photo that would change the way we see and think about our world." In choice A, the word "fragility" is the wrong word. Choices B and D are absolutely true and for that reason might be tempting, however, they don't have the above quote to support them. And for that reason, they are out.

48. **A. The effects of climate change can be altered.** This is the best answer because why else would President Obama announce his new climate change policy? Choice B is not the best answer because most scientists do agree with the President. Hurricane Sandy was not a direct result of global warming. Obama stated in lines 32-33, "that no single weather event is caused solely by climate change." Choice D is incorrect because it is stated in lines 27-28, "The 12 warmest years in recorded history have come in the last 15 years." That's not the same thing as saying **the last** 12 years have been the warmest in history. Close, but no cigar!

49. **D. Lines 76 -80 ("So the ... grandchildren").** This is the best answer because the President states that if we act (take measures to reduce carbon pollution} it will have a "profound impact on the world..."

50. **D. condition of being resolved.** All of the choices are meanings for the word rest. (One time I looked up the word "bear" in the dictionary and found about 20 different meanings!) So what we have to do to figure this out is to go to the passage to see how the word is used in context. Let's go back and take another look. Ahh! See what I mean.

51. **C. support the idea that severe weather is influenced by global warming.** This is the best answer because in lines 34-36, it states, "... we also know that in a world that's warmer than it used to be, all weather events are affected by a warming planet." The President here uses Hurricane Sandy as an example of just that. It was a destructive storm, in part, because global warming had raised the sea levels. For this reason, both A and B are out. Although Choice D makes a good point, it's not the one we are looking for here.

52. **B. Human activity has contributed to the rising levels of carbon pollution in our atmosphere.** This is the best answer because it is stated in lines 21-23 of the passage and shown on the far right of the graph. There is no evidence to support choices A or C. Choice D is a true statement and supported by both the passage and the graph, but it does not address the central issue of climate-change.

Reading Test 3

65 MINUTES, 52 QUESTIONS

DIRECTIONS

Each passage or pair of passages below is followed by a number of questions. After reading each passage or pair, choose the best answer to each question based on what is stated or implied in the passage or passages and in any accompanying graphics (such as a table or graph).

Questions 1 - 10 are based on the following passage.

The following excerpt is adapted from Nathaniel Hawthorne's "The Minister's Black Veil."

THE SEXTON stood in the porch of Milford meeting-house, pulling busily at the bell-rope. The old people of the village came stooping along the street. Children, with bright faces, tripped merrily beside their
5 parents, or mimicked a graver gait, in the conscious dignity of their Sunday clothes. Spruce bachelors looked sidelong at the pretty maidens, and fancied that the Sabbath sunshine made them prettier than on week days. When the throng had mostly streamed into the porch, the
10 sexton began to toll the bell, keeping his eye on the Reverend Mr. Hooper's door. The first glimpse of the clergyman's figure was the signal for the bell to cease its summons.
  "But what has good Parson Hooper got upon his
15 face?" cried the sexton in astonishment.
  All within hearing immediately turned about, and beheld the semblance of Mr. Hooper, pacing slowly his meditative way towards the meeting-house. With one accord they started, expressing more wonder than if
20 some strange minister were coming to dust the cushions of Mr. Hooper's pulpit.
  "Are you sure it is our parson?" inquired Goodman Gray of the sexton.
  The cause of so much amazement may appear
25 sufficiently slight. Mr. Hooper, a gentlemanly person, of about thirty, though still a bachelor, was dressed with due clerical neatness, as if a careful wife had starched his band, and brushed the weekly dust from his Sunday's garb. There was but one thing remarkable in his
30 appearance. Swathed about his forehead, and hanging down over his face, so low as to be shaken by his breath, Mr. Hooper had on a black veil. On a nearer view it seemed to consist of two folds of crape, which entirely concealed his features, except the mouth and chin, but
35 probably did not intercept his sight, further than to give a darkened aspect to all living and inanimate things. With this gloomy shade before him, good Mr. Hooper walked onward, at a slow and quiet pace, stooping somewhat, and looking on the ground, as is customary with
40 abstracted men, yet nodding kindly to those of his parishioners who still waited on the meeting-house steps. But so wonder-struck were they that his greeting hardly met with a return.
  "I can't really feel as if good Mr. Hooper's face was
45 behind that piece of crape," said the sexton.
  "I don't like it," muttered an old woman, as she hobbled into the meeting-house. "He has changed himself into something awful, only by hiding his face."
  "Our parson has gone mad!" cried Goodman Gray,
50 following him across the threshold.
  Such was the effect of this simple piece of crape, that more than one woman of delicate nerves was forced to leave the meeting-house. Yet perhaps the pale-faced congregation was almost as fearful a sight to the
55 minister, as his black veil to them.
  A rumor of some unaccountable phenomenon had preceded Mr. Hooper into the meeting-house, and set all the congregation astir.
  Mr. Hooper had the reputation of a good preacher, but
60 not an energetic one: he strove to win his people heavenward by mild, persuasive influences, rather than to drive them thither by the thunders of the Word. The homily that he now delivered was marked by the same characteristics of style and manner as the general series

65 of his pulpit oratory. But there was something, either in the sentiment of the discourse itself, or in the imagination of the auditors, which made it greatly the most powerful effort that they had ever heard from their pastor's lips. It was tinged, rather more darkly than usual,
70 with the gentle gloom of Mr. Hooper's temperament. The subject had reference to secret sin, and those sad mysteries that we hide from our nearest and dearest, and would fain conceal from our own consciousness, even forgetting that the Omniscient can detect them. A subtle
75 power was breathed into his words. Each member of the congregation, the most innocent girl, and the man of hardened breast, felt as if the preacher had crept upon them, behind his awful veil, and discovered their hoarded iniquity of deed or thought. Many spread their clasped
80 hands on their bosoms. There was nothing terrible in what Mr. Hooper said, at least, no violence; and yet, with every tremor of his melancholy voice, the hearers quaked. An unsought pathos came hand in hand with awe. So sensible were the audience of some unwonted
85 attribute in their minister, that they longed for a breath of wind to blow aside the veil, almost believing that a stranger's visage would be discovered, though the form, gesture, and voice were those of Mr. Hooper.

1. Which of the following best describes what happens in the story?

   A) Several characters suspect another character of illicit activities.
   B) One character questions his faith.
   C) Several characters criticize another character for his unusual behavior.
   D) Several disparate characters join as one congregation.

2. The main purpose of the first paragraph (lines 1-13) is to

   A) foreshadow future events.
   B) suggest a sense of unease.
   C) indicate the importance of the sexton's responsibilities.
   D) provide a contrast with the succeeding paragraphs.

3. The immediate response of the people of the town to the minister's black veil was

   A) surprise.
   B) disbelief.
   C) anger.
   D) fright.

4. Which choice provides the best evidence for the answer to the previous question?

   A) Lines 14-15 ("But what … astonishment")
   B) Lines 22-23 ("Are you … sexton")
   C) Lines 46-47 ("I don't … meeting-house")
   D) Lines 49-50 ("Our parson … threshold")

5. As used in the line 5, the word "graver" most nearly means

   A) solemn.
   B) joyful.
   C) earnest.
   D) favorable.

6. The minister's usual preaching style can best be considered

   A) persuasive.
   B) unremarkable.
   C) fiery.
   D) dramatic.

7. It can reasonably be assumed that the minister's black veil is likened to

   A) sunglasses.
   B) a Halloween mask.
   C) skeletons in the closet.
   D) a death bed.

8. Which choice provides the best evidence for the answer to the following question?

   A) Lines 32-36 ("On a ... things")
   B) Lines 46-48 ("I don't ... face")
   C) Lines 69-70 ("It was ... temperament")
   D) Lines 70-74 ("The subject ... them")

9. As used in line 66, "discourse" most nearly means

   A) sermon.
   B) dialog.
   C) feeling.
   D) plot.

10. Which choice is not supported by evidence from the passage?

    A) The minister has taken on a disturbing appearance.
    B) The minister is hiding some secret sin.
    C) The addition of the veil has made Hooper's preaching more interesting.
    D) There is a definite turn in how the townspeople perceive their minister.

Questions 11 - 21 are based on the following passages.

Passage One comments on an extended quote from Thoreau's Walden. *Passage two comments on the previous author's comments.*

Passage 1

"As I preferred some things to others, and especially valued my freedom, as I could fare hard and yet succeed well, I did not wish to spend my time in earning rich carpets or other fine furniture, or delicate cookery, or a
5 house in the Grecian or the Gothic style just yet. If there are any to whom it is no interruption to acquire these things, and who know how to use them when acquired, I relinquish to them the pursuit. In short, I am convinced, both by faith and experience, that to maintain one's self
10 on this earth is not a hardship but a pastime, if we will live simply and wisely. It is not necessary that a man should earn his living by the sweat of his brow, unless he sweats easier than I do." **Henry David Thoreau**

"Now, the one thing that is entirely fatal to leading
15 the simple life is the desire to stimulate the curiosity of others in the matter. Thoreau, who is by many regarded as the apostle of the simple life, is the most conspicuous example of this. He was a man of extremely simple tastes, it is true. He was deeply interested in the
20 contemplation of nature, and he loved to disembarrass himself of all the apparatus of life. It was really that he hated trouble more than anything in the world... He found that by working six weeks he could earn enough to allow him to live in a hut in the woods for the rest of the
25 year. But Thoreau was indolent rather than simple, and what spoiled his simplicity was that he was forever hoping that he would be observed and admired; he was forever peeping out of the corner of his eye to see if inquisitive strangers were hovering about to observe the
30 hermit at his contemplation." **Arthur C. Benson**

Passage 2

"Now this sort of criticism not only exhibits Mr. Benson as totally incapacitated by his academic "environment" for understanding the simple life, but convicts him of complete ignorance of the charm of
35 Thoreau's career. Is it believable that a man who was "forever hoping to be observed and admired" should have taken a course such as Thoreau took, which cut him off from all possibility of recognition during his lifetime—that of spending a great portion of his life in
40 solitary rambles, and entirely ignoring all the avenues that lead to what is known as "success?" Mr. Benson presumably imagines that the diaries in which Thoreau jotted down his thoughts were written with a view to

publication, but this was not the case; indeed, as Mr.
45 Sandborn has recently pointed out, "it was never
Thoreau's intent to print these Journals as they now
appear, still less as they were partially published by his
editor after 1876." When Thoreau died in 1862, a
practically unknown man, with only two of his books,
50 "The Week" and "Walden," published, nothing seemed
more certain than that he had deprived himself of all
likelihood of fame by his entire indifference to public
opinion; and if it was his desire to stimulate the curiosity
of his fellow-countrymen, he stultified himself
55 completely by taking the utmost pains to secure the
contrary result.

How far Mr. Benson is competent to discuss the
question of simplification may be judged from his
complaint that "it is almost true to say that the people
60 who are most in love with simplicity are often the most
complicated natures." I should say it is not "almost,"
but *wholly* true, and the reason is obvious. It is precisely
because the spiritual needs of mankind are so complex
that it is necessary to simplify our bodily needs, and
65 therefore the most complex natures, such as Shelley's
and Thoreau's, are those that have the strongest tendency
to simplification. "Plain living" and "high thinking" of
necessity go together. "Your physical wants," says
Shelley, "are few, whilst those of your mind and heart
70 cannot be numbed or described, from their multitude and
complication. To secure the gratification of the former,
you have made yourselves the bond slaves of each
other." This is, of course, the very corner-stone of the
whole principle of simplification; yet Mr. Benson has
75 overlooked it." **Henry Stevens Salt**

11. What does Thoreau mean by the "pursuit" in line 8 ?

    A) desire for material goods
    B) seeking of social acceptance
    C) yearning for fame
    D) accomplishments

12. Thoreau sees the houses "in the Grecian or Gothic style" as being

    A) expensive.
    B) imposing.
    C) austere.
    D) gratuitous.

13. As used in line 22, "trouble" most nearly means

    A) effort.
    B) police problems.
    C) interference.
    D) anxiety.

14. Benson pretty much characterizes Thoreau as a

    A) brilliant thinker.
    B) mystic.
    C) hermit.
    D) fake.

15. Which choice provides the best evidence to the answer in the previous question?

    A) Lines 14-16 ("Now the … matter")
    B) Lines 16-19 ("Thoreau, who … true")
    C) Lines 18-21 ("He was … life")
    D) Lines 25-30 ("But Thoreau … contemplation")

16. The tone of all three authors (Thoreau, Benson and Salt) is

    A) indifferent.
    B) instructive.
    C) irreverent.
    D) sardonic.

17. Salt disagrees with all of the following of Benson's reactions to Thoreau EXCEPT

    A) Benson sees him as lazy.
    B) Benson thinks Thoreau was just "posturing" and not really living the simple life.
    C) Benson thinks he did what he did just for publication.
    D) Benson saw Thoreau as a man of extremely simple tastes.

18. Salt mentions the Shelley quote to

    A) indicate why Thoreau was incapable of true solitude.
    B) argue that Thoreau was so complicated that he would never have enjoyed the simple life.
    C) imply that some people just cannot accept the simple life.
    D) suggest the essential relationship between plain living and complicated thinking.

19. Which three authors mentioned seem most closely aligned in their thinking on the relationship between the need for the simple life and a complex nature?

    A) Thoreau, Salt, Shelley
    B) Thoreau, Benson, Shelley
    C) Benson, Shelley, Salt
    D) Thoreau, Benson, Salt

20. Salt's response to "he (Thoreau) was forever hoping that he would be observed and admired" is

    A) agreement because Thoreau published Walden.
    B) disagreement because Thoreau did suffer peer pressure.
    C) surprise because Thoreau spent so many years in solitude and published just two books on the subject.
    D) that an academic scholar is never capable of understanding solitude.

21. Which of the following accurately describes the difference between the two commentators?

    A) Benson mentions far more details of Thoreau's life.
    B) Salt does not really look up to Thoreau.
    C) Salt feels that Thoreau had much purer motives for seeking the simple life than does Benson.
    D) Benson sees Thoreau as more the "apostle of the simple life" than does Salt.

Questions 22 - 31 are based on the following passage and supplementary material.

The following is taken from remarks made by President Barack Obama at the 2010 National Medal of the Arts and National Humanities Medal Ceremony.

The fact is that works of art, literature, works of history, they speak to our condition and they affirm our desire for something more and something better.
It was the writings of Thomas Paine that General
5 Washington ordered his men to read before crossing the Delaware. It was spirituals sung by slaves around a campfire that helped to keep hope alive. We can think of the protest songs that tell the story of the civil rights movement, the photographs from the Great Depression
10 that showed how folks were suffering, but also how they were striving.
Time and again, the tools of change, and of progress, of revolution, of ferment—they're not just pickaxes and hammers and screens and software, but they've also been
15 brushes and pens and cameras and guitars.
And the arts and the humanities help us through the hard times and they remind us of what make the good times worthwhile. After all, the goal doesn't always have to be so lofty. Sometimes, we just need a break, a chance
20 to laugh or escape from the moment.
So all of the individuals that we honor today are part of this tradition. We can point to their performances—on stage or on film—that we carry with us forever because we've been so moved. We can think of the novels that
25 have chronicled the American experience—from the streets of Newark to the courts of Alabama. How many young people have come to see the senseless cruelty of racism—and the importance of standing up for what's right—through the eyes of a girl named Scout? How
30 many young people have learned to think by reading the exploits of Portnoy and his complaints? (Laughter.)
We also remember the art that challenged our assumptions; the scholarship that brought us closer to the events of our history; the poetry that we loved—or at
35 least the poetry that we might recite to a girlfriend to seem deep. Of course, we still hum the great songs by the musicians in this room—songs that in many cases have been the soundtrack of our lives over decades.
And that's why I'm so proud to have this opportunity
40 to celebrate the contributions that all of you have made to our country. It's why we have to remember that our strength as a people runs deeper than our military might; it runs deeper than our GDP—it's also about our values and our ideals that each generation is called to uphold,
45 and that each artist helps us better understand.
And it's also about the capacity of the arts and the humanities to connect us to one another. In a nation as

big as ours, as diverse as ours, as full of debate and consternation as it sometimes is, what the people we
50 honor here today remind us of is that kernel of ourselves that connects to everyone else and allows us to get out of ourselves, to see through somebody else's eyes, to step in their shoes. And what more vital ingredient is there for our democracy than that?
55 In 1962, in the last months of his life, the poet Robert Frost was dispatched by President Kennedy to visit the Soviet Union. And it was a gesture of goodwill. Frost traveled and gave readings, filling venues all across Russia. What he really wanted to do, though, was have a
60 chance to talk to Khrushchev. Frost was a poet, but he was also a pretty tough guy.
It wasn't until the end of his trip that the meeting was arranged. And when they met, even though Frost was frail and sick, he decided he had to speak his mind to the
65 Soviet leader. And Frost stood up and he said, "A great nation makes great poetry." And then he told Khrushchev that he should reunite East and West Berlin. A great nation should make great poetry. Like so many artists and musicians and writers and poets before hi—
70 and so many that came after him—Robert Frost wasn't afraid to say his piece or speak truth to power. He wasn't afraid to tell what was on his mind. He wasn't held back by convention or what was considered normal or acceptable.
75 And that is an incredible power, an incredible resource. And we're seeing that power all across the world today. That's what challenges us. That's what pushes us to be better, to be more faithful to the sense of humanity that so often can be lost in the experiences of
80 our daily lives.
Pissarro once said, "Blessed are they who see beautiful things in humble places." That is the blessing of those that we honor here today, and we are blessed that they are able to share what they see and what they
85 hear and say.

22. The main purpose of the passage is to

A) discuss Frosts' legacy as our poet laureate.
B) discuss the effect of protest songs, pictures and the arts in general for moving the masses to change.
C) describe how the arts help to affirm who we are and to structure our dreams of who we can be.
D) demonstrate how the arts help us to relax and enjoy ourselves.

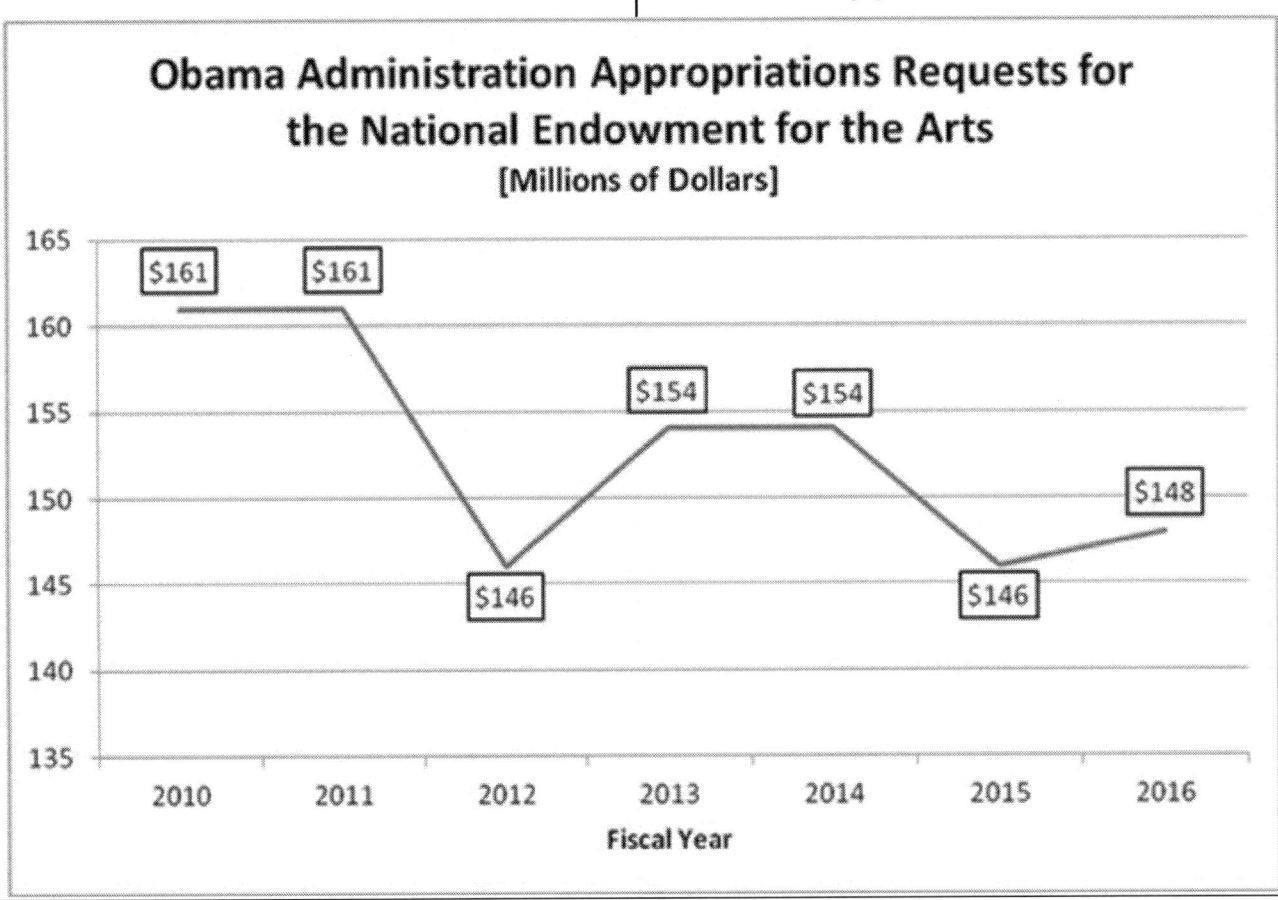

23. Which choice provides the best evidence for the answer to the previous question?

    A) Lines 1-3 ("The fact…better")
    B) Lines 4-6 ("It was…Delaware")
    C) Lines 16-20 ("And the…moment")
    D) Lines 55-74 ("In 1962…acceptable")

24. In lines 34-36 ("… the poetry….deep") the tone of the president is

    A) serious.
    B) profound.
    C) light-hearted.
    D) insightful.

25. As used in line 50, "kernel" most nearly means

    A) core.
    B) rank.
    C) modicum.
    D) plurality.

26. The main rhetorical effect of lines 62-67 is to

    A) emphasize the weak condition of Frost.
    B) stress the power of poetry.
    C) demonstrate Frost's courage to speak up.
    D) contrast the ideals of East and West Berlin.

27. As used in line 73, "convention" most nearly means

    A) constraints of society.
    B) legal regulations.
    C) political imperatives.
    D) bureaucracy.

28. The President would most likely agree that artists should

    A) abide by the dictates of society.
    B) confer with other artists before they finalize their work.
    C) speak out against injustice.
    D) help to lighten our daily load by their talents.

29. Which choice provides the best evidence for the answer to the previous question?

    A) Lines 4-6 ("It was … Delaware")
    B) Lines 12-15 ("Time and … guitars")
    C) Lines 21-24 ("So all … moved")
    D) Lines 46-54 ("And it's … that")

30. It can be inferred that Pissarro (line 81) is a(n)

    A) politician.
    B) artist.
    C) explorer.
    D) Soviet leader.

31. According to the chart, which of the following statements is true?

    A) The Obama administration's appropriation requests have continued to decline since 2010.
    B) The year 2012 saw an all-time low in appropriation requests.
    C) $161,000,000 is the most money ever requested by the Obama administration.
    D) The appropriations for the year 2017 will be greater than in 2016.

Questions 32 - 42 are based on the following passage.

The following passage, taken from an essay published in 1929, explores the theme of women and fiction.

When you asked me to speak about women and fiction I sat down ... and began to wonder what the words meant. They might mean women and what they are like; or they might mean women and the fiction that
5 they write; or they might mean women and the fiction that is written about them; or they might mean that somehow all three are inextricably mixed together and you want me to consider them in that light. But when I began to consider the subject in this last way, which
10 seemed the most interesting, I soon said that it had one fatal drawback. I should never be able to come to a conclusion. I should never be able to fulfill what is, I understand, the first duty of a lecturer – to hand you after an hour that – one cannot hope to tell the truth. One can
15 only show how one came to hold whatever one does hold. One can only give one's audience the chance of drawing its own conclusions as they observe the limitations, the prejudices, the idiosyncrasies of the speaker. Fiction here is likely to contain more truth than
20 fact. Therefore, I propose, making use of all the liberties and licenses of a novelist, to tell you the story of the two days that preceded my coming here – how, bowed down by the weight of the subject which you have laid upon my shoulders, I pondered it, and made it work in and out
25 of my daily life...

Here then was I (call me Mary Beton, Mary Seton, Mary Carmichael or by any name you please—it is not a matter of any importance) sitting on the banks of a river a week or two ago in fine October weather, lost in
30 thought. That collar I have spoken of, women and fiction, the need of coming to some conclusion on a subject that raises all sorts of prejudices and passions, bowed my head to the ground. To the right and left bushes of some sort, golden and crimson, glowed with
35 the colour, even it seemed burnt with the heat, of fire. On the further bank the willows wept in perpetual lamentation, their hair about their shoulders. The river reflected whatever it chose of sky and bridge and burning tree, and when the undergraduate had oared his boat
40 through the reflections they closed again, completely, as if he had never been. There one might have sat the clock round lost in thought. Thought—to call it by a prouder name than it deserved—had let its line down into the stream. It swayed, minute after minute, hither and thither
45 among the reflections and the weeds, letting the water lift it and sink it until—you know the little tug—the sudden conglomeration of an idea at the end of one's line: and then the cautious hauling of it in, and the careful laying of it out? Alas, laid on the grass how small, how
50 insignificant this thought of mine looked; the sort of fish that a good fisherman puts back into the water so that it may grow fatter and be one day worth cooking and eating. I will not trouble you with that thought now, though if you look carefully you may find it for
55 yourselves in the course of what I am going to say.

32. The first paragraph primarily serves to

    A) suggest how the task at hand might not be as simple as first thought.
    B) emphasize the impossibility of the proposed task.
    C) demonstrate how the weight of the topic was wearing on the speaker.
    D) imply that a lecturer's main concern is to his or her audience alone.

33. Which choice provides the best evidence for the answer to the previous question?

    A) Lines 1-3 ("When you ... meant")
    B) Lines 3-8 ("They might ... light")
    C) Lines 8-19 ("But when ... speaker")
    D) Lines 20-25 ("Therefore, I ... life")

34. The author of the passage mentions the three Mary's in lines 26-27 in order to

    A) reflect a multifaceted approach.
    B) emphasize the significance of the name.
    C) remind us of past women writers.
    D) underscore the insignificance of the narrator's identity.

35. The narrator is probably sitting on the bank of the river because

    A) she is absorbing the natural beauty of the scene.
    B) she enjoys fishing.
    C) she is reflecting on a subject.
    D) she is waiting for someone.

36. Which choice provides the best evidence for the answer to the previous question?

    A) Lines 26-30 ("Here then ... thought")
    B) Lines 33-39 ("To the ... tree")
    C) Lines 49-53 ("Alas, laid ... eating")
    D) Lines 53-55 ("I will ... say")

37. The word "collar" on line 30 suggests a

    A) connection.
    B) seizure.
    C) predicament.
    D) band.

38. The literary device used in lines 36-37 is a(n)

    A) simile.
    B) alliteration.
    C) personification.
    D) onomatopoeia.

39. The "Thought" mentioned in line 42 seems

    A) confused.
    B) premature.
    C) sophisticated.
    D) ponderous.

40. As used in line 47, "conglomeration" most nearly means

    A) dilution.
    B) enervation.
    C) coalescence.
    D) distraction.

41. The main rhetorical effect of lines 44-49 ("It swayed ... out") is that it

    A) implies a bothersome distraction.
    B) suggests a guilty conscience.
    C) indicates a fish's jerk on the line.
    D) indicates an abrupt knowledge of an idea.

42. It can be reasonably inferred from the passage that the author

    A) feels women authors to be superior to men.
    B) would rather be fishing than lecturing.
    C) is a writer herself.
    D) recognizes her responsibility to her.

Questions 43 - 52 are based on the following passage and supplementary material.

NASA and an international team of planetary scientists have found evidence in meteorites on Earth that indicates Mars has a distinct and global reservoir of water or ice near its surface. Since water is such a crucial
5 element to a planet having life, this is certainly an important piece of evidence.

Though controversy still surrounds the origin, abundance and history of water on Mars, this discovery helps resolve the question of where the "missing Martian
10 water" may have gone. Scientists continue to study the planet's historical record, trying to understand the apparent shift from an early wet and warm climate to today's dry and cool surface conditions.

The reservoir's existence also may be a key to
15 understanding climate history and the potential for life on Mars. The team's findings are reported in the journal Earth and Planetary Science Letters.

"There have been hints of a third planetary water reservoir in previous studies of Martian meteorites, but
20 our new data require the existence of a water or ice reservoir that also appears to have exchanged with a diverse set of Martian samples," said Tomohiro Usui of Tokyo Institute of Technology in Japan. "Until this study there was no direct evidence for this surface reservoir or
25 interaction of it with rocks that have landed on Earth from the surface of Mars."

Researchers from top institutes around the world have studied three Martian meteorites. The samples revealed water comprised of hydrogen atoms that have a
30 ratio of isotopes distinct from that found in water in the Red Planet's mantle and current atmosphere. Isotopes are atoms of the same element with differing numbers of neutrons.

While recent orbiter missions have confirmed the
35 presence of subsurface ice, and melting ground-ice is believed to have formed some geomorphologic features on Mars, this study used meteorites of different ages to show that significant ground water-ice may have existed relatively intact over time. This, of course, gives some
40 credence to the hypotheses of researchers such as Ann Vickery and Jay Melosh, who have maintained for years that the presence of streambeds on Mars are a strong indication that there was once life there. "There exists on
45 Mars a valley networks that look like terrestrial valley networks and don't look like any other kind of feature found anywhere else in the solar system" Vickery points out.

Researchers emphasize that the distinct hydrogen
50 isotopic signature of the water reservoir must be of sufficient size that it has not reached isotopic equilibrium with the atmosphere.

"The hydrogen isotopic composition of the current atmosphere could be fixed by a quasi-steady-state
55 process that involves rapid loss of hydrogen to space and the sublimation from a widespread ice layer," said coauthor John Jones, a JSC experimental petrologist.

Curiosity's observations in a lakebed, in an area called Mount Sharp, indicate Mars lost its water in a
60 gradual process over a significant period of time.

"In the absence of returned samples from Mars, this study emphasizes the importance of finding more Martian meteorites and continuing to study the ones we have with the ever-improving analytical techniques at

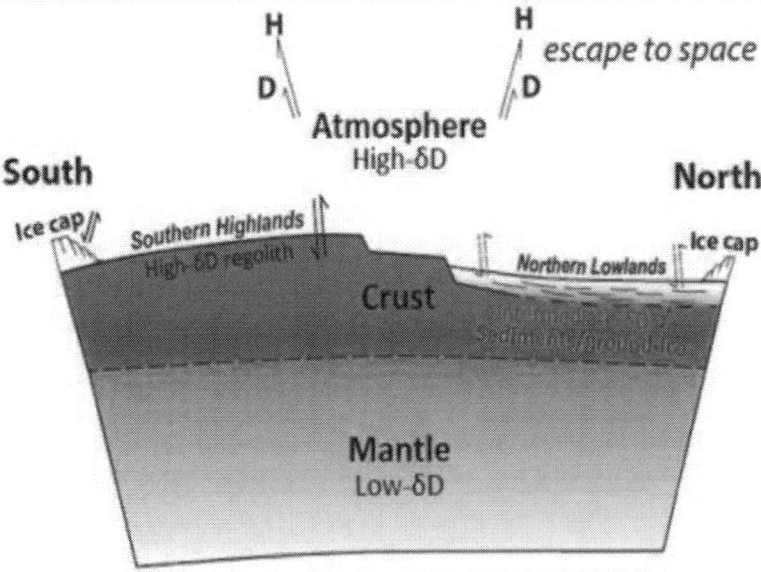

This illustration depicts Martian water reservoirs. Recent research provides evidence for the existence of a third reservoir that is intermediate in isotopic composition between the Red Planet's mantle and its current atmosphere. These results support the hypothesis that a buried cryosphere accounts for a large part of the initial water budget of Mars. Image Credit: NASA

our disposal," said co-author Conel Alexander, a
cosmochemist at the Carnegie Institution for Science.
   In this investigation, scientists compared water, other
volatile element concentrations and hydrogen isotopic
compositions of gases within the meteorites, which may
have formed as the rocks erupted to the surface of Mars
in ancient volcanic activity or by impact events that hit
the Martian surface, knocking them off the planet.
   "We examined two possibilities, that the signature for
the newly identified hydrogen reservoir either reflects
near surface ice interbedded with sediment or that it
reflects hydrated rock near the top of the Martian crust,"
said coauthor and JSC cosmochemist Justin Simon.
"Both are possible, but the fact that the measurements
with higher water concentrations appear uncorrelated
with the concentrations of some of the other measured
volatile elements, in particular chlorine, suggests the
hydrogen reservoir likely existed as ice."
   The information being gathered about Mars from
studies on Earth, and data being returned from a fleet of
robotic spacecraft and rovers on and around the Red
Planet, are paving the way for future human missions on
a journey to Mars in the 2030s. Perhaps then, we will
finally get an answer to the age old quandary about life
on Mars. We will certainly learn a lot more about the
closest planet to Earth with conditions that might have
allowed some form of life to exist.

43. The central idea of the passage is primarily concerned with

   A) how new discoveries may lead to an understanding of climate conditions on Mars.
   B) the importance of finding and studying more Martian meteorites.
   C) the new discovery of an additional water source on Mars.
   D) controversial evidence suggesting an abundance of water on Mars.

44. Which choice provides the best evidence for the answer to the previous question?

   A) Lines 1-4 ("NASA and ... surface")
   B) Lines 7-10 ("Though controversy ... gone")
   C) Lines 14-16 ("The reservoir's ... Mars")
   D) Lines 83-87 ("The information ... 2030s")

45. As used in line 3, "distinct" most nearly means

   A) clear.
   B) conspicuous.
   C) separate.
   D) uncertain.

46. It can be reasonably inferred from the passage that

   A) Martian meteorites are scarce.
   B) Some Martian meteorites have been returned by robotic spacecraft.
   C) All Martian meteorites contain evidence of water.
   D) More Martian meteorites have been found in Japan than anywhere else.

47. Which choice provides the best evidence for the answer to the previous question?

   A) Lines 18-23 ("There have ... Japan")
   B) Lines 28-31 ("The samples ... atmosphere")
   C) Lines 61-66 ("In the ... Science")
   D) Lines 83-87 ("The information ... 2030s")

48. The author's attitude about this new study is best described as one of

   A) apathy.
   B) optimism.
   C) reflection.
   D) skepticism.

49. According to the passage, the meteorites used in this study

   A) were from different areas on Mars.
   B) were about the same age.
   C) contained unique hydrogen atoms.
   D) contained chlorine.

50. As used in line 36, "geomorphologic" most nearly means

    A) surface.
    B) situational.
    C) changing.
    D) local.

51. According to information from both the passage and the chart

    A) there is no evidence of water in the Martian mantle.
    B) there exists the possibility of surface water on Mars.
    C) there are at least three ice caps on Mars.
    D) there is evidence of water in both the mantle and atmosphere of Mars.

52. The author of the passage would most likely consider the information in the chart to be

    A) an excellent representation of the findings of the new study.
    B) compelling, but too controversial.
    C) a possible, but crude, representation.
    D) interesting, but inaccurate.

Explanations

1. **C. Several characters criticize another character for his unusual behavior.** This is the best answer because when the minister suddenly appears wearing the veil, the old woman and Goodman Gray both disapprove. Choice A is not the best answer because there is nothing unlawful about the veil. Choice B is incorrect because we cannot judge whether anyone is questioning his or her faith from this brief excerpt. You could probably make a weak case for D, but it is certainly not what the story is about.

2. **D. provide a contrast with the succeeding paragraphs.** This is the best choice because in the first paragraph the reader encounters phrases like "bright faces," "tripped merrily," "Sabbath sunshine," and "pretty maidens." The succeeding paragraphs suggest an ominous tone. Choices A and B are both incorrect for the same reason: there is nothing threatening in the paragraph. Although the sexton is mentioned in the paragraph, the story is not about him or his job. So choice C is out.

3. **A. surprise.** All of the sentiments expressed as answers were experienced by the townspeople, but the first was expressed by the sexton in the second paragraph: "astonishment."

4. **A. Lines 14-15 ("But what … astonishment").** This is the best answer for the same reason mentioned above. The other lines do not apply.

5. **A. solemn.** We need a word that is the opposite of "merrily." Solemn or serious is clearly the best choice. You might have entertained "earnest," but sincere is not the meaning we want here.

6. **B. unremarkable.** This is an easy one. Just look to lines 59 to 60 for your answer. "Mr. Hooper had the reputation of a good preacher, but not an energetic one…" Yes, I do see the word "persuasive" in the next line, but I also see "mild," (which, if you'll notice, comes first in that construction) and that coupled with "not … energetic" makes "unremarkable" the better choice.

7. **C. skeletons in the closet.** This is the analogy question. C is the best answer because the minister's black veil is like a mask hiding someone or something, and "skeletons in the closet" are secrets we don't want anyone to see. Sunglasses are used to filter the sun, so that's not a possible answer. Now, a Halloween mask does hide the wearer, but it's meant to "scare" as children trick or treat on a fun holiday. Choice D just doesn't fit.

8. **D. Lines 70-74 ("The subject … them").** The phrase "secret sin" says it all. Case closed.

9. **A. sermon.** This is appropriate because Mr. Hooper is preaching to his congregation from the pulpit, and he is giving his "homily" or "sermon." A dialog, choice B, is a conversation, which is not applicable in this situation. Choices C and D are clearly unsuitable as well.

10. **B. The minister is hiding some secret sin.** This may well be, but it is not supported by any evidence in the passage. All of the other choices are true according to the passage.

11. **A. desire for material goods.** Thoreau tells us in the first four lines of the second paragraph that he was more interested in pursuing his freedom than in material trappings like "rich carpets," "fine furniture," etc.

12. **D. gratuitous.** Thoreau lived in a hut in the woods, so wouldn't it follow that he thought the big, ornate houses unnecessary? While it is true that such houses are expensive and imposing, that's not the idea here. Choice C is inappropriate. This is difficult because the word "gratuitous" is not one that some of you will know, but you can eliminate the others because they don't really fit the sense of the sentence.

13. **A. effort.** Benson states, "Thoreau was indolent rather than simple." In other words, he was lazy. He just does not want to make the effort. The other choices are clearly not appropriate here.

14. **D. fake.** Benson consistently paints a picture of Thoreau as a man who was posturing, trying to call attention to himself, but not truly what he purported to be. We see this in the final few sentences of the Benson excerpt.

15. **D. Lines 25-30 ("But Thoreau …contemplation").** The use of the words "observed and admired" and "hovering about" support this choice very well. The others just do not address this topic.

16. **B. instructive.** Each seems to believe in what he is saying and is trying to put forth his thoughts in an instructive manner.

17. **D. Benson saw Thoreau as a man of extremely simple tastes.** Both Benson and Salt seem to agree that Thoreau was a man of simple tastes.

18. **D. suggest the essential relationship between plain living and complicated thinking.** He goes on to explain that exact relationship at length.

19. **A. Thoreau, Salt, Shelly.** What eliminates choices B, C, and D is Benson.

20. **C. surprise because Thoreau spent so many years in solitude and published just two books on the subject.** He makes this point very cogently when he explains the discrepancy between living in the woods for a good deal of time only to publish two works towards the end of his life.

21. **C. Salts feels that Thoreau had much purer motives for seeking the simple life than does Benson.** Salt spends a fair amount of his essay describing the need that Thoreau had for the simple life. He says those with complex natures require the life of contemplation far more than others. Again, this is the only true statement. Choice A is incorrect because of the phrase "far more." Choice B is also incorrect because Salt is defending Thoreau. As for choice D, Benson is the one who sees Thoreau as fake.

22. C. describe how the arts help to affirm who we are and to structure our dreams of who we can be. This is the best answer because it is stated in the opening or topic sentence of the passage. It is a very positive sentiment. Choice A is not the best answer because it is too narrow. Choice B sounds like propaganda and is rather ambiguous. Change how? Choice D is too superficial.

23. A. Lines 1-3 ("The fact...better"). As we pointed out earlier, this is the main idea of the entire passage. Choice B is far too specific. Choice C is also too narrow. Choice D is only one example, although a good one, of the main idea of the entire passage.

24. C. lighthearted. This is the best answer because the President is joking when he refers to "poetry that we might recite to a girlfriend to make us sound deep." In other words, we were using poetry, not for the sake of edification, but to impress our girlfriends! Choices A, B, and D, one could argue, all mean the same thing, and for that reason alone eliminate them as possible answers. They, also, miss the joke.

25. A. core. This is the best answer because the word "kernel" as used here means that central or fundamental part of our being. Choice B refers to the word, "colonel." Choice C "modicum" means a small amount, while D "plurality" means a large amount. Both are inappropriate here.

26. C. demonstrate Frost's courage to speak up. This is the best answer because in line 65 it states that even though Frost's health was suffering he still "stood up" to Khrushchev. The author, here, is speaking figuratively, not literally. In other words, Frost courageously confronted Khrushchev, the most powerful Communist leader at the time. The other choices have nothing to do with the idea of "standing up" for what you believe.

27. A. constraints of society. This is the best answer because "constraints," as used in this context, refer to what is considered normal or acceptable. Choice B is incorrect because there was nothing illegal about what Frost was saying. The same can be said for "political imperatives." Choice D is egregiously erroneous.

28. C. speak out against injustice. This is the best answer because the President mentions in the third paragraph, lines 12-15, that the "tools of progress, of revolution" include the "brushes, pens and cameras and guitars" (of the artist). Later, he uses the anecdote about Robert Frost's confrontation with Khrushchev as a specific example. Choice A is incorrect because Frost wasn't held back by the dictates or "conventions" of society. Choice B was never mentioned. Choice D is too superficial.

29. B. Lines 12-15 (Time and...guitars"). This is the best answer for the same reasons as mentioned previously.

30. B. artist. This is the best answer because since the entire passage is about the continuing contributions of artists to our society, it would seem fitting to conclude with a quote from a famous artist. The other choices don't make sense.

31. C. $161,000,000 is the most money ever requested by the Obama administration. This is the best answer because the chart clearly indicates this in the years 2010 and 2011. Choice A is incorrect because although the appropriation requests have declined twice, they have always risen the following year. Choice B is incorrect because the same low in 2012 was repeated in 2015. Choice D may be true, but there is no way to tell.

32. **A. suggest how the task at hand might not be as simple as first thought.** This is the best answer because of at least four reasons, all of which are spelled m-i-g-h-t. The emphasis on this one word tells us that the author is having difficulty getting to the nub of the issue. Choice B is not the best answer because even though she states that *she* may never come to a conclusion, the audience will. Choice C is not the best because although at the end of the paragraph the author does make mention of the weight of the subject, it is not the main stress. As for choice D, the word "alone" makes it too extreme.

33. **B. Lines 3-8 ("They might … light").** This is the best answer because these lines contain the four might's mentioned above. Choice A stresses the word "wonder," which is not what we are looking for. Choice C is concerned with the "duty of the lecturer." Choice D is not the best answer because these lines express the author's intent to use her skills as a novelist to illuminate the topic.

34. **D. underscore the insignificance of the narrator's identity.** The author actually tells us that the names are unimportant on lines 27-28. Indeed, the passage is about the germination of an idea and not the question of authorship. That being said, the other choices miss the mark.

35. **C. she is reflecting on a subject.** This is the best answer because it captures the main idea. Choice A does have some merit. The author seemingly enjoys the natural beauty of the surrounding scene, but the answer falls short because it's not the main idea of the passage. Choice B is incorrect because she is not actually fishing, but rather "fishing" for an idea. Choice D is never mentioned.

36. **A. Lines 26-30 ("Here then … thought").** This is the best answer because the author states that she is "lost in thought." Choice B is not the best answer because they address the beauty of the scene, which is not the main focus. Choice C is tempting because the lines mention "line" and "fish," but remember fishing is just a metaphor. Choice D is inappropriate.

37. **C. predicament.** The "collar" refers to the **weight** on her **shoulders** as mentioned in the previous paragraph. Here in the second paragraph, she speaks of the **need** of coming to a conclusion. Clearly, she is having difficulties with the topic. Choice A is not the correct answer because although there is an obvious connection between women and fiction, it's the "prejudices and passions" that present the problem. Choices B and D are there to mislead you. They are both definitions of the word "collar," but they are not the meanings in context.

38. **C. personification.** This is the best answer because this figure of speech attributes human (person) qualities to inanimate objects, nature, or animals, which is what the author is describing: "willows wept in perpetual lamentation." The other choices do not apply. Choice A is a comparison. Choice B has to do with sound repetition; "onomatopoeia" also refers to sound.

39. **B. premature.** Follow the metaphor of "fishing" for an idea that turns out to be "small and insignificant" - the kind that a "good fisherman puts back into the water so that it may grow fatter."

40. **C. coalescence.** Here is a wonderful illustration of the importance of those Latin prefixes. Remember: **co** and **con** both mean come together.

41. **D. indicates an abrupt knowledge of an idea.** Well, if "while fishing" you were to feel a "tug" on the line, it means you have caught something. In this case, a sudden inclination of an idea.

42. **C. is a writer herself.** This is an easy one because the author says she is a writer in the first paragraph, "…I propose making use of all the liberties … of a novelist, to tell the story…" Enough said.

43. C. the new discovery of an additional water source on Mars. This is the best answer because according to the passage this was the result of the new study. The meteorites mentioned in choice B are important, but only as a means of finding collaborating evidence to support what scientists already surmise. Choice A is correct as stated, but notice the word "also" in the first sentence of the third paragraph. So, that understanding is a possibility derived from the new study. The controversy mentioned in D, which according the passage exists, is barely touched upon in this essay.

44. A. Lines 1-4 ("NASA and ... surface"). These are the lines that directly refer to the new evidence. The other choices do not apply to the central idea.

45. C. separate. "Distinct" is used here to mean separate from the other two water sources: the mantle and atmosphere. Choices A and B can both mean clear, but in a different context. They are not the precise definitions we need here. Choice D misses the mark completely.

46. A. Martian meteorites are scarce. The writer states that we need to discover more Martian meteorites for further study, or use the ones we have with improving scientific techniques. So, if we need to discover more, then we don't have enough. (Interestingly, I read somewhere that scientists have identified less than 100 Martian meteorites here on earth.) Choice B has never happened. Choice C is too extreme: there is no evidence to support this claim or the one made in Choice D.

47. C. Lines 61-66 ("In the ... Science"). This is the best answer because these lines confirm the above explanation. The other choices do not.

48. B. optimism. This is the best choice because of what the author says in the final paragraph. Take a look. Choice A would never be the answer: why would the author bother to write the article in the first place if he didn't care. "Reflective" or thoughtful doesn't fit here: the passage is much more informational. "Skepticism" is simply too negative.

49. C. contained unique hydrogen atoms. This is the best answer because it is in keeping with what we pointed out in the explanation for question 43. What made these meteorites special was the fact that they contained evidence of water from a totally different place than the two scientists had already located. We have no idea where on the planet the meteorites came from. Also, the passage states that the new study did use meteorites of different ages. Choice D is incorrect because what's different about the meteorites is that they lack chlorine.

50. A. surface. At first glance this might seem like a difficult question, but if you think about for a few seconds, the answer sinks in and becomes as apparent as the Grand Canyon!

51. D. there is evidence of water in both the mantle and atmosphere of Mars. This is the best answer because it says so in the passage, and because all of the other choices are false. The only quandary you might have is with choice B. The passage suggests that there probably was surface water in the distant past, but certainly not now.

52. C. a possible, but crude, representation. This is the best choice because while the evidence of the new study indicates a third water source, this chart is hardly exact. It gives the reader an idea of what the reservoir might look like. The emphasis here is on the word "might." The word "excellent" in choice A eliminates it as a possibility. There is nothing really compelling or controversial about the chart. As for choice D, it is interesting, but not completely inaccurate.

Reading Test 4

65 MINUTES, 52 QUESTIONS

DIRECTIONS

Each passage or pair of passages below is followed by a number of questions. After reading each passage or pair, choose the best answer to each question based on what is stated or implied in the passage or passages and in any accompanying graphics (such as a table or graph).

Questions 1 - 11 are based on the following passage.

The following excerpt is from A Study in Scarlet by Sir Arthur Conan Doyle as narrated by Dr. Watson.

He was not studying medicine. Neither did he appear to have pursued any course of reading which might fit him for a degree in science or any other recognized portal which would give him an entrance into the learned
5 world. Yet his zeal for certain studies was remarkable, and within eccentric limits his knowledge was so extraordinarily ample and minute that his observations have fairly astounded me. Surely no man would work so hard or attain such precise information unless he had
10 some definite end in view. Desultory readers are seldom remarkable for the exactness of their learning. No man burdens his mind with small matters unless he has some very good reason for doing so.

His ignorance was as remarkable as his knowledge.
15 Of contemporary literature, philosophy and politics he appeared to know next to nothing. Upon my quoting Thomas Carlyle, he inquired in the naivest way who he might be and what he had done. My surprise reached a climax, however, when I found incidentally that he was
20 ignorant of the Copernican Theory and of the composition of the Solar System. That any civilized human being in this nineteenth century should not be aware that the earth travelled round the sun appeared to be to me such an extraordinary fact that I could hardly
25 realize it.

"You appear to be astonished," he said, smiling at my expression of surprise. "Now that I do know it I shall do my best to forget it."

"To forget it!"
30 "You see," he explained, "I consider that a man's brain originally is like a little empty attic, and you have to stock it with such furniture as you choose. A fool takes in all the lumber of every sort that he comes across, so that the knowledge which might be useful to him gets
35 crowded out, or at best is jumbled up with a lot of other things so that he has a difficulty in laying his hands upon it. Now the skillful workman is very careful indeed as to what he takes into his brain-attic. He will have nothing but the tools which may help him in doing his work, but
40 of these he has a large assortment, and all in the most perfect order. It is a mistake to think that that little room has elastic walls and can distend to any extent. Depend upon it there comes a time when for every addition of knowledge you forget something that you knew before. It
45 is of the highest importance, therefore, not to have useless facts elbowing out the useful ones."

"But the Solar System!" I protested.

"What the deuce is it to me?" he interrupted impatiently; "you say that we go round the sun. If we
50 went round the moon it would not make a pennyworth of difference to me or to my work."

I was on the point of asking him what that work might be, but something in his manner showed me that the question would be an unwelcome one. I pondered over
55 our short conversation, however, and endeavored to draw my deductions from it. He said that he would acquire no knowledge which did not bear upon his object. Therefore, all the knowledge which he possessed was such as would be useful to him. I enumerated in my own
60 mind all the various points upon which he had shown me that he was exceptionally well-informed. I even took a pencil and jotted them down. I could not help smiling at

114

the document when I had completed it. It ran in this way—SHERLOCK HOLMES—his limits.
65 1. Knowledge of Literature.—Nil. 2. Philosophy.—Nil. 3. Astronomy.—Nil. 4. Politics.—Feeble. 5. Botany.—Variable. Well up in belladonna, opium, and poisons generally. Knows nothing of practical gardening. 6. Geology.—Practical, but limited. Tells at a glance
70 different soils from each other. After walks has shown me splashes upon his trousers, and told me by their colour and consistency in what part of London he had received them. 7. Chemistry.—Profound. 8. Anatomy.—Accurate, but unsystematic. 9. Sensational Literature.—
75 Immense. He appears to know every detail of every horror perpetrated in the century. 10. Plays the violin well. 11. Is an expert boxer, and swordsman. 12. Has a good practical knowledge of British law.
  When I had got so far in my list I threw it into the fire
80 in despair. "If I can only find what the fellow is driving at by reconciling all these accomplishments and discovering a calling which needs them all," I said to myself, "I may as well give up the attempt at once."

1. The author is shocked at the revelation that Holmes

   A) plays the violin.
   B) is a detective.
   C) is unaware of the Copernican Theory.
   D) is so politically uninformed.

2. As used in line 4, "portal" most nearly means

   A) area.
   B) gateway.
   C) introduction.
   D) arena.

3. The narrator's remarks, on lines 21-30, about "any civilized human being in this nineteenth century should not be aware that the earth travelled round the sun..." primarily demonstrate

   A) a closer understanding of his friend.
   B) confusion as to why he is acting in this manner.
   C) surprise that he knows so much but not this.
   D) alarm at such an epiphany.

4. The friend suggests in line 37 that the "skillful workman" does which of the following?

   A) He remembers only that information that will help him in his endeavors.
   B) He understands the "lumber of every sort."
   C) He knows furniture very well.
   D) He knows a lot about all aspects of life.

5. Which choice provides the best evidence for the answer to the previous question?

   A) Lines 26-28 ("You appear ... it")
   B) Lines 32-37 ("A fool ... it")
   C) Lines 42-44 ("Depend upon ... before")
   D) Lines 48-51 ("What the ... work")

6. As used in line 42, "distend" most nearly means

   A) stretch.
   B) blow-up.
   C) turn into.
   D) absorb.

7. Which of the following words LEAST describes the friend's attitude towards acquiring new information?

   A) pragmatic
   B) utilitarian
   C) purposeful
   D) unfocused

8. It can be reasonably inferred from the passage that

   A) Watson is an extremely meticulous person.
   B) Watson and Holmes are not particularly impressed with one another.
   C) Holmes has no formal education whatsoever.
   D) Holmes is too laid back to have a career.

9. Which choice provides the best evidence for the answer to the previous question?

   A) Lines 5-8 ("Yet his ... me")
   B) Lines 18-21 ("My surprise ... System")
   C) Lines 37-38 ("Now the ... brain-attic")
   D) Lines 65-78 ("1. Knowledge ... law")

10. The tone of the passage is best described as

    A) annoyed.
    B) inquisitive.
    C) befuddled.
    D) angry.

11. Why is the final sentence ironic for anyone who knows who Sherlock Holmes is?

    A) Watson's list, from our perspective of modern detective work, epitomizes which qualities a perfect detective has.
    B) Watson is so serious that he missed the obvious humor in his statement.
    C) Watson is himself a detective.
    D) Watson is unaware what great friends they will become.

Questions 12 - 22 are based on the following passages and supplementary material..

Passage 1 is adapted from a book written by George Fitzhugh, a Virginia lawyer, writer, and slave owner. Passage 2 is from a speech by abolitionist, William Lloyd Garrison.

Passage 1

We not only boast that the White Slave Trade is more exacting and fraudulent (in fact, though not in intention) than Black Slavery, but we also boast that it is more cruel, in leaving the laborer to take care of himself and
5 family out of the pittance which skill or capital have allowed him to retain. When the day's labor is ended, he is free, but is overburdened with the cares of family and household, which make his freedom an empty and delusive mockery.
10 But his employer is really free, and may enjoy the profits made by others' labor without a care or a trouble as to their well-being. The Negro slave is free, too, when the labors of the day are over, and free in mind as well as body, for the master provides food, raiment, house, fuel,
15 and everything else necessary to the physical well-being of himself and family. The master's labors commence just when the slave's end. No wonder men should prefer white slavery to capital, to Negro slavery, since it is more profitable, and is free from all the cares and labors
20 of black slave-holding.
  The Negro slaves of the South are the happiest, and, in some sense, the freest people in the world. The children and the aged and infirm work not at all, and yet have all the comforts and necessaries of life provided for
25 them. They enjoy liberty, because they are oppressed neither by care nor labor. The women do little hard work, and are protected from the despotism of their husbands by their masters. The Negro men and stout boys work, on the average, in good weather, not more than nine hours a
30 day. The balance of their time is spent in perfect abandon. Besides, they have their Sabbaths and holidays. White men, with so much of license and liberty, would die of ennui, but Negroes luxuriate in corporeal and mental repose. With their faces upturned to the sun, they
35 can sleep at any hour, and quiet sleep is the greatest of human enjoyments. "Blessed be the man who invented sleep." 'Tis happiness in itself — and results from contentment with the present, and confident assurance of the future. We do not know whether free laborers ever
40 sleep. They are fools to do so, for whilst they sleep, the wily and watchful capitalist is devising means to ensnare and exploit them. The free laborer must work or starve. He is more of a slave than the Negro because he works longer and harder for less allowance than the slave and
45 has no holiday, because the cares of life with him begin

when its labors end. He has no liberty, and not a single right.

Passage 2

The abolitionism which I advocate is as absolute as the law of God, and as unyielding as his throne. It admits of
[50] no compromise. Every slave is a stolen man; every slaveholder is a man stealer. By no precedent, no example, no law, no compact, no purchase, no bequest, no inheritance, no combination of circumstances, is slaveholding right or justifiable. While a slave remains in
[55] his fetters, the land must have no rest. Whatever sanctions his doom must be pronounced accursed. The law that makes him a chattel is to be trampled underfoot; the compact that is formed at his expense, and cemented with his blood, is null and void; the church that consents
[60] to his enslavement is horribly atheistical; the religion that receives to its communion the enslaver is the embodiment of all criminality. Such, at least, is the verdict of my own soul, on the supposition that I am to be the slave; that my wife is to be sold from me for the
[65] vilest purposes; that my children are to be torn from my arms, and disposed of to the highest bidder, like sheep in the market. And who am I but a man? What right have I to be free, that another man cannot prove himself to possess by nature? Who or what are my wife and
[70] children, that they should not be herded with four-footed beasts, as well as others thus sacredly related?

1790 Census Records: Chart of Slave Populations

State	Total Population (1790)	Slave Population	
Connecticut	237,655	2,648	1%
Delaware	59,096	8,887	15%
Georgia	82,548	29,264	35%
Maryland	319,728	103,036	32%
Massachusetts	378,556	0	0%
New Hampshire	141,899	157	0.1%
New Jersey	184,139	11,423	6%
New York	340,241	21,193	6%
North Carolina	395,005	100,783	26%
Pennsylvania	433,611	3,707	0.8%
Rhode Island	69,112	958	1%
South Carolina	247,073	104,094	42%
Virginia	747,550	292,627	39%

12. The main purpose of Passage 1 is to

    A) examine the purpose and necessity of slavery.
    B) illustrate the benefits of one system against the liabilities of another.
    C) argue that capitalism is a relative term.
    D) question the profitability of two distinct systems.

13. Which choice provides the best evidence for the answer to the previous question?

    A) Lines 3-6 ("… it is … retain")
    B) Lines 17-20 ("No wonder … slave-holding")
    C) Lines 28-31 ("The Negro … abandon")
    D) Lines 42-47 ("The free … right")

14. As used in line 5, "pittance" most nearly means

    A) livelihood.
    B) trifle.
    C) fortune.
    D) salary.

15. The author's tone in the first paragraph of Passage 1 can best be described as

    A) rational.
    B) somber.
    C) truculent.
    D) persuasive.

16. The central claim of Passage 2 is that

    A) there is no possible rationale for slavery.
    B) slavery goes against the laws of God.
    C) every man is entitled to secure his wife and children.
    D) man is not an animal.

17. Which choice provides the best evidence for the answer to the previous question?

    A) Lines 48-50 ("The abolitionism … compromise")
    B) Lines 51-54 ("By no … justifiable")
    C) Lines 62-67 ("Such, at … market")
    D) Lines 67-71 ("And who, … related")

18. As used in line 55, "fetters" most nearly means

    A) shackles.
    B) sovereignty.
    C) location.
    D) employment.

19. The rhetorical device employed by the author of Passage 2 in lines 69-71 implies that

    A) women and children sometimes behave like animals.
    B) women and children should be considered holy.
    C) slaves are not animals.
    D) slaves are like women and children.

20. The attitude of the author of Passage 2 can best be described as

    A) amenable.
    B) compliant.
    C) concerned.
    D) adamant.

21. Which statement best describes the relationship between the passages?

    A) Passage 2 amplifies the proposal put forth in Passage 1.
    B) Passage 2 refutes a central claim advanced in Passage 1.
    C) Passage 2 expresses reservations about the situation described in Passage 1.
    D) Passage 1 more realistically discusses the situation manifested in Passage 2.

22. The data in the table supports all of the following statements EXCEPT

    A) only one state had a slave population of 0%.
    B) Virginia had the greatest slave population.
    C) Delaware was the least populated state in 1790.
    D) only New Hampshire and Pennsylvania had a slave population of less than 1%.

Questions 23 - 32 are based on the following passage.

This passage is taken from an introduction to a book on dream psychology published in 1920.

Freud's theories are anything but theoretical. He was moved by the fact that there always seemed to be a close connection between his patients' dreams and their mental abnormalities, to collect thousands of dreams and to
[5] compare them with the case histories in his possession. He did not start out with a preconceived bias, hoping to find evidence which might support his views. He looked at facts a thousand times "until they began to tell him something." His attitude toward dream study was, in
[10] other words, that of a statistician who does not know, and has no means of foreseeing, what conclusions will be forced on him by the information he is gathering, but who is fully prepared to accept those unavoidable conclusions.
[15] This was indeed a novel way in psychology. Psychologists had always been wont to build, in what Bleuler calls "autistic ways," that is through methods in no wise supported by evidence, some attractive hypothesis, which sprung from their brain, like Minerva
[20] from Jove's brain, fully armed. After which, they would stretch upon that unyielding frame the hide of a reality which they had previously killed. It is only to minds suffering from the same distortions, to minds also autistically inclined, that those empty, artificial structures
[25] appear acceptable molds for philosophical thinking.
   The pragmatic view that "truth is what works" had not been as yet expressed when Freud published his revolutionary views on the psychology of dreams. Five facts of first magnitude were made obvious to the world
[30] by his interpretation of dreams. First of all, Freud pointed out a constant connection between some part of every dream and some detail of the dreamer's life during the previous waking state. This positively establishes a relation between sleeping states and waking states and
[35] disposes of the widely prevalent view that dreams are purely nonsensical phenomena coming from nowhere and leading nowhere. Secondly, Freud, after studying the dreamer's life and modes of thought, after noting down all these mannerisms and the apparently insignificant
[40] details of his conduct which reveal his secret thought, came to the conclusion that there was in every dream the attempted or successful gratification of some wish, conscious or unconscious. Thirdly, he proved that many of our dream visions are symbolical, which causes us to
[45] consider them as absurd and unintelligible; the universality of those symbols, however, makes them very transparent to the trained observer. Fourthly, Freud showed that sexual desires play an enormous part in our unconscious, a part which puritanical hypocrisy has
[50] always tried to minimize, if not to ignore entirely. Finally, Freud established a direct connection between the symbolic visions of our sleep and the symbolic actions of the mentally deranged.
   There were, of course, many other observations which
[55] Freud made while dissecting the dreams of his patients, but not all of them present as much interest as the foregoing nor were they as revolutionary or likely to wield as much influence on modern psychiatry.

23. The main idea of this passage is that

   A) Freud's ideas were not really revolutionary.
   B) Freud's hypotheses were indeed popular in his time.
   C) there is a direct connection between philosophy and dreams.
   D) Freud employed a practical approach to his work on dream psychology.

24. Which choice provides the best evidence for the answer to the previous question?

   A) Line 1 ("Freud's theories … theoretical")
   B) Lines 9-14 ("His attitude …conclusions")
   C) Lines 51-53 ("Finally, Freud … deranged")
   D) Lines 54-58 ("There were … psychiatry")

25. According to the passage, the "statistician" mentioned in line 10

   A) probably has a preconceived bias.
   B) has a background in psychology.
   C) studies the evidence until it tells him something.
   D) impatiently searches for answers.

26. As used in line 16, "wont" most nearly means

   A) disinclined.
   B) accustomed.
   C) desirous.
   D) suffered.

27. The reference to "Minerva" in line 19 supports

   A) the idea that the basis for dream psychology can be traced to Greek mythology.
   B) the common belief that dream theory is an attractive hypothesis.
   C) the "autistic ways."
   D) Freud's approach to dream psychology.

28. Before Freud's novel approach to dream interpretation, dreams were most often considered by psychologists of the time as

   A) mental abnormalities.
   B) significant connectives to reality.
   C) autistic.
   D) nonsense.

29. According to Freud, every dream reveals

   A) secret thoughts.
   B) sexual desires.
   C) symbols.
   D) gratification.

30. Which choice provides the best evidence for the answer to the previous question?

   A) Lines 30-33 ("First of ... state")
   B) Lines 37-43 ("Secondly, Freud ...unconscious")
   C) Lines 43-47 ("Thirdly, he ... observer")
   D) Lines 51-53 ("Finally, Freud ... deranged")

31. The tone of the passage as a whole can best be characterized as

   A) informative.
   B) facetious.
   C) philosophical.
   D) contentious.

32. As used in line 58, "wield" most nearly means

   A) exhibit.
   B) expose.
   C) exert.
   D) emphasize.

Questions 33 - 42 are based on the following passage.

Religion and Society

Religious beliefs (or non-beliefs) are at the center of what most people consider among their most private thoughts.

Max Weber (1864 – 1920) was a scientist who
5 studied human social behavior and wrote about how those internal beliefs might have dramatic effects on social movements, specifically the modern notion of capitalism.

Weber saw that capitalism, as an economic system,
10 started and flourished in northwestern Europe, in areas that were predominantly populated by Protestants in stark contrast to areas that were mostly Catholic. Capitalism did not start in other nations or continents, only in Europe. As a scientist he not only asked why, but
15 he also looked for causality. The result was his book: *The Protestant Ethic and the Spirit of Capitalism*.

The Protestant Reformation was a religious/political overthrow of the Catholic Church's monopoly of Christian faith in Europe. Beginning in the early 1500's
20 entire nations broke away from the doctrinal hegemony of Rome. Religious persecutions shook the fabric of society, as personal beliefs were suddenly required to give way to the requirements of the state. Religious reformers started by making their case to individuals, but
25 ultimately it was the will of the government that settled what beliefs would be tolerated or punished. King Henry VIII was a prototype of the Protestant reformation when he declared himself head of the Church of England (Defender of the Faith) in addition to his temporal
30 powers. Anywhere Henry ruled, Catholics were forced to renounce allegiance to the Pope under pain of death. Without the restraints of the Catholic Church, society was more free to explore different ways of developing business models.

35 John Calvin was a prominent protestant reformer who preached that God was all-powerful, all knowing, had no beginning and no end. Calvin concluded that humans were too concerned with trying to convince God that they were worthy of eternal salvation. Christians were
40 wasting their time doing "good works," praying for salvation, or paying for indulgences. God already knew which humans would be saved and which would be damned even before they were born. This was called the doctrine of predestination, the belief that nothing an
45 individual does today can change the knowledge that God already had from all eternity. This belief was never allowed in the Catholic Church that believed humans were created with free will and could choose between many options.

50 In some ways Calvin was talking himself out of a job. But as a successful preacher he had a corollary to the raw doctrine of predestination. He also preached that God was just and that in the present He gives each individual an insight into whether he is one of the saved or one of
55 the damned. Calvin preached that this preview of salvation would be manifested in how economically successful a person became throughout life. The opposite would also be true, a person who was economically disadvantaged would be getting the message that the bad
60 fortune now would continue into the next life. Catholics, in contrast, had no such beliefs. Repentance for sins at one's deathbed was all that was required to enter into an eternal reward.

Martin Luther also ushered in many of the changes in
65 the Church, which would result in a population more prone towards thinking for themselves. He eschewed Latin opting for all prayers and hymns to be in the German vernacular. The congregation instead of being mesmerized by the massive cathedrals, which were in
70 stark juxtaposition to the hovels that many of them lived in, now had simpler churches. The Gregorian Chant, which awed them, was now sung in German and the people were asked what they thought about various aspects of the Church. Choosing a different form of
75 Christianity encouraged people to think for themselves and this certainly made them more successful.

Weber concluded that where Protestantism was prevalent a spirit arose of conscious rational origin: work hard, make profits, reinvest profits and repeat.
80 Reinvesting and repetition were key because success was not seen as complete until one died successful. Spending for pure pleasure, therefore, was seen as antithetical to success and ultimate salvation. This attitude magnified millions of times throughout society became the critical
85 mass and eventually the core driving principle that is the hallmark of capitalism. Without this impetus, capitalism may never have flourished.

33. The purpose of the passage is primarily to

   A) explain the origin of capitalism.
   B) establish John Calvin as the founder of capitalism.
   C) explain why non-Europeans are not open to capitalism.
   D) explain how King Henry became the "defender of the faith."

34. Which choice provides the best evidence for the answer to the previous question?

    A) Lines 4-8 ("Max Weber… capitalism")
    B) Lines 9-12 ("Weber saw… Catholic")
    C) Lines 23-34 ("Religious reformers … models")
    D) Lines 55-57 ("Calvin preached … life")

35. As used in line 29, the word "temporal" most nearly means:

    A) temporary.
    B) spiritual.
    C) worldly.
    D) absolute.

36. The tone of the passage is:

    A) inquisitive.
    B) argumentative.
    C) indifferent.
    D) informative.

37. Based on the passage, the emergence of capitalism was most likely due to

    A) King Henry VIII becoming head of the Church of England.
    B) people's religious convictions.
    C) freedom of choice coupled with a correlation of success with eternal bliss.
    D) Luther's campaign against indulgences.

38. Which choice provides the best evidence for the answer to the previous question?

    A) Lines 9-12 ("Weber saw …Catholic")
    B) Lines 30-34 ("Anywhere Henry…models")
    C) Lines 55-57 ("Calvin preached… life")
    D) Lines 77-81 (Weber concluded… successful")

39. What does the author mean when he says that "Calvin was talking himself out of a job?"

    A) He did not seem to know what he was talking about.
    B) The Church members did not need him if their fates were already sealed.
    C) His going against church doctrine would alienate him from his congregation.
    D) Repentance at one's deathbed was all one needed to enter paradise.

40. As used in line 51 "corollary" most nearly means

    A) argument.
    B) solution.
    C) caution.
    D) addition.

41. It can be inferred that John Calvin believed in all of the following EXCEPT

    A) God is omnipotent.
    B) humans have free will.
    C) people need not pray for salvation.
    D) a strong work ethic.

42. According to the passage, which of the following was NOT something that Luther did that prepared people for capitalism?

    A) having simpler churches.
    B) hymns were written in the common language, German, rather than Latin.
    C) the congregation were encouraged to ask questions.
    D) he did away with indulgences.

Questions 43 - 52 are based on the following passage and supplementary material.

For many decades now, our media, economists, politicians and philosophers have freely exercised their penchant for doom and gloom. Chicken Little's "The sky is falling" has never been so in vogue. From our now 70
5 year rant that we have placed nuclear immolation in the hands of fanatics to our fear of being hit by a super comet, to Al Gore's Nobel Prize warning us of global warming and the havoc that will bring to our weather, we are constantly besieged with the fear of final immolation.
10 Perhaps our most recent candidate for world destruction is the honeybee along with the apocryphal quote from Einstein that if we destroyed the honeybee, mankind would certainly die within four years. No definitive research has been able to validate that Einstein
15 ever said that, but many entomologists have **surmised** that thousands of species of plants would perish were it not for the honeybee. The list of plants ranges from hundreds to many thousands, so there is a lot of disagreement here.
20 Although the ebb and flow of bee populations has been documented for centuries, no definitive culprit has emerged as the cause for the now 15 year radical decrease in its population. So called "colony collapse disorder" has been ascribed to the use of pesticides,
25 fungicides, parasitic mites, viral pathogens, and, of course, global warming. Some have pointed the finger at bee farmers who overwork their bees by transporting them around the country to pollinate almond orchards in California and other crops in different states.
30 Europe has recently banned neonicotinoids, pesticides believed to contribute to this sharp decrease in bee populations, which has been as high as fifty percent in some areas. However, the use of those pesticides in both Canada and Australia has not witnessed any such decline
35 in population, so again the source of the problem remains foggy. There has been very little substantive effort in the United States to curtail this sharp decline since the true cause remains enigmatic.
Other countries feel that ecological farming is a
40 system that can be used to stabilize human food production, preserve wild habitats and ultimately save the bees. This panacea has been used successfully in many parts of the world such as Bhutan, which has led the world in adopting a 100% organic farming policy. In
45 our part of the world, Mexico has banned genetically modified corn to protect its native corn varieties. Indian scientist Vandana Shiva and his group of farmers have built an organic farming system resistant to industrial agriculture over two decades. Some European countries
50 have burned thousands of acres of corn contaminated with GM varieties. Many other countries in Europe have banned GM crops altogether.

In essence, what these countries are doing is going back to the way farming has been done for centuries
55 before GM technology came about. This age old system of farming resists insect damage by doing away with large mono-crops in order to create bio-diversity. The advantages of this system range from avoiding soil loss from wind and water erosion, avoiding pesticides and
60 chemical fertilizers, and restoring soil nutrients with natural composting technology.
All of this is essential to restoring the health of our bee population, which has already been decimated in so many places in the world. This will ultimately allow us
65 to restore the farm yields that we will need to feed an ever-growing world population. We will also have to divert most or our farm yield to people rather than to feeding livestock and use as bio-fuels.
The most current findings indicate that insecticides
70 accumulate in individual bees and within entire colonies, including the honey that bees feed to infant larvae. Those that do not die right away, have sub-lethal effects, development defects, loss of orientation and overall weakness. When so many die off, it leaves the work of
75 the bees to smaller numbers, which have to now support the depleted habitat. This results is colony collapse.
Yes, we have seen some forward thinking people such as the famous actor, Morgan Freeman, planting clover and a variety of plants on his 124 acre Mississippi ranch
80 and bringing in 20 hives to pollinate those plants, but it is going to take a much more concerted effort if we are to save our waning bee population. If we cannot agree to change our farming systems, and decrease our use of pesticides, fertilizers and GMOs, we may be joining
85 Chicken Little soon and telling everyone that the sky is falling. Only this time, it might actually be true.

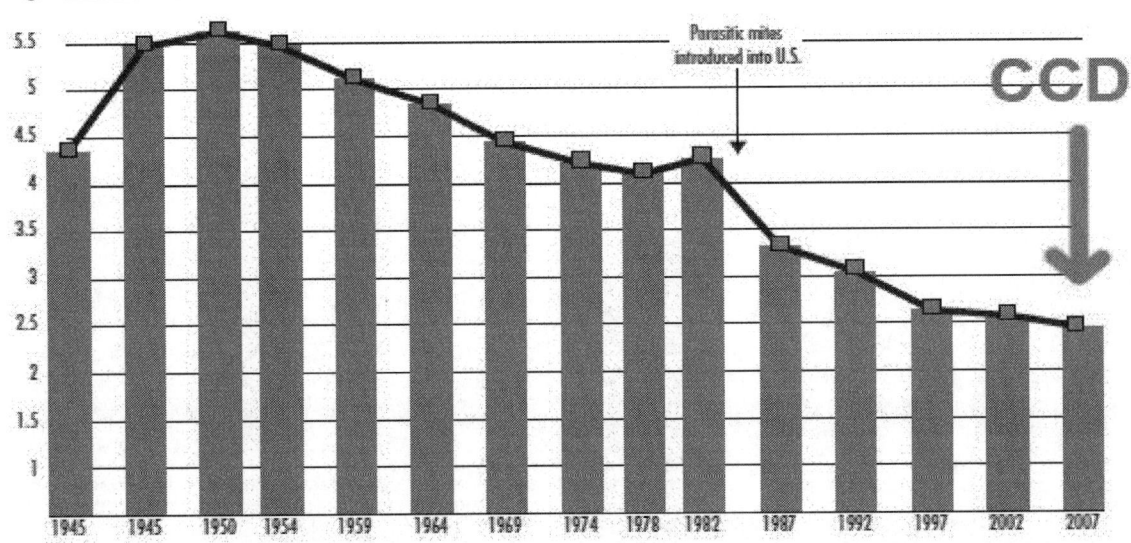

Figure 4: US honey-producing colonies

Data source: U.S. Department of Agriculture's (USDA) National Agricultural Statistics Service (NASS) NB: Data collected for producers with 5 or more colonies. Honey producing colonies are the maximum number of colonies from which honey was taken during the year. It is possible to take honey from colonies which did not survive the entire year.

43. The purpose of this passage is to

    A) discuss different farming techniques that would allow farmers to feed more people.
    B) compare and contrast ecological and GMO farming techniques.
    C) examine the causes and effects of a shrinking bee population.
    D) consider some of the factors that could cause our world to end.

44. Which choice provides the best evidence for the answer to the previous question?

    A) Lines 23-26 ("So called.... warming")
    B) Lines 39-42 ("Other countries…bees")
    C) Lines 53-55 ("In essence…about")
    D) Lines 77-82 ("Yes, we…population")

45. "Entomologists" in line 15 most probably specialize in

    A) lizards.
    B) words.
    C) insects.
    D) farms.

46. In the first paragraph, the author accuses the media, economists, etc. of all of the following EXCEPT

    A) exaggeration.
    B) negativity.
    C) pessimism.
    D) insight.

47. As used in line 11, "apocryphal" most nearly means

    A) unauthentic.
    B) brilliant.
    C) insightful.
    D) memorable.

48. What has cast some doubt on some pesticides as the culprit?

    A) GMOs are not affected by them.
    B) Bees show no sign of them in their blood.
    C) Other countries using these pesticides have not had declines in bee populations.
    D) Many bees are not affected by these same insecticides.

49. Which of the following was **not** mentioned as something that other countries are doing to reverse this trend of bee loss?

    A) Burning thousands of acres of corn
    B) Using older methods of farming
    C) Banning the use of GMOs
    D) Developing bee farms

50. All of the following are considered possible causes for "colony collapse disorder" EXCEPT

    A) parasite mites.
    B) insecticides.
    C) other insects.
    D) overworking of bees.

51. As used in line 36, "substantive" most nearly means

    A) tangible.
    B) concerned.
    C) agreed on.
    D) announced.

52. According to both the passage and the chart,

    A) there has been an ebb and flow of honey bee populations.
    B) the introduction of parasitic mites has contributed to a decrease in bee producing colonies.
    the years from 2008 to the present will continue to see a drop in honey bee populations.
    C) CCD or "colony collapse disorder" is not a factor in honey bee decline.

125

Explanations

1. **C. is unaware of the Copernican Theory.** This is the best answer because it says so in lines 19 and 20. You can't argue with that! Choice A is not shocking. Since Watson was Holmes' friend, he would know if Holmes was a detective or not. Eliminate choice B. Choice D is probably true, but the passage gives no indication that this shocked Watson.

2. **B. gateway.** This is the best answer because of the word entrance, which appears on the same line. Choice A is too broad, while choice D is inappropriate. "Introduction" is not bad, but "gateway" is better.

3. **C. surprise that he knows so much but not this.** The evidence for this answer can be found in the first paragraph. Choices A and B clearly miss the mark. You might be tempted to pick D, but the word "alarm" is too extreme.

4. **A. remembers only that information that will help him in his endeavors.** This is the correct answer because Holmes only considers "useful" facts. Choices B and D are not the best answers because Holmes has no desire to understand "lumber of every sort" or **all** aspects of life. Choice C is not the best answer because Holmes does not mean "furniture" in a literal sense. He is speaking metaphorically.

5. **C. Lines 42-44 (Depend upon ... before").** This is the best answer because these lines best corroborate the previous answer when Holmes states, "It is of the highest importance, therefore, not to have useless facts elbowing out the useful ones." The other quotes just do not apply.

6. **A. stretch.** This is the best answer because of the word "elastic," which is on the same line. Enough said.

7. **D. unfocused.** Be careful. Remember you are looking for the answer that is **not** true of Holmes. Considering all we have already said about Holmes, this should be an easy one.

8. **A. Watson is an extremely meticulous person.** Just look at Watson's list! Choice B is out because Watson is impressed with other aspects of Holmes' character. As for C, who knows? Choice D is obviously incorrect as Holmes was a famous detective.

9. **D. Lines 65-78 (1. Knowledge ... law").** This is the best answer because of the aforementioned list, which demonstrates just how scrupulous Watson could be. The other choices are inapt.

10. **C. befuddled.** Considering Watson's "surprise" and "astonishment," this is the best answer. Watson was not really as annoyed as perplexed. "Angry" would be too strong. Choice B doesn't apply.

11. **A. Watson's list, from our perspective of modern detective work, epitomizes what qualities a perfect detective has.** Makes sense doesn't it? Choice B is not the best answer because we are talking about Holmes, not Watson. That can be said for the other choices as well.

12. **B. illustrate the benefits of one system against the liabilities of another.** This is the best choice because the author of Passage 1 is making a comparison between capitalism and slavery. Choice A is never addressed and it is just too big for a three-paragraph passage. You would need several books or even an entire library to answer it. Choice C is easily to eliminate. As for choice D, it is true that profit is a part of this passage, but not the main purpose.

13. **D. Lines 42-47 ("The free …right").** This is the best answer because here the author clearly compares the two systems using the free laborer and the slave; and as you can tell, he believes slavery is the better one. The other choices are inappropriate.

14. **B. trifle.** In this case, we need a negative word because of context clues such as "cruel," "allow," "overburdened," and "mockery." Trifle means "a small amount," which is the only negative choice.

15. **C. truculent.** This is the best answer because of the word "boast," which the author uses twice in this paragraph. By using it twice he is getting "in the face" of his opponents—those who are opposed to slavery. "Truculent" means belligerent, and is he ever! The other choices are all positive, and thus incorrect.

16. **A. There is no possible rationale for slavery.** This should be obvious from the tone of the passage: the writer is very forceful with his words. All of the other choices are mentioned, but they are not the central claim. Remember: the author is an abolitionist.

17. **B. Lines 51-54 ("By no … justifiable").** This is a hard question. Many of you may have picked choice A. The reason that B is better is because it more accurately addresses the question of "rationale." Choice A, lines 48-50, makes it unequivocally clear that the author is against slavery, but choice B just as lucidly states that there is no justification or rationale for slavery. It's a fine distinction, but one we sometimes have to make. The other choices miss the point.

18. **A. shackles.** This is the best answer because "shackles" mean manacles or chains, which makes sense in this context. That is why "the land must have no rest." Choice B carries the idea of being free, like in sovereign nation, which is the opposite of what we are looking for. The other choices do not fit.

19. **C. slaves are not animals.** This is an easy one because the author is speaking of slaves, not women and children. Choice C is the obvious answer. Choice A is so ridiculous, it's silly. Choice B misses the point. Choice D is also ridiculous.

20. **D. adamant.** As we mentioned earlier, the author's tone is very forceful in his condemnation of slavery. He evens states there is "no compromise." That being said, choices A and B are not in play. Choice C, "concerned" is simply not strong enough. "Adamant," or unyielding, is the best answer.

21. **B. Passage 2 refutes a central claim advanced in Passage 1.** This is the best answer because Passage 2 does rebut the claim that "slaves of the South are the happiest … and freest people in the world," which is one of the central claims of Passage 1. The other choices are inappropriate.

22. **D. Only New Hampshire and Pennsylvania had a slave population of less than 1%.** This is the best choice if you look carefully. Massachusetts also had a slave population off less than 1%: 0%. Choices A, B, and C are all true according to the passage.

23. D. Freud employed a practical approach to his work on dream psychology. This is the best answer because it is implied in the first two lines with the phrase, "... anything but theoretical." Also, in line 26, the author speaks of Freud's "pragmatic view." Choice A is not the best answer because Freud's work was truly novel. Choice B is incorrect because as with any new idea, it takes time for popular acceptance. Choice C is incorrect as well because the passage states that there is a connection between dreams and the dreamer's life, not philosophy.

24. A. Line 1 ("Freud's theories … theoretical"). We have already seen the rationale for this answer in the explanation to the previous question. The other quotes do not apply.

25. C. studies the evidence until it tells him something. This is the best answer because in lines 7 and 8 the author states, "He (Freud) looked at the facts … until they began to tell him something." Furthermore, in the next sentence, the author compares Freud to that statistician. Choices A and D express the opposite idea. Choice B was never stated.

26. B. accustomed. Remember to always bring the word in context back to the passage to see exactly how it was used. In this case, when you do so, the only choice that makes sense is "accustomed." (Keep in mind that for this particular question, the most obvious answer is usually wrong. The ETS wants you to bite on "desirous," but that answer does not make sense here.)

27. C. the "autistic ways." This is the best answer because the "autistic ways" are those **not** supported by any evidence - just "sprung" from the brain "fully armed" like Minerva. Choice A is silly. Choices B and D are not mentioned.

28. D. nonsense. This can clearly be seen in lines 33-36: "This (connection) … disposes of the widely prevalent view that dreams are purely nonsensical … leading nowhere." Enough said.

29. D. gratification. This question demonstrates the importance of one word, "every." Although all of the choices are mentioned in Freud's "five facts" about dreams, the word "every" only applies to "attempted or successful gratification" in line 42.

30. B. Lines 37-43 ("Secondly, Freud … unconscious"). This is the best answer because of the rationale mentioned in the previous explanation. The other choices are inappropriate.

31. A. informative. This is the best answer because the passage did impart a plethora of interesting information. I sure learned something. Choice B is incorrect because there is nothing amusing about the passage. Choice C is an interesting answer, but it is not exactly what the passage does, which is to discuss how Freud revolutionized dream analysis. "Contentious" means argumentative and there is no argument here about Freud's revolutionary and influential contributions to psychiatry.

32. C. exert. This is the best answer because of the word "influence." "Exert" means "bring to bear," which captures the idea. Choices A and B simply don't fit. Choice D would be a stretch at best, so let's not.

33. A. explain the origin of capitalism. This is the best answer because this main idea pervades the passage from the beginning to the end. Just look to the start and the conclusion of the essay. Choice A may or may not be true, but it was never definitely stated. Choice B is incorrect because capitalism **did** begin in Europe. Choice D is too specific.

34. B. Lines 9-12 ("Weber saw ... Catholic"). This is the best answer since it clearly supports the previous one because in the third paragraph it states that capitalism **started** in Europe. The other choices are inapt.

35. C. worldly. This is the best answer because the passage states that King Henry made himself the spiritual leader of England in addition to his temporal powers. Well, then, temporal is the opposite of spiritual. Plug in the other choices and none really make sense.

36. D. informative. This is the best answer because of the pedagogical nature of the passage. Choices A and B are incorrect because the author never really questions or argues about anything. "Indifferent," as we have stressed earlier, is never the correct answer.

37. B. people's religious convictions. This is the best answer because from the beginning to the conclusion of the passage, the narrator makes the point that Protestantism and capitalism went hand in hand. While choice A does have some merit, it's not the main idea. "Eternal bliss" eliminates choice C. Choice D was never mentioned.

38. D. Lines 77-81 ("Weber concluded ... successful"). This is the best answer because these lines corroborate our answer when they refer to Protestantism's spirit of hard work and profits. The other choices do not apply.

39. B. the Church members did not need him if their fate was already sealed. This is the best answer because John Calvin was a religious theologian and pastor. By preaching predestination, he was making his services obsolete. Why would his congregation need him if their fate was predetermined? The narrator mentions that Calvin was a successful preacher, so he must have known what he was talking about. That eliminates A. The narrator also states that Calvin was "a prominent Protestant reformer," so his congregation would not be "alienated." There goes choice C. Choice D refers to Catholicism, not Protestantism.

40. D. addition. This is the best answer because if you go back to the passage and look at how the word is used, it's the only answer that makes sense. Why? Look at the next sentence. Do you see the word "also?" That's why.

41. B. humans have free will. This is the best answer because in the fifth paragraph it mentions that Catholics believed in free will, not Protestants. If you go back and look, all of the other choices are tenets that Calvin agreed with.

42. D. he did away with indulgences. This choice was never mentioned in connection with Luther and, therefore, is the best answer. Choices A and B were clearly stated in the seventh paragraph. In the same paragraph, the author states that Luther "ushered in many ... changes in the Church, which would result in a population more prone towards thinking for themselves." He also says, "the people were asked what they thought about various aspects of the Church." These two quotes would eliminate C as a NOT.

43. C. examine the causes and effects of a shrinking bee population. Although the other choices were mentioned, they were not evident throughout the passage as C certainly was.

44. A. Lines 23-26 ("So called ... warming"). This excerpt goes right to the heart of the matter listing very specific examples of what scientists believe might be causing the decline in bee population. None of the others are this specific.

45. C. insects. Since they specialize in bees, their field of study must be insects.

46. D. insight. Once you see that the "sky is falling," exaggeration is out and that is negative and therefore pessimistic, so insight is the only choice left.

47. A. unauthentic. Again, you have to read the sentence after the one containing the word in context, but, if you do, it clearly states that "no definitive research has been able to validate that Einstein ever said that." So, it must be unauthentic.

48. C. other countries using these pesticides have not had declines in bee populations. This is specifically stated in lines 33-36 and all of the others are either refuted by the text or not mentioned.

49. D. developing bee farms. Again, all of the others are specifically mentioned except for this one.

50. C. other insects. Each of the other choices is mentioned, but other insects are never brought up.

51. A. tangible. When something is tangible, it is able to be touched. You can see it at work. None of the other choices fits this at all.

52. B. The introduction of parasitic mites has contributed to a decrease in bee producing colonies. This is the best answer because it says so in the third paragraph. In addition, the chart illustrates a pronounced downward trend since the use of parasitic mites. Choice A is not the answer because of the aforementioned downward trend. There is no real ebb and flow – mainly just ebb. There is no way to substantiate choice C. As for choice D, "colony collapse disorder" is definitely a factor both in the passage and the chart.

GRAMMAR

English, like many languages, has its own way of doing things. This, of course is a great way to learn how a culture thinks by carefully analyzing its language. Interestingly, most grammar tests avoid questioning students on the subtleties and niceties of the language because, depending on the situation or interpretation, either choice could be correct.

That is why you sometimes see an answer on the SAT or PSAT crossed out. This is because they realized too late that the question was left up to interpretation and two answers were acceptable.

Example 1: The jury was/were informed that they could come in late tomorrow.

If we are considering the entire jury, then "was" is correct. If we are considering each member being informed, then it is "were."

None is another example.

Example 2: None of the team members was/were performing well.

"Was" both sounds better and indicates that "not one member is doing well." However, how about the sentence "Almost none of them was/were moral?" Here, "were" sounds better and indicates the plural nature of the sentence.

So, we will assume that you will not be tested on any esoteric distinctions and will avoid any of these in this book.

Some of you have been weaned on grammar from your private school experience and others might have only been exposed to it for a few weeks in fifth grade. For the latter, perhaps a brief definition of some basic terms would come in handy.

Basic Definitions

Noun: A group of words that refer to things and people and nameable things such as: book, ostrich, Galileo, hoodlum, Tennessee. Abstract things are also nouns: fear, joy, beauty, sin.

Pronoun: A word that takes the place of or "sits in" for a noun:

Personal pronouns: he, she, it, they, I, you, we us, etc.

Possessive pronouns: ours, yours, theirs, his, her, mine, etc.

Question and relative pronouns: who, whom, which where, why, when, what, whose, etc.

Verb: words that are actions or states. ex. kick, grapple, climb, wonder, think, explore, remind.

Linking verbs: to be, is, are, was, were, has, have and had been, will or shall be, etc.

A verb is active when the subject does the action—John captured the prize. It is passive when the object appears as the subject and the subject as the object. The prize was captured by John.

Adjective: A word that describes a property or state.

ex. ornery, haphazard, blue, obvious, gracious, cancerous, etc. They are used to describe nouns.

ex. She is **rich.**

ex. The **elegant** bachelor was pursued by many.

Adverb: A word that describes verbs, adjectives and other adverbs.

ex. He walked **vigorously.**

ex. She was **fabulously** rich.

ex. He walked **very** slowly.

Conjunction: (The terms coordinator and subordinator are sometimes used.) A word that connects two phrases. Coordinating ones connect two complete thoughts: and, or, nor, but, yet, so. Subordinate ones begin a dependent clause: if, whether, despite, although, whereas, etc.

Preposition: A word that typically expresses time or spatial relationships. They are followed by a few words forming a phrase that always ends with a noun or pronoun and are used to describe a noun or help clarify a concept. ex: by, from, around, across, during, through, under.

Tense

Some grammar manuals spend as much as 14 pages to explain rules, exceptions and exceptions to exceptions for tense. It is better to understand some guidelines and apply them than to memorize countless rules and variations. With that in mind, here are a few basics.

Keep all verbs in a sentence in the same tense.

ex. After he had broken his leg, he walked down the aisle on crutches.

ex. Because he likes fresh ingredients in his dishes, he grows many of the herbs and vegetables himself.

If you have two past tenses and one of the actions must have occurred earlier than the other, express the earlier one in the past perfect. This means that you must use the word "had" before the verb.

ex. The doctor suspected that I had torn my Achilles tendon.

If you express something that is always true, it is called the universal present and must be expressed in the present tense.

ex. My teacher told us yesterday that Acadia National Park is in Maine. To say that it "was" in Maine might cast some doubt as to where it is now.

If you use a conditional, if or wish, you must use the verb "were' instead of "was."

ex. If she were there yesterday, I think we would have won.

ex. I wish Tesla were alive today to observe so many of his visions becoming reality.

Never begin your if clause with "If I would have." Use "If I had" instead.

ex. If Alan Turing had not been successful in decoding the German communications system (Enigma), millions of people would have died.

Subject – Verb Agreement

This has always accounted for almost 40% of all errors on the SAT. However, it should be a good deal less on the new test because both punctuation errors and redundancies will probably be added to the mix. The following are some indications that should help you to deal with any agreement errors on the exam:

1. Always try to find the central verb right away. Then, backtrack to see what the subject is. What they will often do is throw one or two prepositional phrases in the way to befuddle you. ex. The general with his soldiers were beaten badly. Since "men" is plural and directly precedes "were," it seems correct. However, the sentence does indicate that the soldiers were not beaten but only the general. So, it should be "was."

2. They might also place a relative pronoun in the way such as that, who, or which. ex. The quarterback, who was injured in the fights that ensued after the vicious fouls, were brought to the emergency room. Twelve words intervene between quarterback and were. This does not alter the fact that quarterback is singular and thus requires a singular verb—was.

3. There is/are, was/were, has/have, etc. Anytime you have one of these variations of the infinitive "to be," you must have the verb agree with the first noun or pronoun that follows. ex. There was/were three divas trying to outdo each other. Since divas is more than one, we must use the verb-were. We have seen occasions when they place that first noun or pronoun considerably away from the "There is, was, have been" construction. ex. There was/were in the olden days, before men were first enlightened about how to devise a plan of attack for war, some ridiculous stratagems that are laughable by today's military standards. Instead of following the "There was" construction with a noun, this sentence places the noun 21 words later (stratagem). This is seldom done, so it will unlikely affect you.

Pronoun Agreement

It is important that we know to whom the author is referring. Look at these examples. (Sometimes, the best way to correct the problem is just to rewrite it.)

ex. Tom's father thinks he's stupid.

We don't know whether Tom's father thinks he himself is stupid or that his son is stupid.

Correction: Tom's father thinks that his son, Tom, is stupid.

On any grammar exam, always be conscious of pronouns and make sure that the word they refer to (its antecedent) agrees in number and person with it.

ex. If a team is destined to follow its leader, he/they has/have to come across as a real person. Since leader is singular, we must choose "he" and "has."

ex. The expense of buying organic vegetables is about four times more today than it was to purchase it/them twenty years ago. Here, we are referring to vegetables, so we need the word "them."

Fragments

A fragment is a group of words that appears to form a sentence, but lacks a central verb and therefore is not a sentence.

ex. In the moonlight, the shimmering waves that pounded the shore like drum beats from afar.

Yes, we do have the verb "pounded", but it is preceded by the relative pronoun "that" resulting in a relative clause but no central clause. If we just remove the word "that," it becomes a sentence.

Run-On Sentences

A run-on sentence is the most egregious grammatical error. It places two complete thoughts next to each other and they therefore "run into" each other. When you see two complete thoughts separated by only a comma and that comma is not followed by a coordinating conjunction, you have a run-on. The easiest way to correct it is to place a semi-colon between the two clauses. You can do that only if the two ideas are very similar.

ex. They were true competitors; they just loved to win.

You can also do it by apposition, use of a relative clause, making it a complex sentence or simply writing two sentences.

ex. Natasha and Brianna will lead the team this year, their leadership was superlative this year. (Run-On)

ex. 1 Natasha and Brianna will lead the team this year because their leadership was superlative.

ex. 2. Natasha and Brianna, who led the team this year, will continue their superlative leadership next year.

ex. 3. Natasha and Brianna, two superlative leaders, will continue their leadership next year.

All of these are acceptable corrections for the run-on sentence.

Parallel Structure

This is an effective writing technique, but you must abide by a few rules or the grammar police will arrest you. There are two basic types. The first is a sequence and this is easy to spot.

ex. She likes to feather step, free spin, and moonwalking.

Once you begin a sequence, you must maintain the same structure. So, just change it to moonwalk and all is well.

The second is harder to pick up and this is the one you will see more commonly on grammar tests. When you have the words "and, than, or and as well as" in a sentence, the structure on both sides must be the same.

ex. A coach's goal is to train his players in a particular system as well as instilling sound sportsmanship in them.

Once you see the words "as well as, or, and, than" you have to make sure that the structure on the right side is the same as that already established on the left. Here, we would have to change it to "as well as to instill."

Transitional Phrases

Often the error on a test will be simply the wrong transitional phrase, so it is important that you pay attention to specific words and what they really mean. So, make sure you know the actual meanings of words like "thus, moreover, however, whereas, and, so forth, consequently," etc. One word that you take for granted could cost you points.

Faulty Comparisons

We have to keep in mind exactly what is being compared. Often the sentence is comparing something animate to something inanimate and that is certainly an error.

ex. Phil appreciated the architectural sketches of his wife more than other architects.

Here, Phil appreciates sketches more than the architects. Don't compare things to people.

ex. He enjoys the novels of Nabokov more than Proust.

Again, he enjoys novels (things) more than Proust (a person.)

Misplaced Modifiers

A modifier is a word or group of words describing or limiting another word or group of words. It must be placed as close as possible to the word it is modifying.

ex. A qualified dentist can only fill cavities.

"Qualified" is our modifier but it seems to be saying that the dentist can only fill cavities, when they can, of course, do bridge work, braces, root canals etc. Merely taking the word "only" and placing it as the first word in the sentence makes it clear and effective.

ex. Many of the sarcastic comments were made by the coach of the team that had a bitter tone.

So, who has the bitter tone, the coach, the team or the comments? The underlined phrase should follow "comments" instead.

Dangling Participles

Participles are verbals, verb forms that act as adjectives or nouns. On most grammar exams, you will see it as the first word in a sentence or clause, usually ending in **ing** but sometimes **ed.**

When you see this, go right to the comma following it and make sure the first noun or pronoun is doing the action of that ing or ed word. If not, you have a dangling participle.

ex. Arriving at the restaurant, it was great to see some old friends.

"It" cannot arrive, so we have to place a person there.

Correction: Arriving at the restaurant, I was glad to see some old friends.

Diction

There will be times when a word is underlined and it is absolutely the wrong word in that context. In that case, look at the choices and opt for the one that most fits the sense of the sentence.

ex. eminent-imminent, contemptuous-contemptible, principal-principle, climatic-climactic, compliment-complement, laudable-laudatory, navel-naval, restive-restless, venal-venial.

These are words that look enough alike that they can be easily confused. You might start by making sure you know the distinctions between each of these words.

Idioms

An idiom is a style or manner of expression peculiar to a given people. On grammar tests, it is usually a matter of a misuse of prepositions, but it can be virtually any word that by custom is always used with another word.

ex. Recently, scientists have discovered that colds can be caused from frigid conditions.

Looks fine, but the correct preposition is caused **by.**

ex. Most of his ideas are inconsistent to current theory.

Again, a very small word, **to,** makes this incorrect. The correct preposition is **with.**

ex. He made a suggestion in the hope to gain a new perspective.

Again, we say **of gaining** rather than **to gain.**

There are countless idioms in our language, so it really comes down to your being more observant both in your reading and conversation during the next few months leading up to your exam so that you are equipped to pick up these idioms.

Double Negative

Today, most of us do not have difficulty with double negatives, but you should keep in mind that the words *scarcely, hardly, barely, only,* and *but* are negatives and should not be used with another negative.

ex. Terry has **scarcely no** money left.

Use **scarcely any,** instead.

ex. I **couldn't hardly** believe her.

Use **could hardly** instead.

Redundancies

These are repetitive phrases or words that make writing heavy.

ex. prestigiously acclaimed, rush in a hurry, trespassers who wrongfully enter, whole entire.

Avoid these in your writing and keep an eye out for them when taking the exam. Sometimes, they are a complete clause or phrase following a comma. If what is being said is so obvious that it is unnecessary, then that is a redundancy and must be deleted.

Punctuation

Although it does not appear that the strong focus on punctuation problems that you will see on the ACT will be evidenced on the SAT, you should see a number of them and therefore should spend some time going over punctuation rules in a good grammar book. That being said, most of the punctuation mistakes you will encounter will be of the indiscriminate kind. For example, "This book, is very helpful." Notice that we do not need a comma after book. (But, I must agree that the book is definitely helpful!)

Particular Question Types

Yes, No: In this type of question you are given a question such as "Should the author delete or add the following sentence from the passage?" If you pay attention to the question and just think about it for ten seconds, it is almost always easy to decide whether the answer is Yes or No. The hard part is deciding why it is Yes or No.

Combining Two Sentences: In this type of question, the first criterion should always be "Does the combined sentence contain all of the essential ingredients of the two sentences?" After that, you must look at which choice most tersely and smoothly combines the two sentences. Most of the time, the briefest sentence will be the answer, but remember, if that sentence contains any grammatical errors, or any awkward phrasing, then it cannot be the answer.

Logical Placement of a Sentence: For this type of question, it is very important that you establish clearly in your mind what exactly the sentence in question is saying and what the key words refer to. Once you have done that, it is just a matter of pinpointing which sentence it must most logically follow. This is generally not a very difficult question as long as you are careful. Take your time on it.

Graphic of Chart Question: The SAT has not been asking difficult questions of this type so far. So, just look for the most common sense answer and that should be it. It is possible that they will eventually start asking the types of questions that are found on the Science part of the ACT, but so far there is no indication that they are going to do that.

Conclusion Question: For this question type there are two possibilities. If the questions just asks which choice best concludes the passage, then the question is quite easy. The harder possibility is when they ask you for the choice that also brings cohesion to the passage by mentioning something that was developed earlier in the passage. In this harder case, you need to make sure that your choice does both.

GRAMMAR PRACTICE PASSAGES

* There are still many minor rules that we have not covered, but we do so in the practice pages in the book. Pay careful attention to those explanations and if you do not understand them, ask your English teachers to go over them with you. **It is very important that you don't just do the practice questions we have provided without going over the explanations. They not only make you sharper for the exam, but also get you ready for college.**

The passages below are designed to make you understand how to take this test more efficiently. At first, you might just want to give up. If you persist, you will start to notice that it gets easier very rapidly. Grammar is fairly logical, so those solid math students out there should have an advantage as math is based on logic.

A good way to work with this format is to pretend that you wrote each of these short essays and that you are taking one last look at them before you submit them to your teacher. For each underlined part, ask yourself "Is that how I would have written it?" "Are there any changes I should make?" "What are those changes?" If you feel that you would not make any changes then simply pick the first choice, which will be NO CHANGE.

If you keep your right hand over the choices and do not allow yourself to see the choices before you make the correction yourself, you will see a very rapid improvement. Keep track of how many you get wrong on each passage and challenge yourself to get at least one better on each succeeding one.

You have ample time to complete the grammar part. Do not rush through it. Be careful and you will be amazed at how good you get in a very short time.

Writing and Language Test 1

35 MINUTES, 44 QUESTIONS

DIRECTIONS

Each passage below is accompanied by a number of questions. For some questions, you will consider how the passage might be revised to improve the expression of ideas. For other questions, you will consider how the passage might be edited to correct errors in sentence structure, usage, or punctuation. A passage or a question may be accompanied by one or more graphics (such as a table or graph) that you will consider as you make revising and editing decisions.

Some questions will direct you to an underlined portion of a passage. Other questions will direct you to a location in a passage or ask you to think about the passage as a whole.

After reading each passage, choose the answer to each question that most effectively improves the quality of writing in the passage or that makes the passage conform to the conventions of standard written English. Many questions include a "NO CHANGE" option. Choose that option if you think the best choice is to leave the relevant portion of the passage as it is.

Questions 1 - 11 are based on the following passage.

This is an excerpt from the book Tai Chi Ch'uan through the Western Gate by Rick Barrett.

The art of Push Hands has been practiced since the sixth century B.C. At its higher level, Push Hands (1) <u>inspire</u> images of the Jedi contests between Yoda and Obi-Wan Kenobi.

1.
A) NO CHANGE
B) inspires
C) "inspires"
D) inspired

(2) <u>At it's worst,</u> it looks more like bad Sumo wrestling between two drunks. Too often, it resembles the latter.

Push hands is a two-person exercise designed to (3) <u>inculcate</u> the skills of the Chinese internal martial art of T'ai Chi Ch'uan. Why is T'ai Chi considered an "internal" martial art? Like the fictional *Star Wars* characters, whose skill depends on mastering "the Force," the internal martial artist cultivates and directs internal energy called ch'i. (4) <u>Thus the use</u> of muscular force actually interrupts the circulation of this energy. Push Hands, therefore, uses the least amount of physical force to produce the biggest effect. It sounds paradoxical that you can become stronger by relaxing your muscles, (5) <u>and it is</u> easily demonstrated by someone who has trained in t'ai chi ch'uan. The hard part is letting go of the security blanket of muscular tension that you have carried with you since infancy. Even when we see a petite woman easily pushing two large, strong men, our minds are unconvinced. It is such an improbable event that we need to rationalize it in some way.

2.
A) NO CHANGE
B) At its worst
C) At its worse
D) At its' worse

3.
A) NO CHANGE
B) introduce
C) establish
D) unleash

4.
A) NO CHANGE
B) Thus, the use
C) Then, the use
D) By this, the use

5.
A) NO CHANGE
B) but it is
C) but they are
D) but, it is

(6) Push Hands is a great sport. At its simplest, the game is to keep one's (7) balance and equilibrium and make one's opponent lose his. Losing your balance—even the threat of losing your balance—provokes a primitive stress response that causes you to tense your muscle as a form of protection. Tension comes from muscles in conflict. We get in our own way. Push Hands helps us overcome that primitive, fearful (8) tightening and we can replace it with something much more effective.

6.
A) NO CHANGE
B) That's where Push Hands comes in.
C) Let's look more seriously at Push Hands.
D) Push Hands gives us a very clear and precise picture of exactly how this works.

7.
A) NO CHANGE
B) balance, and equilibrium
C) balance
D) balance or equilibrium

8.
A) NO CHANGE
B) tightening thus we
C) tightening, and we
D) tightening, and so we

141

At its best, Push Hands is done with (9) seeming effortless grace, like walking a tightrope or diving from a high board or (10) to juggle five balls. It allows us to overcome our fears to perform more calmly and effectively in anything we choose. (11) Push Hands comes very close to being the national pastime of China in that a very high percentage of its people has engaged in it over the years.

9.
 A) NO CHANGE
 B) seeming effortlessly
 C) seemingly effortless
 D) effortless

10.
 A) NO CHANGE
 B) juggling
 C) , to juggle
 D) having to juggle

11. Where should this sentence be placed?

 A) at the beginning of the paragraph
 B) first sentence in the passage
 C) where it is
 D) delete it

Questions 12 - 22 are based on the following passage.

The following passage was written by Barbara Gatti, a long-time dancer and former Rockette.

On the island of Manhattan in the City of New York, there are many entertainment (12) productions. One of the largest and definitely one of the most visited is Radio City Music Hall. The biggest attraction at Radio City Music Hall (13) are a line of thirty-six precision dancers known as The Rockettes. This precision was achieved the hard way—rehearsals. (14) Also, every show was observed by either the choreographer, assistant choreographer, or line captain.

12.
- A) NO CHANGE
- B) cites.
- C) venues.
- D) shows.

13.
- A) NO CHANGE
- B) was a line of thirty-six precision dancers
- C) is a line of thirty-six precision dancers
- D) were a line of thirty-six precision dancers

14.
- A) NO CHANGE
- B) However
- C) Remarkably
- D) In contrast

Entertaining for more than fifty years, (15) four shows a day, seven days a week, fifty-two weeks a year, the Rockettes worked. The obvious question is how? Of course, attrition and audition played a role, and the key element was that there were not thirty-six Rockettes. There were forty-six: thirty-six on stage, and ten on vacation each week. Once that is realized, another question arises. Remember that the Rockettes are a line of precision dancers (16) precisely placed and positioned in the line according to height; what happened if, when a vacationing dancer returned to work, her spot was occupied? The answer is "That's what a rehearsal hall is for!" (17) Everyone in the line rehearsed in their new spot. This situation is complicated by another mind-boggling statistic. Radio City Music Hall used to change shows every month or so. Rehearsals for the next show (18) had took place while the old show was still running. And sometimes there were special events that required extra rehearsal time as well.

15.
A) NO CHANGE
B) worked the Rockettes, four shows a day, seven days a week, fifty-two weeks a year.
C) fifty-two weeks a year, seven days a week, four shows a day, the Rockettes worked.
D) the Rockettes worked four shows a day, seven days a week, fifty-two weeks a year.

16.
A) NO CHANGE
B) precisely placed and situated in the line
C) precisely placed in the line
D) precisely and placed in the line

17.
A) NO CHANGE
B) Everybody in the line rehearsed in their new spot.
C) Everyone in the line rehearsed in there new spot.
D) Everyone in the line rehearsed in her new spot.

18.
A) NO CHANGE
B) had taken place
C) took place
D) takes place

Who would ever want to do this job? Hundreds of women from all over the country lined up to audition for each place in line whenever there was an open call! Besides being able to perform tap, modern jazz, and ballet (at one time in Radio City Music Hall's history, there was a twenty-four-member ballet corps that, at times, needed extra dancers and Rockettes would be required to fill in), potential dancers had to have the necessary stamina required (19) <u>for</u> a lengthy high kick segment that was the staple of every Rockette routine.

These "Dancing (20) <u>Daughters", as their</u> founder, Russell Markert, dubbed them, have served as ambassadors of goodwill for not only Radio City Music Hall, but for the entire country as well. (21) They participated in USO Tours during World War II, entertained thousands of American troops, performed in Super Bowl Halftime shows with more than 150 viewers watching, and even (22) <u>appearing with</u> the 2001 Presidential Inauguration Ceremony, dancing on the White House lawn.

Although the Rockettes are no longer in residence year-round at Radio City Music Hall, they still entertain over five thousand people per show for four shows a day for six weeks during their "Christmas Spectacular" there. And, because of the enormous popularity of this holiday event, the Rockettes have taken their show "on the road," delighting audiences in Arizona, California, Colorado, Florida, Illinois, Massachusetts, Missouri, Nebraska, and Texas.

19.
   A) NO CHANGE
   B) by
   C) in
   D) as

20.
   A) NO CHANGE
   B) Daughters," as their
   C) Daughters", as there
   D) Daughters," as they're

21. At this point, the writer is considering adding the following sentence.

   They made a lot of extra money by performing these shows.

   Should the writer make this addition here?

   A) Yes, because we need to understand what motivated them and this certainly does that.
   B) Yes, because we need to know this important fact about the Rockettes.
   C) No, because it breaks up the discussion of their being goodwill ambassadors with the fine example in the following sentence with information that is not considered in the rest of the passage.
   D) No, because the passage has already discussed their financial incentives.

22.
   A) NO CHANGE
   B) appearing in
   C) appeared in
   D) appeared at

Questions 23 - 33 are based on the following passage and supplementary material.

Garlic

This glorious vegetable has been around for more than 4,000 years. (23) Its (24) rich pungency and smell has been both extolled and vilified during the course of human history. The ancient Egyptians used it as a medicine for more than 20 different ailments including heart disease and tumors. They even fed it to their slaves to give them more strength to build their pyramids. (25) Many doctors today still recommend garlic supplements. Interestingly, the only slave revolt in Egypt was because of a lack of (26) garlic which happened because the Nile flooded the garlic fields that year.

23.
  A) NO CHANGE
  B) It's
  C) Its'
  D) Their

24.
  A) NO CHANGE
  B) rich pungency, and smell has
  C) rich pungency has
  D) rich pungency and smell have

25. What would be the best way of dealing with this sentence?
  A) NO CHANGE
  B) Insert it after sentence 3.
  C) Delete it.
  D) Combine it with the preceding sentence using ", and" before "many."

26.
  A) NO CHANGE
  B) garlic, which happened
  C) garlic; which happened
  D) garlic, that happened

(27) It was a valuable commodity and a source of (28) currency, as matter of fact, King Tut, as well as many other (29) pharaohs, was sent to the afterlife with cloves of garlic at his side.

In the Mishnah, which is part of the Talmud, the ancient Israelites were referred to as "garlic eaters." During the time when the Egyptians subjugated them, their diet, as with all slaves, included garlic. So it is no surprise that in the Bible (Numbers 11:5) it was written that they missed the vegetable on their escape to the Promised Land.

In ancient Greece and Rome garlic was used for dog bites and bladder infections as well as a cure for asthma and leprosy. It was also given to Greek warriors for courage in battle. It's also been recorded that Greek Olympic athletes ate garlic to enhance their performance. Even Romans used poultices of moss, garlic, and wine to treat wounded soldiers. Also, since the times of Homer, garlic has been purported to be a powerful aphrodisiac. Hippocrates, also known as the "father of medicine," agreed that (31) ingesting garlic would contribute to sexual potency.

27. In context, which of following phrases would most appropriately be inserted at the beginning of this sentence?

   A) For instance,
   B) Furthermore,
   C) In addition,
   D) Incidentally,

28.
   A) NO CHANGE
   B) currency, as a matter of fact;
   C) currency. As a matter of fact;
   D) currency; as a matter of fact,

29.
   A) NO CHANGE
   B) pharaohs was sent
   C) pharaohs, were sent
   D) Their pharaohs were sending

30. In paragraph 3, which writing correction is not warranted?

   A) Delete the needless repetition of the word "also" from so many sentences.
   B) Rewrite sentence 1 to read "Ancient Greeks and Romans used garlic," thus switching to active voice.
   C) Change sentence 2 to "Greek warriors used it for courage in battle."
   D) Capitalize "father of medicine."

31.
   A) NO CHANGE
   B) devouring
   C) swallowing
   D) drinking

(32) In 1858, Louis Pasteur documented that garlic killed bacteria. And I read that Albert Schweitzer used garlic as an antiseptic in his jungle hospital. During World War II, when penicillin and other sulfur drugs were limited, garlic was utilized successfully as a treatment for open wounds and to prevent gangrene. Garlic was recently used in a test study as an ingredient in mouthwash. The mouthwash was clinically proven to be effective in killing bacteria, but the participants in the study complained of halitosis.

As a matter of fact, (33) most negative references to garlic center on its smell. It is often referred to as "the stinking rose." King Alfonso of Castile was so offended by the odor of garlic that he would banish any of his knights from his court for a month if they were found to have garlic breath. Even today no one in the British Royal Family eats garlic so as not to have offensive breath. In the United States garlic took a while to catch on because it was also considered vulgar and low class. Now, California produces 250 million pounds of the stuff every year. There is even a restaurant in San Francisco that sells garlic ice cream. Not to be outdone, there is a restaurant in Helsinki, Finland, that offers garlic cheesecake and garlic beer!

32. What would be the best way to combine sentences 1 and 2 of this paragraph?

   A) bacteria, and I read
   B) bacteria, but I read
   C) bacteria; and I read
   D) bacteria, I read

33.
   A) NO CHANGE
   B) most negative references to garlic center on its smell.
   C) most negative references to garlic, center on its smell.
   D) most negative references to garlic center on their smell.

Questions 34 - 44 are based on the following passage and supplementary material.

I graduated from Stuyvesant High School, just a few blocks from the World Trade Center in New York City. It is the top high school in New York and perhaps one of the most (34) prestigiously acclaimed public schools in the country. I lettered in three different sports and played percussion in the award winning band. I was fortunate to become a national merit scholar; this is a distinction that only 1000 students receive each year. (35) So, it would seem that I must by now be a successful doctor, lawyer, engineer or entrepreneur. I am none of these.

For the past fifteen years, I have taught math to junior high and high school students in private schools making only a living wage. What a failure- or so it would seem to many.

(38) [1] In Finland, the highest ranked academic country in the world, almost 80% of the top 10% of graduating students vie to become teachers, forgoing the wealth they could (36) attain in almost any other field. [2] Why do they do this? [3] The answer is that they do not define themselves by how much money they make or how nice a car they drive or (37) the place they live. [4] They define themselves by

34.
 A) NO CHANGE
 B) prestigious acclaimed
 C) prestigiously recognized
 D) acclaimed

35.
 A) NO CHANGE
 B) Incidentally,
 C) Moreover,
 D) Finally,

36.
 A) NO CHANGE
 B) have attain
 C) have attained
 D) had attained

37.
 A) NO CHANGE
 B) where they live
 C) how they live
 D) their living conditions

how much better they can make their community and their country. [5] That is their motivation. [6] They know that they will be working each day to mold young minds and to develop strong character in their students. [7] They instill confidence in their students, many of whom never believed that they could (39) have achieve what they had done. [8] They share every day in the wonderful accomplishments of their students and count many of them among their friends (40) for years to come. (41)

38. To make this paragraph most logical, sentence 5 should be

    A) placed before sentence 1.
    B) placed before sentence 8.
    C) placed after sentence 8.
    D) left where it is.

39.
    A) NO CHANGE
    B) have achieved
    C) never achieve anything
    D) achieve

40.
    A) NO CHANGE
    B) down the line.
    C) many years later.
    D) in some future time.

41. At this point, the writer is considering adding the following sentence.

    > Did you know that many experts consider Finland the top country in the world for both education and general quality of life?

    Should the writer make this addition here?

    A) Yes, because it reinforces that Finland not only places a high priority on education, but is also a very good place to live.
    B) Yes, because it demonstrates that placing a strong emphasis on education pays rich dividends.
    C) No, because this information is not germane to the topic, which deals solely with the quality of education.
    D) No, because the essay is not really about Finland but uses it only as an example.

Many feel that (42) to use the best and brightest students as teachers will result in decreased productivity for their country. So far, this has not proven true in Finland, which enjoys a standard of living envied by much of our world.

For the past twenty-five years in the United States, teachers have been drawn from the lower echelons of graduating students. If this pattern persists, we will not have enough educated students to run our country. The graph below is a stark indicator of this pattern. Countries that have consistently drawn teachers from the top graduating students have not only seen superior academic performance but generally better quality of life. Having better educated students has translated into better performance in the workforce, healthier citizens and lower crime rates. That is why I hope the best students (44) to consider a career in teaching. They will probably never be rich financially, but their daily lives and what they do for their world will be almost unmatched.

42.
A) NO CHANGE
B) having used
C) using
D) by using

43. According to the graph below, which area of the world can expect to see very low performance in the workforce and less healthy citizens?
A) Hong Kong
B) USA
C) Middle East
D) Finland

44.
A) NO CHANGE
B) will consider
C) are considering
D) considered

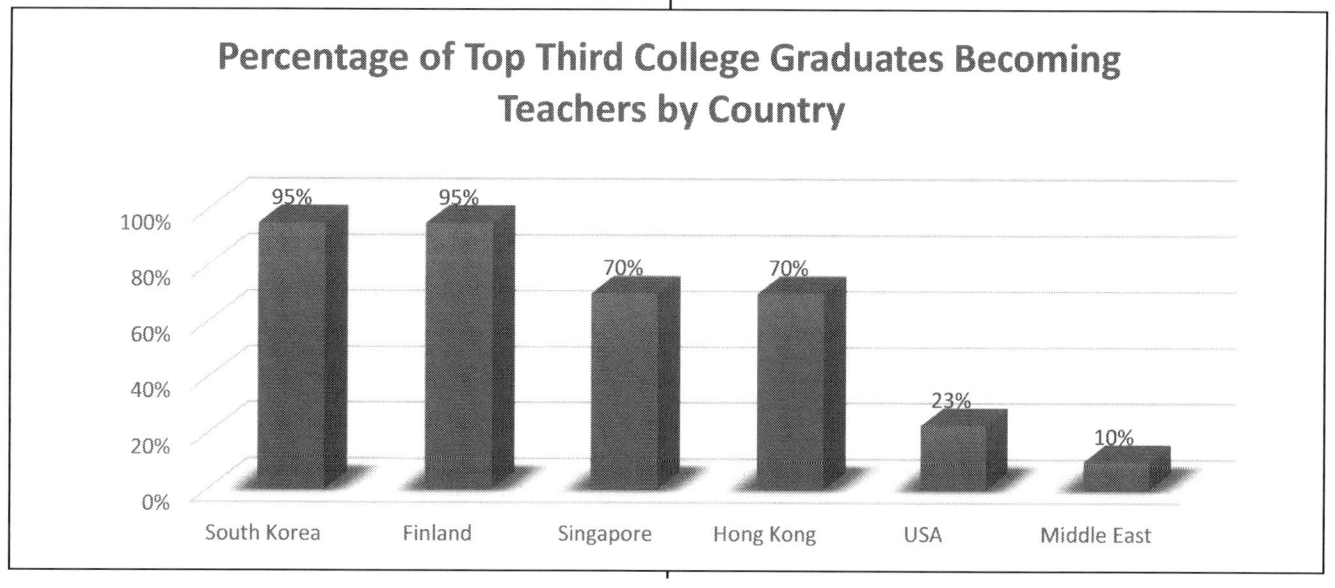

Explanations

1. **B. inspires.** The subject of the verb **inspires** is the collective noun Push Hands, which is **one** type of martial arts. Remember that we add an s to a noun to make it plural, but we add an s to a verb to make it singular. Choice A is obviously incorrect; we don't need the plural form of the verb. Answer C is wrong because there is no reason for the quotation marks. If you notice, all of the other verbs in this paragraph are in the present tense, so inspired, the past tense, is incorrect.

2. **B. At its worst.** It's is the contraction for It is, and we do not need that contraction in this sentence. (The apostrophe confuses us because it does suggest possession at other times—just not with contractions. With contractions an apostrophe is an indication that letter(s) have been left out.) Its is the possessive form of it, and is what is needed here. So, A is out. Choice C is incorrect because the words it and worse are inappropriate. For choice D there is no such animal as its'.

3. **A. NO CHANGE.** The word inculcate means "to instill" or "teach through repetition," and this is exactly the idea the author means to convey. It should be clear that the other word choices are unsuitable.

4. **B. Thus, the use.** Thus is an adverb meaning "consequently" or "therefore," which makes sense here. Also, since it is used at the beginning of the sentence, we need the comma. Therefore, A is out. "Then," which refers to time, doesn't make sense. Choice D, "By this," is also inappropriate—by what?

5. **B. but it is.** But suggests the contrast that is needed in this sentence because of the word **paradoxical.** The conjunction, and, suggests agreement rather than contrast, so A, NO CHANGE, doesn't work. C is incorrect because of "they are." We do not need the plural form. D doesn't work because the comma should precede the conjunction.

6. **B. That's where Push Hands comes in.** A is incorrect because it is just a general statement and does not connect the two paragraphs at all. C is not terrible, but it does not indicate the connection. D is just too wordy. The answer is B because this shows the connection and continues in the same style.

7. **C. balance.** Balance and equilibrium mean the same thing. This sort of mistake is called redundancy. I'm certain and sure that you "get it!"

8. **C. tightening, and we.** This would be the best way to fix this run-on sentence with the comma and conjunction. Choice A is unacceptable because the sentence is a run-on. B is incorrect as "thus" is inappropriate and so is the lack of commas. Actually, for the same reasons choice D is wrong.

9. **C. seemingly effortless.** This is the best choice because we need both words. **Effortless**, the adjective, describes grace and, **seemingly**, the adverb describes **effortless.** It's an effective marriage. Choice A is incorrect because **seemingly** is an adverb and should have the "ly" ending. In answer B, the "ly" is attached to the wrong word. As for choice D, **effortless** is not, by itself, incorrect, but **seemingly effortless** is more precise.

10. **B. juggling.** What we have here is an error in parallel structure. The words **walking** and **diving** demand we use juggling. It's a matter of balance. That being said, the other choices are inappropriate.

11. **C. where it is.** If we were to place this sentence at the beginning of the paragraph, it would not connect with the preceding paragraph. Also, we have an appropriate opening sentence so choice B is eliminated. We should not delete it because it does tie in with that first sentence. It wraps things up.

12. **C. venues.** This is the best answer because Radio City Music Hall is a locale used for large gatherings, which is the definition of a **venue.** Choice A is incorrect because Radio City Music Hall is not a **production** or a show; rather, it is a building where productions and shows take place. That would eliminate choices A and D. As for choice B, don't confuse the word cites with sites. Cite means to quote or to honor.

13. **C. is a line of thirty-six precision dancers.** This is the best choice because the verb **is** is in the correct number and tense. Choice A uses the verb **are,** which is plural; whereas the subject line is singular. Answer B uses the verb **was,** which is incorrect because it insinuates that the Rockettes are defunct when we know they are alive and "kicking." Choice D is again incorrect because the verb is plural.

14. **A. NO CHANGE.** This is the best choice because the precision mentioned is achieved by rehearsals and the observations of the choreographer, assistant choreographer, or line captain. Choices B and D suggest a contrast when there is none. There is nothing remarkable about having someone like a choreographer observing a dance routine; it's quite natural. So, C is out.

15. **D. the Rockettes worked four shows a day, seven days a week, fifty-two weeks a year.** Who has been entertaining us for more than fifty years? The Rockettes have, not **four shows, worked** or **fifty-two weeks.** The Rockettes do not dangle their participles!

16. **C. precisely placed.** This is the best answer because the word **placed** is sufficient. Choices A and B are redundant. Choice D is incorrect because the adverb **precisely** would never modify a conjunction. Adverbs modify or describe verbs, but also adjectives and other adverbs.

17. **D. Everyone in the line rehearsed in her new spot.** This is the best answer because the word **everyone** is singular and the word **her** is also singular. This is the correct agreement of the pronoun and its antecedent. In other words, **her** refers to **everyone,** so both have to agree in number. Choice A doesn't work because the word **their** is plural and **everyone,** as we said, is singular. Choice B substitutes the word **everybody** for everyone, which doesn't help, because **everybody** is also singular. We can eliminate choice C because it contains the word **there.**

18. **C. took place.** This is a matter of tense. We need the simple past tense in this sentence. Choice A is not the best answer because there is no such animal as **had took:** the helping verb **had** would require the past participle **taken.** Choice B does use the verb **had** with the correct verb **taken,** but this construction creates the past perfect tense, which we don't need here. Choice D is incorrect because **takes** is in the present tense.

19. **A. NO CHANGE.** This is the best answer because it is idiomatically correct. It's as simple or complicated as that. We just would not say **required by, in** or **as** in this context. The same way we would say **prior to** instead of **prior for** or **prior as.**

20. **B. Daughters," as their.** This is the best answer for a couple of reasons. First, periods and commas should always go inside the quotation marks. Second, we need the possessive adjective **their.** Only choice B conforms to both of these requirements. Choice A uses the comma outside the quotation marks, which is incorrect. Choices C and D use the wrong word **their. There** means place and **they're** is the contraction for they are.

21. **C. No, because it breaks up the discussion of their being goodwill ambassadors with the fine example in the following sentence with information that is not considered in the rest of the passage.** C is the answer because it discusses the important concept of cohesion and indicates that this would be lost. A is incorrect because we are not discussing motivation at this point. B is far too general. D is incorrect because the passage does not discuss this at all.

22. **D. appeared at.** This, again, is correct for a couple of reasons. First, in order to maintain parallel structure, we need the word **appeared** to go along with **participated** and **performed.** That eliminates choices A and B. Although choice C has the correct tense, the idiom requires "at" rather than "in."

23. **A. NO CHANGE.** Here we want the possessive pronoun since the pungency does belong to the garlic. Choice B is the contraction for "it is," which is not needed here. There is no such animal as **its'**, so C is out. **Their** is the possessive plural while garlic is singular.

24. **C. rich pungency has.** This description suffices. All of the other answers are redundant because a rich pungency is a sharp smell.

25. **C. Delete it.** While it is true that doctors today recommend garlic supplements, this sentence is out of place in a paragraph about ancient Egypt. All of the other choices are incorrect for the same reason.

26. **B. garlic, which happened.** The word **which** is used to introduce a non-restrictive clause such as this. A what?!? I know what you're thinking, but it really is not all that complicated. Non-restrictive clauses are those that can be left out without changing the meaning of the sentence. It simply supplies additional information. These clauses are usually surrounded by or (as in this case) preceded by a comma. The adjective **that,** on the other hand, is used in restrictive clauses, which are integral to the sentence and, therefore, cannot be left out. This is the reason choice D is incorrect. Choice A is wrong because we need the comma before the word **which**. Choice C contains the semi-colon. That is too strong a punctuation mark to use here.

27. **D. Incidentally.** The word incidentally means while we're on the subject—and we are! Choice A means for example, and we are not giving an example here. Answers B and C mean the same thing, don't they? So, it can't be one because it could be the other—double elimination!

28. **D. currency; as a matter of fact,.** As written, this sentence is a run-on, which is why A is incorrect. Choice B contains the needed semi-colon, but it's in the wrong place. The same can be said for C.

29. **A. NO CHANGE.** This is correct as is; everything is in agreement. Choice B is wrong because we need that comma to set off the parenthetical phrase. Choice C is incorrect because the verb **were** is plural, when the subject, King Tut, is singular. The same can also be said of choice D.

30. **D. Capitalize "father of medicine."** There is no reason to capitalize "father of medicine." Since there is no reason to use passive voice in either of those sentences, this would be a good change to make. Needless repetition of also would also tighten this paragraph.

31. **A. NO CHANGE.** Ingesting is a synonym for eating, so it works well. B, devouring, does mean eating, but it's too strong; it suggests eating voraciously or ravenously. Choice C does not necessarily mean eating. I suppose swallowing is technically eating, but it's a stretch. Choice D, drinking, does not work here.

32. **A. bacteria, and I read.** Using a comma with the conjunction **and** does the trick. **Because** is a great joining word, but there is no cause and effect between these two sentences. So, D is out. B is incorrect because **but** is inappropriate; there is no contrast here. The semi-colon in choice C would work, but not with the conjunction **and.**

33. **A. NO CHANGE.** Remember to add an s to a noun to make it plural and an s to a verb to make it singular. Here the subject is **references,** so the verb **center** does **not** have the s. B is incorrect because the verb does have the s. There is no reason for the comma in choice C. Choice D contains **their,** which is plural, while smell is singular.

34. **D. acclaimed.** A, B, and C are all redundant. If something is prestigious, it is already acclaimed.

35. **A. NO CHANGE.** This is the answer because we are looking for a conjunction that says "as a result" or "consequently" or the like. "So" does this but the others do not.

36. **C. have attained.** This is the answer because it indicated an action begun in the past but is still going on. A and B both indicate an action taking place in the present and the sentence demands a past tense. D is past perfect, but there is no indication of an action completed in the past before another action taking place in the past.

37. **C. how they live.** A, B, and D violate parallel structure, because whenever you start a series, you must use the same construction throughout. "How" is used only in C.

38. **D. left where it is.** This is the answer because it comments on the previous two sentences and makes sense of them. It serves no strong purpose in any of the other spots.

39. **B. have achieved.** This is the answer because it is an action that began in the past and is still going on. A and D are both present tense; C is awkward.

40. **A. NO CHANGE.** This is the only one that makes sense out of the sentence. The others are also awkwardly expressed.

41. **D. No, because the essay is not really about Finland but uses it only as an example.** D is the answer, as it indicates the specific reason that it would not be fitting to add it here. C is also a fairly good answer, but it is not as succinct an answer as D.

42. **C. using.** It is a matter of the correct idiom. Yes we could use the infinitive as a subject, but idiom (the way we as a culture have agreed to use words) specifies a gerund (ing) here. This is perhaps the hardest part of the grammar exam in that it rewards those with a good ear.

43. **C. Middle East.** Since the graph indicates that the Middle East draws only 10% of the highest graduating students into teaching, this is the clear answer.

44. **B. will consider.** This is the answer because she wants this action in the future. A makes no sense. C is present, and D is past.

Writing and Language Test 2
35 MINUTES, 44 QUESTIONS

DIRECTIONS

Each passage below is accompanied by a number of questions. For some questions, you will consider how the passage might be revised to improve the expression of ideas. For other questions, you will consider how the passage might be edited to correct errors in sentence structure, usage, or punctuation. A passage or a question may be accompanied by one or more graphics (such as a table or graph) that you will consider as you make revising and editing decisions.

Some questions will direct you to an underlined portion of a passage. Other questions will direct you to a location in a passage or ask you to think about the passage as a whole.

After reading each passage, choose the answer to each question that most effectively improves the quality of writing in the passage or that makes the passage conform to the conventions of standard written English. Many questions include a "NO CHANGE" option. Choose that option if you think the best choice is to leave the relevant portion of the passage as it is.

Questions 1 - 11 are based on the following passage.

The following passage is about Ultimate Frisbee, a very popular college sport played by many in leagues after they graduate college.

Ultimate Frisbee is a sport that incorporates all the best that sport can offer, (1) <u>but it had not yet</u> ascended to the pinnacle of Olympic Sports.

1.
   A) NO CHANGE
   B) but has not yet
   C) but hasn't of yet
   D) and has not yet

(2) Every college has an Ultimate team, and a large percentage of players continue to play even after college. (3) To combine the constant movement and athletic endurance of soccer with the aerial passing skills of football, Ultimate is played by two teams with a frisbee on a field with end zones, similar to football. The object of the game is to score by catching a pass in the opponent's end zone. A player must stop running while in possession of the (4) disc, he may pivot and pass to any of the other receivers on the field. It is a transition game in which players move quickly from offense to defense on turnovers that occur with an interception, a dropped pass, a pass out of bounds, or when a player is caught holding the disc for more than ten seconds.

2.
   A) NO CHANGE
   B) Consistently every
   C) Ordinarily every
   D) Virtually every

3.
   A) NO CHANGE
   B) Combining
   C) In an attempt to combine
   D) Trying to combine

4. Which of the following is NOT acceptable?
   A) disc, he may pivot
   B) disc; he may pivot
   C) disc, but he may pivot
   D) disc. He may pivot

What epitomizes the sport is that it is self refereed and always has been. Players decide among themselves what the call should be and use observers in tournaments to determine the call only in major matches. This is the essence of Ultimate and what makes it in the eyes of the participants a great sport. Although it is a fiercely competitive sport, it is closer to golf in its sportsmanship. Remember that in golf, the players often call infractions on themselves. They want to win, of course, but are unwilling (5) to do so at the cost of losing their integrity. The integrity of Ultimate depends on each (6) player's responsibility to uphold the spirit of the game; this responsibility is not taken lightly. Competitive play is encouraged, but never at the expense of respect between players, sticking to the rules, and (7) the basic joy of play.

Another interesting aspect is that no physical contact is allowed between players. A foul occurs when contact is made, but an intentional foul is considered cheating and a strong offense against the spirit of sportsmanship. Often a player is in a position where it would be advantageous to foul or commit some violation, but he or she is morally bound to (8) obey and adhere to the rules.

5.
 A) NO CHANGE
 B) to commit a foul at
 C) to perform that infraction at
 D) doing so at

6.
 A) NO CHANGE
 B) players
 C) players'
 D) Player's

7. Which of the following is NOT acceptable?
 A) the basic joy of play.
 B) enjoyment of play.
 C) the pursuit of play.
 D) allowing yourself to enjoy.

8. Which of the following is NOT acceptable?
 A) NO CHANGE
 B) obey
 C) obey and stick to
 D) obey, and adhere to

Although it is played on a 40- to 70-yard field, with end zones of 25 yards each, somewhat similar to football, its injuries, although common because of the athleticism required, are not generally as debilitating as in football. (9)

Another big difference in Ultimate is the time of play and the scoring. Games generally run about 90 minutes, and play to a score of 13 or 15. (10) However, if the game is running late, a gong goes off and then the winning score becomes two points more than the leading team currently has.

No referees, no definite time limits or final scoring, coed teams, a strong emphasis on moral integrity—(11) these allow Ultimate to embody all the true elements of sport.

9. At this point, the writer is considering adding the following sentence.

> Perhaps, if the National Football League were not so intent on making bundles of money, it would transform football into a more benign sport by handing down more severe penalties for hits to the head.

Should the writer make this addition here?

A) Yes, because it would further develop the idea of Ultimate as a benign sport.
B) Yes, because more young people might opt for Ultimate since it is less violent.
C) No, because this sounds like a personal diatribe against football rather than a fuller explanation of Ultimate.
D) No, because, even though they are both played on a large, rectangular field, football and Ultimate are two very different sports.

10.
    A) NO CHANGE
    B) Therefore,
    C) On that account
    D) Because of that

11.
    A) NO CHANGE
    B) these allow,
    C) this will allow
    D) these are the things that allow

Questions 12 - 22 are based on the following passage and supplementary material.

Recently, the U.S. Fish and Wildlife Service determined threatened status for the polar bear (*Ursus maritimus*) under the Endangered Species Act. The Service found, based upon the best available scientific and commercial information, that the polar bear habitat, principally sea ice, is declining throughout the species' range, and that this decline is expected to continue for the foreseeable future. It is this loss that threatens the species (12) throughout all of its range.

Therefore, (13) it was found out by scientists that the polar bear is likely to become an endangered species within the near future. Throughout the Arctic, polar bears are known by a variety of common names, including nanook, nanuq, ice bear, sea bear, isbjorn, and white bear. They are considered marine mammals because their primary habitat is the sea ice. (14) They are the largest of the bear species. In addition to their large body size, they are usually stocky in form, with fur color ranging from white to yellow. The weight of an average male can be more than 1,400 pounds. (15) The nose, lips, and skin of the bears are black.

12.
  A) NO CHANGE
  B) throughout,
  C) throughout
  D) through

13.
  A) NO CHANGE
  B) it will be found out by scientists
  C) scientists find
  D) scientists founded

14. Which choice most effectively combines the underlined sentences?

  A) Because they are the largest bear species, they are often very bulky with colors ranging from white to yellow.
  B) Since they are one of the largest bear species, they are often found to have both white and yellow fur.
  C) The largest of bear species, they are usually stocky in form, with fur color ranging from white to yellow.
  D) They are the largest bear species, very stocky in form, and with colors ranging from white to yellow.

15. Which of the following words best fit at the beginning of this sentence?

  A) Consequently,
  B) Interestingly,
  C) Outstandingly,
  D) However,

(16) During the course of their evolution, these bears have used the Arctic sea ice niche and are found throughout most ice-covered seas of the Northern Hemisphere. Over most of their range, polar bears remain on the sea ice year-round or spend only short periods on land. In the absence of ice during the summer season, some populations remain on land for extended periods until ice again forms and provides a platform for them to move to sea.

[1] Polar bears are evolutionarily adapted to life on sea ice. [2] They need sea ice as a platform for hunting, for seasonal movements, (18) traveling to terrestrial denning areas, for resting, and for mating. [3] Open water is not considered an essential habitat type for polar bears because life functions such as feeding, reproduction, or resting do not occur in open water. [4] However, open water is a fundamental part of the marine system that supports the seal species, the principal prey of the polar bears, and seasonally refreezes to form ice needed by the bears. [5] Further, the open water interface with sea ice is an important habitat (19) used to a great extent by polar bears.

16.
   A) NO CHANGE
   B) During the evolution
   C) During the course of its evolution
   D) As they evolved

17. The writer wants to add the following sentence to paragraph 4. After which sentence should he add it?

   These are fundamental needs.

   A) sentence 1 (after "on sea ice")
   B) sentence 2 (after "and for mating")
   C) sentence 3 (after "in open water")
   D) sentence 4 (after "needed by the bears")

18.
   A) NO CHANGE
   B) to travel to
   C) having traveled to
   D) for travel to

19.
   A) NO CHANGE
   B) for them.
   C) use to a great extent by them.
   D) used to a great extent by it.

The relationship (20) among the well-being of the polar bear and adequate sea ice is a critical one. Unfortunately, the extent of Arctic sea ice has been declining for many years due to several factors including global warming. Prior to the early 1970's, ice extent was measured with visible-band satellite imagery and aircraft and ship reports. With the (21) advent of passive microwave (PM) satellite observations, beginning in 1972 with a single channeled instrument and then reliably in 1978 with a multi-channeled instrument, we have a deterioration of Arctic sea more accurate, three-decade record of this decline. Over the period from

20.
A) NO CHANGE
B) amongst
C) between
D) as well as

21.
A) NO CHANGE
B) passing
C) elimination
D) exclusion

1978 to 2015, (22) successive studies by various agencies have documented an overall downward trend in Arctic sea ice extent and area. Unless progressive conservation efforts are put into place and enforced, the polar bear will most certainly become endangered.

22. Which choice completes the sentence with accurate data based on the graph?

A) NO CHANGE
B) there has been a complete deterioration of Arctic sea ice.
C) the National Snow and Ice Data Center warns about the effects of global warming.
D) the National Snow and Ice Data Center documents an overall reduction of Arctic sea ice.

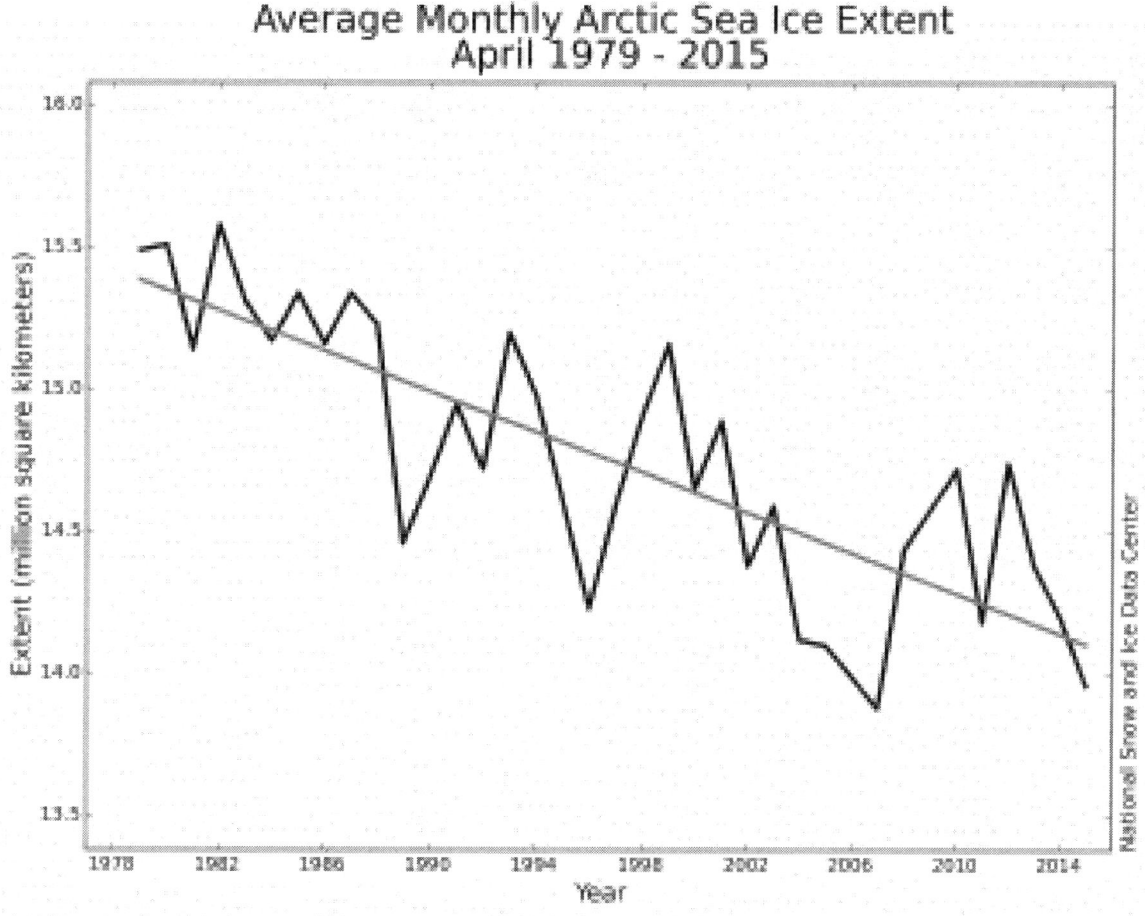

Questions 23 - 33 are based on the following passage

Edison and Tesla were two very different inventors. Thomas Edison, "the Wizard of Menlo Park," could not have been more different (23) than Nicola Tesla, an immigrant from Yugoslavia. Yes, they both had the ability to go days without sleep to develop an invention, but that is where the similarities ended. Edison is credited with over 1,000 inventions. (24) However, the vast majority of these were the results of trial and error. Tesla was often amused by what he called Edison's "empirical dragnets." As Tesla saw it, "If Edison had a needle to find in a haystack, he would proceed at once with the diligence of the bee to examine straw after straw until he found the object of his search. I was a sorry witness of such doings, knowing that a little theory and calculation would have saved him 90% of his labor."

Perhaps this is the (25) spirit of their difference. Edison developed his inventions through pure empiricism. This method is based on experiment and observations. He used an army of (26) assistants and aides to pursue his trial-and-error methods. Tesla, on the other hand, would not even begin the experiment until he had worked out most of the problem through mathematical and scientific techniques and used few assistants, if any. Tesla initially worked for Edison when he first arrived in America. However, after Edison repeatedly cheated him out of money and stole his copyrights, Tesla walked away despite (27) that jobs were very scarce.

23.
A) NO CHANGE
B) from
C) then
D) to

24.
A) NO CHANGE
B) Moreover,
C) Therefore,
D) However

25.
A) NO CHANGE
B) cause
C) symptom
D) essence

26.
A) NO CHANGE
B) friends
C) assistants
D) assistants and associations

27.
A) NO CHANGE
B) scarcity of jobs at the time.
C) many people were busily looking for jobs at this time.
D) the greatest problem of job shortage when he left.

The irreconcilable difference, however, emanated from the use of Tesla's alternating current (AC). Edison had always used DC (direct current) to power his light bulbs, his major source of income. He used his considerable financial power and backing to sway newspapers against this new threat of AC current. Tesla's way of using AC current (28) being much safer and more efficient. Thus, in time, it won out, but not before setting him back financially for many years. Edison was a very practical businessman who hated Tesla whom he found to be (29) an intellectual, a theoretician, and cultured. He would often "steal" other scientists' ideas and then rush them to the patent office. Tesla, however, was so fascinated by his own ideas and visions that he often lost interest once the ideas (30) was worked out. He had so many ideas that he was eager to pursue that he was often unwilling to spend the tedious time it took to get an invention approved. He once gave George Westinghouse what would today be almost $2 billion in patents to save the company because he felt that Westinghouse would support him in future endeavors and would have gone bankrupt had he not done so.

28.
A) NO CHANGE
B) has been
C) would be
D) was

29.
A) NO CHANGE
B) intellectual, theoretical, and cultured.
C) an intellectual theoretician and cultured.
D) , an intellectually cultured theoretician.

30.
A) NO CHANGE
B) had been
C) were
D) have been

Although more people (31) knows and reveres the name Edison, Tesla was certainly a far more profound thinker and scientist. (32) He refined AC into a far more efficient system, and invented fluorescent bulbs, radio, remote control, electronic motors, robotics, lasers, and wireless communication (the cloud). He also played a key role in the invention of X-rays.

31.
A) NO CHANGE
B) knew and revered
C) know and revere
D) have known and revere

32. Which choice most effectively combines the underlined sentences while maintaining accuracy?

A) Not only did he play an important role in the invention of X-rays, but he also refined AC into an efficient system and invented fluorescent light bulbs, the radio, remote control, electronic motors, robotics, lasers and wireless communication (the cloud).

B) While he only played a key role in the invention of X-rays, he actually invented AC, fluorescent light bulbs, radio, remote control, electronic motors, robotics, lasers, and wireless communication, which many of you know today as the cloud.

C) This is seen in his many inventions such as X-rays, AC, fluorescent light bulbs, the radio, remote control systems, electronic motors, robotics, lasers, and wireless communication, which we can comfortably say was a forerunner of what we call today the cloud.

D) Tesla was famous for his part in the invention of X-rays, AC and for his invention of fluorescent light bulbs, the radio, remote controls, electronic motors, robotics, lasers, and the wireless communication that is commonly referred to today as the cloud.

No inventor has ever had such vision and influence.

33. Which choice best concludes the essay and recalls a point made earlier?

   A) He was truly one of the great thinkers to walk the planet in the twentieth century.
   B) His theories and ability to do scientific calculations enabled him to surpass the best inventors of his day.
   C) No other scientist has ever transformed the world as Tesla did.
   D) We can see that he was in essence a far greater scientist than Edison and should be honored as such.

Questions 34 - 44 are based on the following passage.

"It has been said that art is a tryst, for in the joy of it maker and beholder meet." ~Kojiro Tomita

All art is ultimately about communication, (34) which is considered a meeting of two minds, two souls who have never met and may never meet. Dancers, musicians, architects, sculptors and painters all have a specific idea of what they wish to get across to a specific audience. (35) Each uses a very precise set of techniques to do this.

Painters look at the world differently (36) than the rest of us. They have trained their eyes to observe more of both the "big picture," large masses of shape and color, (37) as well as the specific details that bring the work into focus for the viewer. An artist who practices seeing forms

34.
A) NO CHANGE
B) which is a meeting of two minds,
C) a meeting of two minds,
D) meetings of two minds,

35.
A) NO CHANGE
B) Furthermore, each
C) On the other hand, each
D) However, each

36.
A) NO CHANGE
B) from
C) to
D) with

37.
A) NO CHANGE
B) and
C) from
D) with

depicted by light and shadow will in time begin (38) viewing all objects around him or her as forms in space. A child does this every day without realizing he or she is doing it. Only as he gets older and has many demands on him to do this and learn that and experience this and that does he forget to look at the world in this very basic way. Every child is an (39) artist, the challenge is how to remain an artist when we grow up.

38.
- A) NO CHANGE
- B) by viewing
- C) to view
- D) with a view of

39.
- A) NO CHANGE
- B) artist and yet the challenge
- C) artist; the challenge
- D) artist, while the challenge

Many great artists have expressed this need to look at the world in a particular way. What the artist wishes to communicate is often very subtle. He often takes the viewer along a path he would not have traversed through caverns unknown and asks the viewer to believe in him as he guides him. We must not forget that a real artist is like a pitcher who tries to convince the batter that the ball is somewhere that it is not. The ball may appear to be in a certain spot, but, when the batter tries to hit it, it will no longer be there. (40) As the great cubist painter, Pablo Picasso, once said, "Art is a lie that makes us realize the (41) authentic truth." Artists have gleaned a truth that few of us know. They share it with us, but make us enter their world in order to understand it. The truth of who we are or why we are here or what (42) life is is experienced by very few.

40. At this point, the writer is considering adding the following sentence.

    > The great knuckle ball throwing pitcher, Hoyt Wilhelm, was a master at this type of pitch, often making batters look quite foolish while trying to hit his elusive pitch.

    Should the writer make this addition here?

    A) Yes, because this extends the pitching metaphor so that the reader will have a clearer picture of what he means by it.
    B) Yes, because the reader will be better able to understand the relationship of sports and art.
    C) No, because this information might fit in well somewhere else, but definitely not here.
    D) No, because, although this might be interesting information, it is tangential to the topic and thus takes the reader away from the focus of the essay.

41.
    A) NO CHANGE
    B) truth
    C) real truth
    D) genuine truth

42.
    A) NO CHANGE
    B) life is, is experienced
    C) life is, has been experienced
    D) life is had been experienced

Artists help us to enhance our powers of observation, to see beyond the obvious implications of things. They observe essential details and abstract those that are not. They don't paint every leaf on the tree, but (43) <u>suggests</u> what is there. They encourage us to use our imaginations. Ultimately, their art is a sharing, a communication, of two souls who could be living thousands of miles apart. At the moment of epiphany, (44) <u>when the viewer does understand it,</u> communication occurs in a powerful way.

43.
A) NO CHANGE
B) suggest
C) have suggested
D) will suggest

44.
A) NO CHANGE
B) as the viewer finally understands it,
C) omit it
D) when the viewer has grasped it,

Explanations

1. **B. but has not yet.** A is past perfect (had) and is unnecessary here; we do not need "of" in C; D is no good as we need a contrast word and "and" is not one.

2. **D. Virtually, every.** This is our answer as virtually means "almost always." A is incorrect because not every college has a team; B, consistently, and C, ordinarily do not mean almost always.

3. **B. combining.** This is a participle and the most succinct of all the choices. C and D are too wordy, and A is just not the correct idiom.

4. **A. disc, he may pivot.** This is not acceptable because you cannot divide two complete thoughts with a comma. You need a semi-colon (B), a comma and coordinating conjunction (and, but, yet, etc.) or period and two distinct sentences.

5. **A. NO CHANGE.** D is wrong because we always follow "unwilling" with an infinitive. B and C are both infinitives but they are excessively wordy.

6. **A. NO CHANGE.** This is our answer because it is a singular subject "each." B does not have an apostrophe and therefore is not possessive; C indicates a plural and D has a capital P, which is unnecessary.

7. **D. allowing yourself to enjoy.** A, B, and C are consistent with parallel structure in that they all use a noun construction—joy and play. D uses a verb construction and therefore breaks the flow. Since "rules" is a noun, a noun must also be used on the other side of "and."

8. **B. obey.** A, C, and D are redundant since both words mean the same thing.

9. **C. No, because this sounds like a personal diatribe against football rather than a fuller explanation of Ultimate.** C is the answer because it indicates the irrelevance of this comment at this juncture. D does not address the real reason it should not be inserted here but just reiterates something already mentioned. A is wrong because every paragraph develops the idea of Ultimate as a benign sport, and so it is not necessary here. B might be true but it still disrupts the flow of the passage if placed here.

10. **A. NO CHANGE.** This is our answer since the sentence requires a contrast. B, C, and D are not contrast words.

11. **A. NO CHANGE.** B is wrong because of the comma. It is unnecessary; C is no good since it is singular and we have listed a number of items; D is far too wordy.

12. **C. throughout.** This is the best answer because as originally written **throughout all** is redundant. The two words mean the same thing; we don't need both. So that knocks out A. Choice B is wrong because of the comma; it's inappropriate. Answer D is not the best answer because it conveys a different meaning.

13. **C. scientists find.** We need the active voice, and that's why C is the best answer. Choice A is in the passive voice, which we should avoid. B is the wrong tense, whereas **founded** has a different meaning.

14. **C. The largest of bear species, they are usually stocky in form, with fur color ranging from white to yellow.** The answer is C as it has the most elegant structure and is brief. A and B show a causal relationship between size and color and thus are incorrect. D is good but the word "and" after the comma breaks the rhythm and is unnecessary.

15. **B. Interestingly.** This is the best choice because it *is* an interesting fact. I, for one, never knew that the nose, lips, and skin of the polar bear are black. **Consequently** indicates cause and effect, which is absent here. There is nothing **outstanding** about this fact, so this choice is out. **However** shows contrast, which is not the case here.

16. **D. As they evolved.** This is the best answer because it's succinct. Choice A is not the best answer because it is too verbose. Why use six words when you can say the same thing in three? Answer B is too ambiguous. Whose evolution? Choice C uses the word **its,** which makes it incorrect because we are speaking of bears, plural.

17. **B. sentence 2 (after "and for mating").** B is the answer as the author has just made a list of basic things that the bears need to survive and this choice follows it with the words "these" and "fundamental."

18. **D. for travel to.** This answer is correct because it maintains the parallel structure of the sentence. Take another look. We have **for** hunting, **for** seasonal movements, **for** resting, and **for** mating, so it follows that to maintain the given balance, we would use **for** travel. All of the other choices are incorrect because they are not parallel.

19. **B. for them.** This is the best answer because it's less repetitious; the words **polar bears** and **bears** are already used three times in this small paragraph. So, choice A is incorrect because enough is enough! In choice C the word **use** is in the wrong tense, and choice D uses the incorrect pronoun **it,** instead of **them.**

20. **C. between.** This is the best answer because this preposition is used when two things are specified. We use **among** for three or more. Thus, A is out. The word **amongst** is synonymous with **among**; so, it doesn't work either. Choice D is not the best answer because the phrase is inappropriate in this sentence.

21. **A. NO CHANGE.** The word **advent** means the arrival of something important. Here it refers to the arrival or coming of a technological advance in satellite imagery. Choices B, C, and D have negative meanings while we need a positive one.

22. **D. The National Snow and Ice Data Center documents an overall reduction of Arctic sea ice.** This is the best answer because the chart clearly reflects this fact. Choice A is not the best answer because of the phrase "various agencies." The word "complete" in choice B is too absolute. The phrase "global warming" eliminates C.

23. **B. from.** The idiom requires "from." This is perhaps the most difficult part of any grammar test in that it depends on one's ear and not all of us have a great ear for language. The problem is eased if one happens to have a musical ear or loves language. A, C, and D are just not acceptable idioms.

24. **A. NO CHANGE.** However, is our answer. B means "in addition" so that does not work; C is no good because it shows a causal relationship, which is not what we are looking for. D appears to be the same as A, but it needs to be followed by a comma and is not. Punctuation is often so small and "seemingly" insignificant that we don't pay much attention to it. Try to pay attention to it on the test.

25. **D. essence.** Essence is the perfect answer. We can't say that Edison's empiricism caused or was a symptom of the difference and it certainly was not the spirit of the difference, so they are out.

26. **C. assistants.** This is the answer because otherwise we would have a redundancy (needless repetition). A and D are certainly repetitive and friends can not necessarily help you in a scientific pursuit.

27. **B. scarcity of jobs at the time.** This is our answer because it uses so few words. In general, look for choices that can pretty much say everything, but use a small number of words.

28. **D. was.** This is the answer because it is the correct tense. A makes it a sentence fragment (incomplete thought) and B tells us this is an ongoing action, which it is not; C shows an element of wish, which does not work here.

29. **B. intellectual, theoretical, and cultured.** This is the answer because it maintains parallel structure. A is wrong because two nouns are followed by an adjective, which is not acceptable since we must use the same part of speech throughout in a series. C has a noun and an adjective. D could possibly work, but it has a comma preceding the phrase and it does not require one.

30. **B. had been.** This is the correct answer because we need a tense that indicates that the past action was completed before another past action in the same sentence; A is singular and we require a plural; C indicates at the same time, which it is not; D is an ongoing process, but does not tell us it was completed before the previous action.

31. **C. know and revere.** This is the correct answer because it is present tense. A is wrong because it is singular and people is plural; B is wrong because there is no indication that we will still feel that way; D is wrong because the second "have" is missing.

32. **A. Not only did he play an important role in the invention of X-rays, but he also refined AC into an efficient system and invented fluorescent light bulbs, the radio, remote control, electronic motors, robotics, lasers and wireless communication (the cloud).** A is the answer because the information is more correct. Tesla did not invent AC but only developed a practical way of using it commercially. To say in B that he "only" played an important role in the invention of X-rays makes this sentence silly.

33. **B. His theories and ability to do scientific calculations enabled him to surpass the best inventors of his day.** B is the best answer because it specifically recalls a point made earlier about using specific calculations to arrive at his conclusions. A is to general and therefore does not answer this question. In C, the word "ever" is a big word and the passage does not lead us to that conclusion. D is a tempting answer but it does not cite a point made earlier.

34. **C. a meeting of two minds,.** C is the answer. A and B are too wordy and D should be meeting, not meetings.

35. **D. However, each.** Choice A does not start the sentence with a contrast word and since that is the sense of this sentence, we need one. B, "furthermore" is an addition word. C, "on the other hand" requires a contrast with a specific thought prior to it and there is none here.

36. **B. from.** That is the correct idiom.

37. **B. and.** This is our answer because we always follow "both" with "and." This is an idiom question and can easily be missed if we do not pay attention to each word.

38. **C. to view.** This is our answer as we always follow begin with an infinitive (to). A, B, and D are not infinitives.

39. **C. artist; the challenge.** This is our answer as a semi-colon is a fine way of correcting a run-on sentence, which this would be without it; you cannot divide it with a comma (A); B would be acceptable without the "yet" if it had a comma; D, "while," is a subordinate conjunction and cannot be used in the second half of a compound sentence.

40. **D. No, because, although this might be interesting information, it is tangential to the topic and thus takes the reader away from the focus of the essay.** D is the answer. C is correct but it does not indicate why it is a bad choice specifically.

41. **B. truth.** This is our answer as it gets rid of "authentic," which makes it redundant. A, C, and D are all redundant.

42. **A NO CHANGE.** This is correct as it does not separate the subject from the verb (the second "is"). The comma in B and C are misleading and unnecessary; the past perfect tense (using "had") in D makes that incorrect.

43. **B. suggest.** This is the best answer because it is plural, and thus, agrees with the subject, "they." A is singular; C and D are the wrong tense.

44. **C. omit it.** This is our answer as the words "when the viewer does understand it" define a word just used-epiphany- and is thus unnecessary. A, B, and D are all redundant.

Writing and Language Test 3

35 MINUTES, 44 QUESTIONS

DIRECTIONS

Each passage below is accompanied by a number of questions. For some questions, you will consider how the passage might be revised to improve the expression of ideas. For other questions, you will consider how the passage might be edited to correct errors in sentence structure, usage, or punctuation. A passage or a question may be accompanied by one or more graphics (such as a table or graph) that you will consider as you make revising and editing decisions.

Some questions will direct you to an underlined portion of a passage. Other questions will direct you to a location in a passage or ask you to think about the passage as a whole.

After reading each passage, choose the answer to each question that most effectively improves the quality of writing in the passage or that makes the passage conform to the conventions of standard written English. Many questions include a "NO CHANGE" option. Choose that option if you think the best choice is to leave the relevant portion of the passage as it is.

Questions 1 - 11 are based on the following passage and supplementary material.

Over the past 10 years, there has been a radical shift in the use of desktop browsing. In fact, as of 2016, users spent more than one trillion minutes online with mobile devices, which (1) <u>are</u> almost twice the time they spent on their desktops. Last year alone, desktop browsing decreased almost 10%. Almost 20 percent of millennials no longer

1.

A) NO CHANGE
B) is
C) has been
D) had been

use a desktop computer, but they don't use their mobile devices exclusively. (2) Most see themselves as multiple platform users. So, even though there is a decline in desktop use, it is still relevant, even among millennials.

(3) [1] Mobiles seem to be their preferred platform for digital consumption. [2] However, when on desktop, Millennials spend more time on each website than when viewing from their mobile devices. [3] However, this is forecast to change within the next two years. [4] This contributes to the fact that desktop currently remains a more profitable platform for ad revenue.

Currently (4) moreover, display ads perform almost ten times better on mobile than on desktop. Meanwhile, native video ads, which have long been proven to be more profitable than display ads, perform two times better than display ads both on mobile and desktop. Regarding video ad completion rates, those viewed on mobile devices garner a 74% completion rate among Millennials while those viewed on desktop reach 67%.

2. Which choice most effectively combines the underlined sentences?

   A) Most see themselves as multiple platform users and so, even though there is a decline in desktop use, it is still relevant, even among millennials.
   B) Despite some decline in desktop use, it is still relevant among millennials, as they see themselves as multi-platform users.
   C) Whereas most millennials see themselves as multi-platform users, desktops are still relevant despite the fact that there has been some decline in desktop use.
   D) Millennials tend to see themselves as multi-platform users, so even though there has been some decline in desktop use, it is still relevant to most of them.

3. To make this paragraph most logical, sentence 4 should be

   A) placed after sentence 1.
   B) placed after sentence 2.
   C) placed after sentence 4.
   D) left where it is.

4.

   A) NO CHANGE
   B) however
   C) alas
   D) therefore

Native advertising is a form of paid media that is frequently (5) adapted by content marketers. By definition, it is any paid content that is "in-feed" and inherently non-disruptive. This includes promoted tweets on Twitter, suggested posts on Facebook, and editorial-based content recommendations from content discovery platforms. Content marketers are increasingly turning to native advertising, (6) as it is understood to be better at building trust and engagement with prospective customers than traditional display ads. They (7) balk and hesitate at going with print ads in newspapers.

Most recently, native content has also become synonymous with sponsored content, which is just one of six native advertising formats. (8) These are likely (9) due to the fact that many publications have made a push to grow their sponsored content units in recent years. According to a recent report on multiscreen video best practices, mobile video is a key way of reaching and impacting Millennials. When it comes to video length, Millennials prefer ads that are shorter in length (10 seconds or less), as they are sensitive to ad clutter. However, ads that

5.
A) NO CHANGE
B) understood
C) associated with
D) adopted

6.
A) NO CHANGE
B) as it seems more likely to build
C) as most observers tend to think it is better at building
D) as it is commonly conceded that it is more conducive at building

7.
A) NO CHANGE
B) hesitate and waffle
C) balk
D) refuse and balk

8.
A) NO CHANGE
B) Some are
C) This is
D) Others are

9.
A) NO CHANGE
B) by virtue of
C) inasmuch as
D) because

try to provide too much information within a few seconds may lead to confusion and minimize message takeaway. So, even among Millennials, 30-second videos should be considered when communicating new or complex information.

Though mobile is the driving force of the future, it still does not mark the end of the road for desktop and laptop computers. It is interesting to note that desktop computers are still used somewhat more at home and on weekends than at work and in transit. They are still vital in business, and will remain so. Technology will continue to evolve, and Millennial users will continue to adapt to it. (10) <u>It remains to be seen how their digital behavior and preferences will shape desktop and mobile platforms in the future.</u>

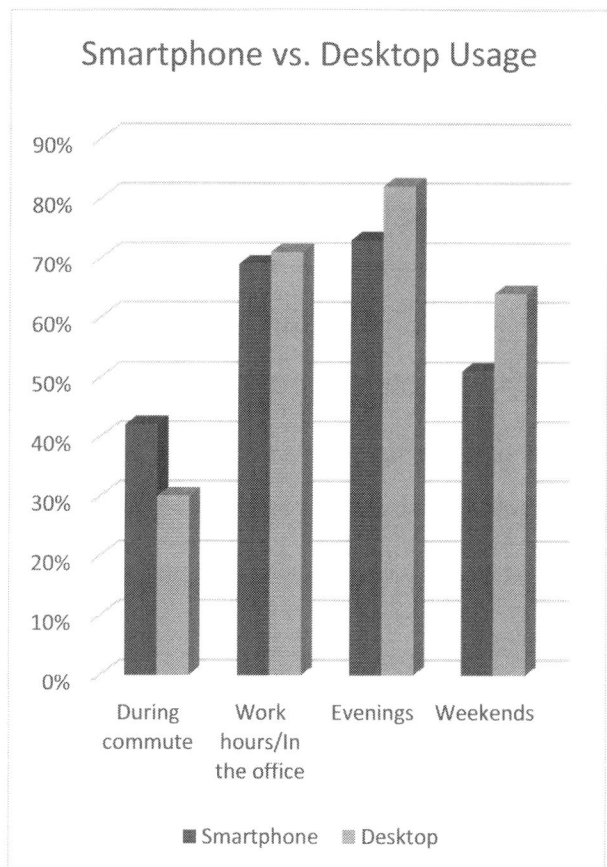

10. Which sentence best concludes this essay?

A) NO CHANGE
B) We will just have to wait and see what unfolds in the future.
C) Millennials are a much different generation than any we have seen in hundreds of years.
D) Millennials have taken the bull by the horns and who knows where they will go with it once they really get going.

11. During further research, the writer finds the graphic shown on the left. Should he include it with the passage?

A) Yes, because it is a very sharp graph that highlights a lot of things in the passage.
B) Yes, because it supports the author's contention of more mobile use in transit and less at home.
C) No, because it weakens a point the passage makes about rising use of mobiles.
D) No, because it lacks clear pertinence to the point the passage makes throughout.

Questions 12 - 22 are based on the following passage.

The electoral college has been a hot topic since the result of the 2016 election. (12) So, let's first get a clear understanding of exactly what it is before we consider whether it should still be.

The Electoral College is a process, not a place. The founding fathers established it in the Constitution as a compromise between election of the President by a vote in Congress and election of the President by a popular vote of qualified citizens. The process consists of the selection of the electors, the meeting of the electors where they vote for President and Vice President, and the counting of the electoral votes by Congress.

The Electoral College consists of 538 electors. A majority of 270 electoral votes is required to elect the President. Your state's entitled allotment of electors (13) equals the number of members in its Congressional delegation: one for each member in the House of Representatives plus two for your Senators. Each candidate running for President in

12.
- A) NO CHANGE
- B) Thus, we must first clear up some of the confusion in order to get a clear understanding
- C) Nevertheless, we must first get an understanding
- D) All things considered, we must first get a clear picture

13.
- A) NO CHANGE
- B) is equal to
- C) is indifferent to
- D) embodies

your state has his or her own group of electors. The electors are generally chosen by the candidate's political party, but state laws vary on how the electors are selected and what their responsibilities (14) will be.

The presidential election is held every four years on the Tuesday after the first Monday in November. You help choose your state's electors when you vote for President because when you vote for your candidate you are actually voting for your candidate's electors. Most states have a "winner-take-all" system that awards all electors to the winning presidential candidate. (15) However, Maine and Nebraska each have "proportional representation." Thus, electoral votes can go to each candidate in those states.

Each state's electoral votes are counted in a joint session of Congress on the 6th of January in the year following the meeting of the electors, (16) whose votes are used for the final vote.

14.
   A) NO CHANGE
   B) are.
   C) has been.
   D) had been.

15. Which choice most effectively combines the underlined sentences?

   A) However, Maine and Nebraska each have a situation that they call "proportional representation, which allows electoral votes to go to each candidate.
   B) However, Maine and Nebraska each have proportional representation, which allows them to give each candidate votes.
   C) By the same token, Maine and Nebraska each have proportional representation, which allows them to give each candidate votes.
   D) Likewise, Maine and Nebraska each have proportional representation, which allows them to give each candidate votes if they choose to.

16.
   A) NO CHANGE
   B) who get to vote for the President.
   C) who are the final arbiters, deciding who becomes the President.
   D) Delete this clause

That's how it is done, but many in our country have been questioning why it is still done that way. Sure, the founding fathers wanted to make certain that a few government officials did not get to make such an important decision. They never dreamed that we would have two elections in sixteen years in which the winner lost the popular vote by two million votes. Al Gore won the popular vote in 2000, but narrowly lost the election. Hillary Clinton won by over two million votes in 2016, but lost by more than 36 electoral votes. Senator Barry Sanders has argued that since most states are either heavily democratic or republican, most states are taken out of the political process during a Presidential election. (17) That leaves it in the hands of the few so-called "swing states." These states then wield far more political clout than they would ordinarily have.

Outgoing Senator, Barbara Boxer, of California has filed a bill to (18) <u>amend</u> the constitution to eliminate the electoral college.

(19) <u>Moreover,</u> the bill is not expected to pass.

17. At this point, the writer is considering adding the following sentence.

    Senator Sanders actually ran against Clinton in the primaries.

    Should the writer make this addition here?

    A) Yes, because that is crucial to understanding his point.
    B) Yes, because it makes no sense without it.
    C) No, because it has already been developed earlier in the passage.
    D) No, because although it might be interesting information, it does not fit and breaks up the point the author is making.

18.
    A) NO CHANGE
    B) fix
    C) alternate
    D) realign

19.
    A) NO CHANGE
    B) Additionally,
    C) However,
    D) Furthermore,

However, though the electors are compelled by tradition to cast their votes based on their state's will, (20) there is no official obligation to do so. A small fine would be levied against them for failing to adhere to the will of the voters in their electorate, but it is possible that some might actually do so if their conscience would not allow them to vote for a candidate they found contemptible. It is unlikely whether such an action would ever be sufficient to overturn the vote.

However, we should keep in mind the words of Thomas Jefferson, one of our great founding fathers. He said. "And what country can preserve (21) it's liberties if their rulers are not warned from time to time that their people preserve the spirit of resistance? Let them take arms. The remedy is to set them right as to facts, pardon and pacify them. What signify a few lives lost in a century or two? The tree of liberty must be refreshed from time to time with the blood of patriots and tyrants." A few electors defecting (22) does not constitute a rebellion, but what if enough electors acted, resulting in the reversal of the original vote?

20.
A) NO CHANGE
B) there is no government obligation to follow this course of action.
C) they are not obliged to do so.
D) nothing in the constitution obliges them to do this.

21.
A) NO CHANGE
B) their
C) its
D) there

22.
A) NO CHANGE
B) do not
C) don't
D) didn't

Questions 23 - 33 are based on the following passage

This speech was delivered by Susan B. Anthony in 1873. She was a great pioneer of Women's Suffrage.

Friends and Fellow Citizens; I stand before you tonight under indictment for the alleged crime (23) of having voted at the last presidential election, without having a lawful right to vote. (24) It shall be my work this evening to prove to you that in thus voting, I not only committed no crime, but, instead, simply exercised my citizen's rights, guaranteed to me and all United States citizens by the National Constitution, beyond the power of any State to deny.

The preamble of the Federal Constitution says: "We, the people of the United States, in order to form a more perfect union, etc."

(25) It was we, the people; not we, the white male citizens; (26) nor yet us, the male citizens; but we, the whole people, who formed the Union. And we formed it, not only to give the blessings of liberty, (27) but to secure them; not to the half of ourselves and the half of our posterity, but to the

23.
A) NO CHANGE
B) voting at
C) to vote at
D) of casting a vote at

24.
A) NO CHANGE
B) I intend
C) It is my ambition
D) I will

25. Which of the following sentences would best be in keeping with the tone of this passage?
A) What were they getting at here?
B) What exactly did they mean when they said that?
C) Let us be clear about this!
D) What exactly did this preamble mean when it said that?

26.
A) NO CHANGE
B) nor yet we,
C) Nor yet us,
D) nor yet we

27.
A) NO CHANGE
B) but even to
C) but also to
D) but again to

184

whole people—women as well as men. It is a mockery to talk to women of their enjoyment of the blessings of liberty (28) while they are denied the use of the only means of securing them provided by this democratic-republican government—the ballot. (29)

For any State to make sex a qualification that must ever result in the disfranchisement of one (30) whole entire half of the people is to pass a bill of ex post facto law, and is therefore a violation of the supreme law of the land. By it the blessings of liberty are forever withheld from women and their female posterity. (31) To them this government has no just powers derived from the consent of the governed. To them this government is not a democracy. It is not a republic; not a democracy. It is an odious aristocracy; a hateful oligarchy of sex; the most hateful aristocracy ever established on the face of the globe; an oligarchy of wealth, where the rich govern the poor. An oligarchy of learning, where the educated govern the ignorant, or even an oligarchy of race, where the Saxon rules the African, might be endured; but this oligarchy of sex, which makes father, brothers, husband, sons,

28.
   A) NO CHANGE
   B) whereas
   C) although
   D) at the same time as

29. At this point, the writer is considering adding the following sentence.

   This is something all women will sacrifice their lives for.

   Should the writer make this addition here?

   A) Yes, because the author knows how much every woman wants this right.
   B) Yes, because she is trying to be persuasive.
   C) No, because this is an exaggeration.
   D) No, because no woman would do this.

30.
   A) NO CHANGE
   B) entirely
   C) wholly entire
   D) entire

31. Which choice most effectively combines the underlined sentences?

   A) To them this government does not have any powers bestowed upon them by those governed, but stills insists that it is a democracy.
   B) To them this government has no just powers derived from the consent of the governed and thus is not truly a democracy.
   C) To them this government has not merited by their actions any right to govern those it is governing and cannot therefore justify calling itself a democracy.
   D) Those in government have not the consent of those it governs and thus should not consider that they are governing a true democracy by any definition of that term.

the oligarchs over the mother and sisters, the wife and daughters of every household—which ordains all men sovereigns, all women subjects, carries dissension, discord and rebellion into every home of the nation. Webster, Worcester, and Bouvier all define a citizen to be a person in the United States, entitled to vote and hold office.

[1] The only question left to be settled now is: Are women persons? [2] And I hardly believe any of our opponents will have the hardihood to say they are not. [3] Being persons, then, women are citizens; and no State has a right to make any law, or (32) enforcing any old law, that shall abridge their privileges or immunities. [4] Hence, every discrimination against women in the constitutions and laws of the several States is today null and void, precisely as in every one against Negroes. (33)

32.
- A) NO CHANGE
- B) to enforce
- C) to be able to enforce
- D) to have enforced

33. To make this paragraph most logical, sentence 2 should be
- A) placed before sentence 1.
- B) placed after sentence 3.
- C) placed after sentence 4.
- D) left where it is.

Questions 34 - 44 are based on the following passage.

Born Edson Arantes do Nascimento on October 23, 1940, in Três Corações, Brazil, Pelé was for many decades the most well-known athlete in the world. Although (34) born and raised in poverty, his top salary in the late 1960s was fully five times the next highest paid athlete. This is amazing when one considers that his sport was only the fifth most popular sport in the United States at the time. How did he become such an unbelievable sports icon? Most often such stories are (35) associated and connected to fairy tales, but not so with him.

Pelé grew up in Bauru in the state of São Paulo. He earned extra money by working in tea shops as a servant. (36) Since he was taught to play by his father, he could not afford a proper football and usually played with either a sock stuffed with newspaper and tied with a string or a grapefruit.

34.
   A) NO CHANGE
   B) he was born and raised
   C) he has been born and raised
   D) he had been born and raised

35.
   A) NO CHANGE
   B) connected by some of these
   C) associated
   D) linked by association

36.
   A) NO CHANGE
   B) Taught
   C) Although he was taught
   D) While he was taught

(37) [1] He is the all-time leading goal scorer for Brazil with 77 goals in 91 games. [2] Pelé began playing for Santos at age 15 and the Brazil national football team at 16. [3] In addition, during his international career, he won three FIFA World Cups—in 1958, 1962 and 1970—being the only player ever to do so. [4] His team lost in 1968 when he broke his leg in the semi-finals. (38)

Pelé's (39) "stunning play and predilection for spectacular goals" made him a star around the world. His team, Santos, toured internationally in order to take full advantage of his popularity.

37. To make this paragraph most logical, sentence 1 should be

A) placed after sentence 2.
B) placed after sentence 3.
C) placed after sentence 4.
D) left where it is.

38. At this point, the writer is considering adding the following sentence.

> One can only imagine what his stature would have become had he been able to win in 1968 also.

Should the writer make this addition here?

A) Yes, because the paragraph is too short.
B) Yes, because it places his great achievement in a larger perspective.
C) No, because it takes away from all of the strong stats in the paragraph.
D) No, because it is irrelevant.

39.

A) NO CHANGE
B) strong play and tendency towards
C) dominant play and amount of
D) notorious play and penchant for

(40) In 1967, there were two factions involved in the Nigerian Civil War in Africa. They were able to agree to a 48-hour ceasefire so they could watch Pelé play an exhibition game in Lagos. During his time at Santos, Pelé played alongside many gifted players.

Many international teams, of course, vied for his services, but the government of Brazil declared Pelé an "official national treasure" to prevent him from being transferred out of the country. This naturally added to his stature as a national hero in Brazil. He did, (41) in addition, play for the New York Generals after his career in Brazil ended. This did much to spur the rise of soccer in the USA.

After he retired, he went into acting, starring in the 1980's hit film *Victory* as a soccer player and soldier among other international movies. He has

40. Which choice most effectively combines the underlined sentences?

  A) In 1967, there were two groups going at it in the Nigerian Civil War in Africa, who were able to halt that terrible war for 48 hours in order to watch Pelé play an exhibition game in Lagos.
  B) Way back in 1967, there happened to be two warring factions doing battle in the Nigerian Civil War in Africa which stopped their squabbling during the time it took to watch Pelé play an exhibition game in Lagos.
  C) In 1967, two factions involved in the Nigerian Civil War agreed to a 48 hour ceasefire so they could watch Pelé play an exhibition game in Lagos.
  D) In 1967, two warring factions involved in the Nigerian Civil War agreed to a 48 hour ceasefire in order to catch an exhibition game featuring Pelé in Lagos.

41.

  A) NO CHANGE
  B) moreover,
  C) understandably,
  D) however,

also had movies made about his spectacular life. He has dedicated himself to (42) philanthropic and charitable work (43) and bettering the lives of his fellow Brazilians. He is active with the charity organization UNICEF and many other children's organizations.

The world eagerly awaited the moment when he would light the Olympic torch in Brazil in 2016, but alas illness prevented him from doing so. Time magazine has named him in their list of 100 most influential people of the 20th century. (44)

42.
A) NO CHANGE
B) philanthropic
C) philanthropic and altruistic
D) altruistic and charitable

43.
A) NO CHANGE
B) thus bettering
C) and because of that bettered
D) and in that way made better

44. Which choice best concludes the essay and recalls a point made earlier in the essay?

A) This really shows how people who grew up impoverished can climb the ladder of success and make it to the top.
B) So, even if you are poor, you should not give up because Pelé serves as a great example of someone who made it to the top of the heap.
C) From humble beginnings, this great man has risen to the pinnacle of his time.
D) Therefore, Pelé serves as a great example for those who have not been given a lot but still want to strive to become the very best they can be.

Explanations

1. **B. is.** C and D are out as they are the wrong tense, but A probably caught some of you. "Users," "minutes," and "devices" are all there to grab your eye and trick you into choosing "are," but the answer is "is" because it really is an amount of time. Yes, I agree, that amount of time is not stated, but it is certainly understood. Tough one!

2. **B. Despite some decline in desktop use, it is still relevant among millennials as they see themselves as multi-platform users.** This is the answer here, as it is the briefest and smoothest choice.

3. **B. placed after sentence 2.** This sentence follows sentence two because "This" refers to the information in that sentence.

4. **B. however.** This is the answer as we need a contrast and the other choices do not provide that at all.

5. **D. adopted.** C looks fine, but when we read the context of the paragraph, we begin to see that they have taken on or adopted this way of doing things.

6. **B. as it seems more likely to build.** A is fine but B is more active and fits better with the rhythm of the sentence.

7. **C. balk.** This is the answer, as the others are all redundant.

8. **C. This is.** The antecedent has to be singular, as it refers to content, not formats.

9. **D. because.** The others choices are far too wordy.

10. **A. NO CHANGE.** This is the most specific and mentions ideas specifically from the passage. The others are just too general.

11. **B. Yes, because it supports the author's contention of more mobile use in transit and less at home.** The graph clearly supports what the writer has established in the passage.

12. **A. NO CHANGE.** Choice A is succinct and connects well to the previous sentence. B, "Thus," is a fine opener but the sentence is unnecessarily long. Remember from the introduction that the test is looking for terse expression in almost every case. C and D are succinct enough, but the opening words are absolutely not the correct words to continue the thought from the previous sentence.

13. **A. NO CHANGE.** Don't avoid this answer just because there are two A answers in a row. There is no reason the test makers will not do that. B is too wordy. C and D are the wrong diction.

14. **B. are.** This is the only choice that keeps the tense of the paragraph consistent.

15. **B. However, Maine and Nebraska each have proportional representation, which allows them to give each candidate votes.** C and D are out right away since we are looking for a contrasting word or phrase to start the sentence and they do not have that. A is fine except for the phrase "that they call," which is not necessary.

16. **D. Delete this clause.** At first, this looks like a tossup between A and B. If that were the case, you would choose B as it uses the active voice (the subject is the doer of the action.) However, it is a smokescreen as this information has already been given in all of the paragraphs preceding it and therefore we do not need to see it again. **D is our answer.**

17. **D. No, because although it might be interesting information, it does not fit and breaks up the point the author is making.** D is the most precise answer as it addresses the problem of continuity. Never insert something into a line or reasoning that does not help to develop that thought. As interesting as that information might be, if it intrudes upon the line of reasoning, you must delete it.

18. **A. NO CHANGE.** This is the correct answer because "amend" is the correct word. We always speak of "amending" a constitution. "Fix" is just too general a word to use here and the others to do fit at all.

19. **C. However,.** This is the correct answer as we are looking for a contrast here and none of the other choices give that.

20. **C. they are not obliged to do so.** This is a tossup between A and C. The other two are far too wordy. However, if we can remember that virtually all of these standardized tests prefer the active voice, we will opt for C as the better answer. "They" beginning choice C also keeps the sentences consistent.

21. **C. its.** "Country" is singular and therefore "their" is out, and, of course, "there" is just an attempt to have you make a very bad error. A, "it's," is a contraction and therefore is incorrect.

22. **A. NO CHANGE.** B and C cancel each other out. They are the same. D is no good as it is the wrong tense.

23. **A. NO CHANGE.** This is the correct answer, as this is a tense question and this is the correct tense. B would mean that she is voting right now; C is the wrong idiom, and D is much too wordy.

24. **B. I intend.** A is too wordy, C contains the wrong word (ambition) and D (I will to prove) is unacceptable English.

25. **C. Let us be clear about this!** This is the answer because it is emphatic and yet keeps the tone of this speech, which the others do not. They are far too post nineteenth century to fit into this speech.

26. **B. nor yet we,.** A and C have the objective case (us) and D has omitted the comma that follows, which is necessary here.

27. **C. but also to.** This is the correct answer because, when you use "not only," you must follow it with "but also." A, B, and D do not and so are wrong.

28. **A. NO CHANGE.** This is because A is briefer than D, and B and C do not mean "at the same time."

29. **C. No, because this is an exaggeration.** Anthony knows that to get her point across strongly there can be no hint of untruth, and an exaggeration would be just that. A is wrong because of the word "every." Remember that extremes are not usually answers because any exception can make them incorrect. B is wrong because the end does not justify the means and Anthony would not sacrifice her goal just to be persuasive. For D, "no" is an extreme and thus a weak choice.

30. **D. entire.** A and C are redundant and B is the wrong part of speech.

31. **B. To them this government has no just powers derived from the consent of the governed and thus is not truly a democracy.** This is the most terse and thus is our choice. C is clear, but is a bit too wordy.

32. **B. to enforce.** We need B because it is an infinitive and we must have the same structure on each side of "and, than, or." The others are not infinitives.

33. **D. left where it is.** It would seem that it should be D and that sentence 3 should follow the opening sentence, but the word "then" makes that a mistake.

34. **B. he was born and raised.** This is the answer because otherwise we would have a dangling participle. C and D are the wrong tense. Once you start a clause or sentence with a participle (born and raised are both participles), you must follow the comma with the person or thing that those participles describe. They describe Pelé, not his top salary.

35. **C. associated.** This is the answer as both words in A mean the same thing and are therefore redundant. B and D are far too wordy.

36. **B. Taught.** This is the answer as it is the briefest and the most accurate. The others present relationships that may or may not have been true.

37. **A. placed after sentence 2.** This is the answer because the last two sentences must obviously follow each other as they are now placed in the paragraph and because of the phrase "in addition," they must follow the information in the underlined sentence.

38. **B. Yes, because it places his great achievement in a larger perspective.** A is out, as there is no rule for how long a paragraph should be.

39. **A. NO CHANGE.** "Stunning" is more intense than "strong" and his stats need such an adjective; therefore B is out. "Dominant" is a great word here, but "amount of" does not fit at all, and so C is out. D is out because "notorious" means "known for a bad reason," and that is certainly not true.

40. **C. In 1967, two factions involved in the Nigerian Civil War agreed to a 48 hour ceasefire so they could watch Pelé play an exhibition game in Lagos.** A and B are out because they use words and phrases such as "were able to halt that terrible war" and "way back in" and "warring." These get in the way of the message and are redundant because being involved in a war already tells us that they are "warring" factions. D is actually a fairly solid rewrite. However, it includes the word "warring," which is unnecessary since we are told they are involved in a war.

41. **D. however,.** This is the answer, as we need a contrast word to explain why he was allowed to play for another country even though he had been listed as an "official national treasure."

42. **B. philanthropic.** This is the answer, as the other choices are redundant.

43. **B. thus bettering.** There is nothing really wrong with A, but B is a better way of showing the relationship to what he has accomplished. C and D are far too wordy.

45. **C. From humble beginnings, this great man has risen to the pinnacle of his time.** Again, as long as the choice is brief, contains no grammatical errors and is not awkwardly expressed, it will be the answer.

Writing and Language Test 4

35 MINUTES, 44 QUESTIONS

DIRECTIONS

Each passage below is accompanied by a number of questions. For some questions, you will consider how the passage might be revised to improve the expression of ideas. For other questions, you will consider how the passage might be edited to correct errors in sentence structure, usage, or punctuation. A passage or a question may be accompanied by one or more graphics (such as a table or graph) that you will consider as you make revising and editing decisions.

Some questions will direct you to an underlined portion of a passage. Other questions will direct you to a location in a passage or ask you to think about the passage as a whole.

After reading each passage, choose the answer to each question that most effectively improves the quality of writing in the passage or that makes the passage conform to the conventions of standard written English. Many questions include a "NO CHANGE" option. Choose that option if you think the best choice is to leave the relevant portion of the passage as it is.

Questions 1 - 11 are based on the following passage.

(1) [1] Leon Termin, a Russian physicist in the 1920s, came up with what he hoped would fulfill that fantasy for many. [2] Many people, especially some of us with tin ears, sometimes like to imagine ourselves as maestros leading a great orchestra or even performing or singing great music ourselves. [3] His classic "theremin" looks much like a

1. To make this paragraph most logical, sentence 1 should be

   A) placed after sentence 2.
   B) placed after sentence 3.
   C) placed after sentence 5.
   D) left where it is.

portable lectern with two antennas sticking out. [4] Early audiences often thought the whole thing pure chicanery. What makes it seem so weird is that the musician does not actually touch the instrument at all. [5] The theremin's uniqueness stems from (2) its being played without physical contact and thus there are no visual or physical cues to indicate when (3) you are hitting the right note. (4)

The thereminist stands in front of the instrument and moves his or her hands (5) in the proximity of two metal antennas. The distance from one antenna determines frequency (pitch), and the distance from the other controls amplitude (volume). Higher notes are played by moving the hand closer to the pitch antenna. Louder notes are played by moving the hand away from the volume antenna.

2.
A) NO CHANGE
B) it's
C) their
D) it

3.
A) NO CHANGE
B) one is
C) they are
D) it is

4. At this point, the writer is considering adding the following sentence.

   Clara Rockmore plays the theremin like a violinist, and nobody else can do that.

   Should the writer make this addition here?

   A) Yes, because it helps the reader to get a sense of what some musicians are doing with this instrument.
   B) Yes, because the reader should know about the best practitioners of this instrument.
   C) No, because there is no context for this information at this point.
   D) No, because Clara Rockmore has not been introduced at this point in the passage.

5.
A) NO CHANGE
B) at an approximation to
C) in the area around the
D) near the

With the theremin, the player has no idea exactly what note will come out. (6) Modern instruments can produce sounds across a wide range. Moving the hand as little as one-sixteenth of an inch can radically change the note. The reality (7) was and is that the theremin, the forerunner of all electronic musical instruments, is considered by many of its fans to be the world's most difficult instrument to play.

Theremin (Termin) was able to sell it in 1929 to RCA, which thought it had figured out how to turn such human (8) yearnings into a profitable business by selling a musical instrument that could supposedly turn the masses into maestros. "Anyone can make exquisitely beautiful music with nothing but his own two hands!" claimed the advertising copy for the instrument. It is "destined to be the universal musical instrument," the advertisements clacked, and people will play it as easily "as they now write or walk."

6. Which choice most effectively combines the underlined sentences?

   A) While modern instruments can produce sounds across a wide range, moving the hand as little as one-sixteenth of an inch can radically change the note.
   B) Modern instruments are designed to produce sounds across a wide range of notes, but moving the hand as little as one sixteenth of an inch can radically change the notes of a therermin.
   C) We can often see a modern instrument produce a sound across a wide range, but with a Theremin, if you move your hand as little as a sixteenth of an inch, you can radically change the notes.
   D) Sometimes a modern instrumentalist can produce a sound across a wide range of notes, but if you move your hand even as little as a sixteenth of an inch with a theremin, it could radically change the notes.

7.
   A) NO CHANGE
   B) was, and is that
   C) was, and is, that
   D) was, and is that,

8.
   A) NO CHANGE
   B) considerations
   C) talents
   D) ambitions

However, the unfortunate coincidence of their purchase and the Great Depression in 1929, added to the fact that it was actually much more difficult to play well than it might have seemed, doomed the early success of their venture. RCA found out the hard way; it sold just 485 of them, at the cost of $175 each (more than $1,700 in 2016 dollars). They had a (9) problem, which needed to be solved.

(10) It was important that they start to find a way of selling for the theremin, which uses simple electronic principles to produce a somewhat eerie sound. If you have listened to the Beach Boys' hit "Good Vibrations," you've heard a theremin riff. The theremin was used to produce the otherworldly music in 1940s and 1950s films like "Spellbound," "The Lost Weekend" and "The Day the Earth Stood Still." Today, devotees gather at conferences and on the Web and small concerts are given around the country. Interest in the instrument is growing.

(11) Consequently we see that, Robert Moog, inventor of the first electronic synthesizer and a theremin enthusiast, has sold more than 4,000 theremins since his company, Big Briar, opened its doors five years ago. Perhaps the future is looking better for this strange instrument.

9.
- A) NO CHANGE
- B) problem that needed a solution.
- C) problem, which was a predicament.
- D) problem.

10. Which of the following provides the best transition from the previous paragraph?
- A) NO CHANGE
- B) Something had to be done soon for the
- C) They had to start looking for different uses for the
- D) But that wasn't the end for the

11.
- A) NO CHANGE
- B) This is evidenced by Robert Moog, inventor of the first electronic synthesizer and a theremin enthusiast, who has
- C) Moreover, we now know that Robert Moog, inventor of the first electronic synthesizer and a theremin enthusiast, has
- D) In any event, Robert Moog, inventor of the first electronic synthesizer and a theremin enthusiast, has

Questions 12 - 22 are based on the following passage and supplementary material.

Coffee: To drink or not to drink—that is the question. Over the years, there (12) have been countless articles on whether this delightful morning pick-me-up is bad for your health or a virtual panacea., decreasing (13) our chances for Parkinson's disease, depression, suicide, type 2 diabetes, Alzheimer's disease, liver cancer, and even death. The naysayers cite problems such as insomnia, nervousness and restlessness, stomach upset, nausea and vomiting, increased heart and breathing rate, and other side effects. Consuming large amounts of coffee, they say, might also cause headache, anxiety, agitation, ringing in the ears, and irregular heartbeats.

So, what's a person to do? The great Greek philosopher, Hippocrates, along with the Stoics and even the Epicureans at the time (14) promulgated "all things in moderation" and that seems always to be good advice. (15) However, we must still address the question as to what exactly is moderation when considering coffee consumption. Recent studies have come up with suggested numbers to combat particular diseases. It is starting

12.
 A) NO CHANGE
 B) has
 C) had
 D) were

13.
 A) NO CHANGE
 B) your
 C) their
 D) someone's

14.
 A) NO CHANGE
 B) charged
 C) indicated
 D) espoused

15. Which choice most effectively combines the underlined sentences?

 A) But we must still consider carefully and look at what exactly moderation is as far as a number for coffee consumption and recent studies have come up with suggested numbers for that.
 B) Recent studies have suggested numbers for this moderate consumption that can help fight particular diseases.
 C) In consideration of what constitutes moderation, recent studies have tried to establish certain amounts that might help to alleviate problems arising from certain diseases.
 D) However, since we still have to try to establish amounts of coffee that can be considered "moderate" to combat each disease, recent studies have set about to discover just exactly what those numbers might be.

to look as if coffee, if not an actual panacea, may have amazing physical and medical benefits.

(16) One of these relates to Alzheimer's disease. This is the most common neuro-degenerative disease in the world and a leading cause of dementia. It is a huge problem these days and there is no good cure for it. Therefore, preventing it is incredibly important. Many studies have supported the correlation between coffee drinking and lower Alzheimer's occurrence. For some reason, coffee drinkers have a much lower risk of Alzheimer's disease.

Many researchers think it may be due to the huge amount of antioxidants found in coffee. (17) There are lots of them. It actually contains more of them than fruits and vegetables. Antioxidants play an important role in overall health. They are natural compounds found in some foods that help neutralize free radicals in our bodies. Free radicals are substances that occur naturally in our bodies but attack the fats, protein and the DNA in our cells, which can cause different types of diseases and accelerate the aging process.

16.
  A) NO CHANGE
  B) Alzheimer's disease is a highly feared disease.
  C) Doctors consider Alzheimer's disease to be one of the worst diseases in the entire world.
  D) Why is Alzheimer's disease considered such a terrible disease?

17.
  A) NO CHANGE
  B) There are many of them.
  C) We find many of them.
  D) Delete the sentence.

Thus, those who consume foods and drinks with more antioxidants (18) tends to be healthier and more upbeat. (19) On balance, a study done by the National Institutes of Health found that those who drink four or more cups of coffee were about 10% less likely to be depressed than those who had never touched the java. And apparently after (20) carefully scrutinizing the data, scientists found that it's not because of the "caffeine high," but the amount of antioxidants in coffee.

So, find how much coffee your body is comfortable with and try not to have more than five cups per day. Chances are you will have a lower risk for suicide, diabetes, and liver failure and will be a better athlete with a healthier brain. (21) Modern research and common sense seem to support the answer to our original question—drink coffee.

18.
   A) NO CHANGE
   B) tended
   C) tend
   D) have tended

19.
   A) NO CHANGE
   B) In the long run,
   C) Nevertheless,
   D) Furthermore,

20.
   A) NO CHANGE
   B) diligently scrutinizing
   C) carefully poring over
   D) delete carefully

21. Which statement most clearly ends the passage with a restatement of the writer's primary claim?
   A) NO CHANGE
   B) It looks like drinking coffee could be the answer to that question.
   C) Maybe some of us should start drinking just a little more coffee.
   D) Drinking coffee seems like the best medicine on the market today.

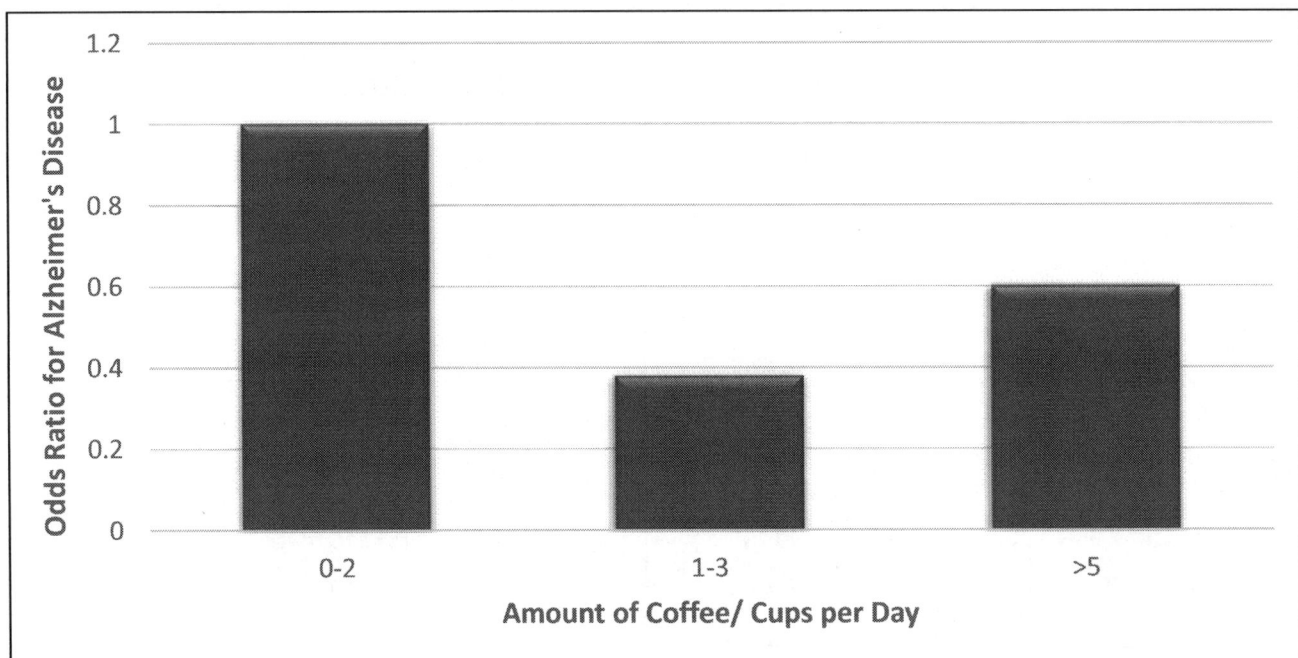

22. During further research, the writer finds the graphic shown above. Should he include it with the passage?

   A) Yes, because the graph clearly supports the assertion from the passage that drinking a moderate amount of coffee each day lowers the incidence of Alzheimer's disease.
   B) Yes, because the graph shows that coffee drinking lowers disease.
   C) No, because the evidence is not obvious.
   D) No, because the passage does not develop this idea at all.

Questions 23 - 33 are based on the following passage

The following essay is about Bobby Fischer, who rose to become the top chess player in the world.

One of the (23) genuinely authentic American geniuses of the 20th century was an extremely troubled person. Bobby Fischer rose to become the top chess player in the country at age 13. The winner each year usually won by the margin of half a point. Fischer, however won all 11 matches one year. (24) In 1972, he battled Boris Spassky, the reigning world champ, in Reykjavík, Iceland. The entire country was riveted to this televised event for two months. Chess teacher Shelby Lyman went from being an unknown to a household name (25) as a result of his live analyses of the matches. Russia had long dominated the chess world and Fisher was a serious threat to this dominance. It was

23.
A) NO CHANGE
B) authentic
C) genuine authentic
D) genuinely, authentic

24. Which choice most effectively combines the sentences in the underlined portion?

A) In 1972, he battled Boris Spassky, the reigning world champ, in Reykjavík, Iceland, with the entire country riveted to their TV sets for two months.
B) In 1972, Fischer battled Boris Spassky, the reigning world champ, in Reykjavík, Iceland, when many in our country were riveted to their television sets for about two months.
C) Fischer battled Boris Spassky, the reigning world champ in 1972, in Reykjavík, Iceland, while many from the States watched on their television sets for two months.
D) In 1972, Fischer battled the reigning world champ, Boris Spassky, in Reykjavík, Iceland, while many watched on their TV sets for about two months.

25.
A) NO CHANGE
B) since
C) for
D) resulting from

a "cold war" battle and people could not get enough. (26) Never before or after has chess had such popularity in our country.

(27) He on occasion showed up late, allowing precious time to elapse from his clock. This and many other gimmicks threw Spassky off his game and he was finally able to defeat him. This was devastating to the Russians because not only did America not have a strong chess tradition, (28) but Fischer was a high school drop-out who was very uneducated despite having two intelligent parents, both with their doctorates. Traditionally, chess champions were cosmopolitan (29) polyglots they had been trained by top grandmasters for many years. How was it possible that Bobby had been able to ascend to such a pinnacle of success without the lessons, the financial support and (30) people to guide him?

26. The author is considering deleting the underlined sentence. Should he do so?

    A) Yes, because it basically says what the previous sentence says.
    B) Yes, it is irrelevant information.
    C) No, because it informs the reader of the significance of this event for Americans.
    D) No, because it makes Americans remember how important this was in the history of their country.

27. Which of the following is the most effective sentence to precede the present one?

    A) Fischer loved to get inside his opponent's heads.
    B) Fischer sometimes showed impatience.
    C) Fischer was a tough competitor.
    D) Fischer was not good at time management.

28.

    A) NO CHANGE
    B) but Fischer had been
    C) but, Fischer was also
    D) but Fischer was also

29.

    A) NO CHANGE
    B) polyglots, they had been
    C) polyglots, who had been
    D) polyglots, which had been

30.

    A) NO CHANGE
    B) professional guidance?
    C) others to help him?
    D) people guiding him?

[1] Fischer began (31) to play at age five and was very much a loner. [2] Having no one to play, he often played against himself. [3] He played a match against the US champ when he was 12 and lost after a close battle. [4] Still, no one has ever been able to explain how he became so great. (32)

After that, he was able to join the Manhattan chess club, the top club in America, and get some solid training, resulting in his being crowned national champion the very next year.

31.
- A) NO CHANGE
- B) playing
- C) trying to play
- D) initially to play

32. To make this paragraph most logical, sentence 4 should be
- A) placed after sentence 1.
- B) placed after sentence 2.
- C) omitted.
- D) left where it is.

Fischer was born in Chicago but raised in Brooklyn, New York by his single parent mother. Although Jewish, he was fiercely anti-Semitic. He was also anti-American as evidenced by his clapping at the film *Pearl Harbor* when the Japanese planes began to bomb the airbase. He had many acquaintances but seemed to have no actual friends. Probably due to an impoverished youth, he demanded (33) exorbitant fees for appearances and felt that people should consider it a privilege to be in his presence. He refused to defend his title a few years after he won it because FIDE, the governing body of chess, would not change one of their rules to accommodate him. He died four years after moving to Reykjavík at age 64, the same number of squares on a chessboard. Sadly, his flame that shone so brightly has been missed by very few.

33.
A) NO CHANGE
B) unfair
C) wild
D) questionable

Questions 34 - 44 are based on the following passage.

Who Am I? A scholar contrasts two approaches to this question.

Psychology and Sociology are both social sciences and there is much overlap in the topics (34) covered by each discipline. In general, (35) on the other hand, the realm of psychology is the individual and of sociology is the group.

So, how does each discipline explain the self, how do they explain the universal question, "Who am I?" Most readers are familiar with the terms *id, ego,* and *superego*, which were first proposed by Sigmund Freud in 1920 to create a theoretical model that (36) explains the totality of the human mind or psyche. (37) The three terms are symbolic and there is no reason to postulate that it exists as

34.
   A) NO CHANGE
   B) covering in
   C) covered with
   D) covered to

35.
   A) NO CHANGE
   B) thus,
   C) however,
   D) but,

36.
   A) NO CHANGE
   B) was explaining
   C) explain
   D) had explained

37. At this point, the writer is considering adding the following sentence.

   Freud is considered to be the founder of modern psychology.

   Should the writer make this addition here?

   A) Yes, because it tells us a crucial piece of information about Freud.
   B) Yes, because the reader needs to have a context to understand why Freud's ideas are so important.
   C) No, because there is no real consensus that Freud founded modern psychology.
   D) No, because it intrudes upon what the writer is saying and thus disrupts the point he is making.

actual, or somatic, structures of the brain. In other words, there is no (38) history where any of the terms physically exist and could be identified.

As a psychologist Freud used the interplay between the conscious and the unconscious to explain how the awareness of self eventually develops inside a human. This awareness then helps to determine the person we identify as our "self." (39) This realization helps us to decide on the person we see as our "self."

Before Freud, sociologist Charles Horton Cooley had offered his own theory in 1902 as to how the self develops within each individual. He called his explanation the "looking-glass Self," using a (now) curiously antiquated name for a mirror. (40) Using a sociologist's point of view, Cooley explained that the self, our own most personal view of who we are, develops not internally independent as might be expected. Rather, he says, it is gradually molded by external forces.

38.
A) NO CHANGE
B) term
C) reason
D) locus

39.
A) NO CHANGE
B) This understanding permits us to decide on the person we will become.
C) This awareness determines how we see our "self."
D) Delete the sentence as it is redundant.

40. Which choice most effectively combines the underlined sentences?

A) Using a sociologist's point of view, Cooley explains that the self, which he sees as our own most personal view of who we are, tends to develop internally independent as we often expect and thus, he believes, it is gradually molded by external forces.
B) Using a sociologist's point of view, Cooley explains that the self, which he sees as our own most personal view of who we are, tends to develop internally independent as we often expect, which he believes it is gradually molded by external forces.
C) Using a sociologist's point of view, Cooley explained that the self, our own most personal view of who we are, develops not internally independent of who we are, as might be expected, but is gradually molded by external forces.
D) Using a sociologist's point of view, Cooley explains that the self, who we are in our eyes, develops not internally independent as one would expect, but is gradually molded by external forces.

Cooley (41) postulates that a newborn has no concept of self but as it grows, though, it gradually becomes aware of other people's perceptions. These perceptions are internalized and the child forms its identity based on how he thinks other people see him. (42) Thus, awareness of others becomes the vehicle for forming and identifying the inner self.

Mother, father, siblings, family, society in general—each and all become a mirror and the child identifies himself as he thinks others see him. This process can be summarized: *I am, who I think you think, that I am.* Since interacting with others never ends while alive, Cooley can thus explain why the question, "Who am I?" continues to (43) revolve throughout one's life.

Although both of these therapists seem to have a similar take on how we develop our perception of who we are, it is interesting to observe how they arrive at it through very different (44) prisms. These allow us to understand the two fields and the different approaches.

41.
A) NO CHANGE
B) understands
C) considers
D) realizes

42.
A) NO CHANGE
B) Nevertheless,
C) However,
D) Because

43.
A) NO CHANGE
B) disburse
C) disperse
D) evolve

44.
A) NO CHANGE
B) attitudes.
C) biases.
D) fields.

Explanations

1. **A. placed after sentence 2.** This is the answer because it adds to the content of sentence two. With sentence two first, the opening sentence presents a hypothetical situation and the second sentence shows how someone tried to make this a reality.

2. **A. NO CHANGE.** This may sound incorrect to many of you, but B is clearly wrong as the sentence calls for a possessive. Since theremin is singular, C is wrong also. D probably "sounds" better to your ear, but you need a possessive here and A is just that.

3. **B. one is.** This is the correct answer as it keeps the right case. A (you) in an unnecessary shift. C is wrong because the plural "they" is not called for. D is wrong because it is being played by a person and it is not a person.

4. **C. No, because there is no context for this information at this point.** D is not a bad answer except that it would be acceptable to introduce her to the passage if the context allowed. Thus, C is a better choice.

5. **D. near the.** This is the correct answer because we always try to be terse when we can.

6. **A. While modern instruments can produce sounds across a wide range, moving the hand as little as one-sixteenth of an inch can radically change the note.** Our rule of thumb of choosing the shortest choice, as long as it is grammatically correct and stays consistent with what the passage is saying, leads us to this answer.

7. **C. was, and is, that.** This is the answer, as it sets off "and is" by commas, which the writer needs to do to make this distinction. There are probably some punctuation problems that many students will still struggle with on this exam because they have just not been exposed to them.

8. **A. NO CHANGE.** This is the answer, as it is the only one that comes close to being the correct diction. None of the other choices really makes much sense here.

9. **D. problem.** This is the correct answer, as it deletes the clause after the comma, which is certainly redundant. A problem is by definition something that needs to be solved, so there is no reason to burden the reader with that useless information.

10. **D. But that wasn't the end for the.** Once again this is the answer because it is the briefest and introduces the contrast that this paragraph provides.

11. **B. This is evidenced by Robert Moog, inventor of the first electronic synthesizer and a theremin enthusiast, who has.** This is the answer as it directly connects to the previous sentence in the last paragraph, thus commenting on it in a way that brings us into this paragraph.

12. **A. NO CHANGE.** Choice A is the answer, as the verb has to agree with the first noun or pronoun that follows the construction: is, are, was, were, has been, have been, etc.

13. **B. your.** This is the best answer, as it is consistent with the person mentioned earlier in the sentence. As you do these grammar passages, always make sure that whatever person (I, me, we, us, you, he, she, it, they) begins the paragraph remains consistent throughout that paragraph. Remember to do this with tense also as this is a very common error in this part of the exam.

14. **D. espoused.** This is the answer, as it is the correct word in this context. A, "promulgated," means to promote or to make widely known. C, "indicated," does not tell us what Hippocrates was actually doing and B, "charged," is wrong in this context.

15. **D. However, since we still have to try to establish amounts of coffee that can be considered "moderate" to combat each disease, recent studies have set about to discover just exactly what those numbers might be.** This is the answer, as it provides all of the essential information and connects the two thoughts most efficiently. A is out because of the redundancy of "consider carefully" and "look at." B does not include enough information from the original sentences. C is far too wordy.

16. **A. NO CHANGE.** This is the best answer here, as it contains the word "these," which connects it so smoothly to the last sentence. Using these demonstrative pronouns (this, that, these, those) is a great way to connect thought. Look out for them on the exam and use them in your own writing.

17. **D. Delete this sentence.** This is the answer because "huge amounts of" from the previous sentence already tells us this so it is redundant.

18. **C. tend.** This is the answer, as it agrees with "Those," which is the subject of that verb.

19. **D. Furthermore,.** This is the answer, as the sentence requires a word that means "in addition" and none of the others have that meaning.

20. **D. delete carefully.** Scrutinize means "to look at very carefully." Thus, in A and B we have a strong redundancy. C is also incorrect because if you are poring over something, the connotation is that you are looking at every detail in a very careful manner and thus this too is redundant.

21. **D. Drinking coffee seems like the best medicine on the market today.** Although none of these is a bad answer, only D incorporates all of the elements of the author's pitch.

22. **A. Yes, because the graph clearly supports the assertion from the passage that drinking a moderate amount of coffee each day lowers the incidence of Alzheimer's disease.** This is the answer, as there is such a clear connection between the graph and what the passage asserts, that moderate drinking lessens the incidence of Alzheimer's disease.

23. **B. authentic.** A is redundant; C is wrong because you must have an adverb to modify an adjective; D is wrong because no comma is necessary.

24. **A. In 1972, he battled Boris Spassky, the reigning world champ, in Reykjavík, Iceland, with the entire country riveted to their TV sets for two months.** This is the best answer because it is the most concise. The others add unnecessary words and phrases that make the answers wordy.

25. **C. for.** A is too wordy; B, "since," is the wrong word; D, "resulting from," is awkward.

26. **C. No, because it informs the reader of the significance of this event for Americans.** D is far too general.

27. **A. Fischer loved to get inside his opponent's heads.** This is the answer because of the word "gimmicks" in the second sentence. Once we realize that Fischer came late in order to throw his opponent off his game, none of the others makes sense.

28. **D. but Fischer was also.** A does not complete the "both … and" requirement and C has a comma after but. You must follow "not only" with "but also"; B, "had been" is the wrong tense as the action had not been completed before another past action.

29. **C. polyglots, who had been.** This choice correctly clears up the run-on sentence; A is incorrect because there is no punctuation separating the two parts of the sentence; B is wrong because you cannot correct a run-on with a comma. Since polyglots are people, we need to use "who" instead of "which." So D is out.

30. **B. professional guidance?** This choice completes the parallel structure. Once you have a grammatical pattern, you must keep it. A, C, and D break that pattern by inserting verbs rather than nouns.

31. **B. playing.** The reason is simple. That is just the acceptable word. Every language has its own idiom and that establishes what is and is not preferred. We prefer "playing" after the verb began.

32. **D. left where it is.** This is the correct choice because it sums up everything in the paragraph. It is where the sense of the paragraph is taking us.

33. **A. NO CHANGE.** Exorbitant is the correct word here. B, "unfair" has nothing to do with being too much. C, "wild" is close but has too many other connotations; D, "questionable" is not what is needed.

34. A. NO CHANGE. This is the best answer because it is the correct idiom. Choice B is incorrect because **covering** is the wrong verb form. We need the past tense. Choices C and D are idiomatically incorrect because they both use an inappropriate preposition.

35. C. however,. This is the best answer because the word however suggests the contrast needed in the context of first two sentences. Choice A is a phrase that introduces an alternate view, which is not the meaning we want. Choice B means **therefore** or **consequently,** which is inappropriate here. The word **but,** choice D, is really used as a conjunction between two sentences.

36. A. NO CHANGE. This is the best answer because it is the correct form of the verb. The subject of the verb **explains** is the noun **model.** Remember that we add an **s** to make a noun plural, but we add an **s** to make a verb singular. This is the same reason why choice C is incorrect. Choices B and D are both inappropriate

37. D. No, because it intrudes upon what the writer is saying and thus disrupts the point he is making. Although this might be interesting information, it certainly does not belong here. It is not crucial information (A) and it does not provide context (B). C is not acceptable as the passage does not consider whether of not Freud is the father of modern psychology.

38. D. locus. This is the best answer because the word **locus** means **place,** which is the correct meaning needed here. The rest of the choices just don't fit.

39. D. Delete the sentence as it is redundant. There is virtually nothing in this final sentence that is not said clearly in the previous sentence and thus none of the rewrites (A, B, or C) are necessary.

40. C. Cooley explained that the self, our own most personal view of who we are, develops not internally independent of who we are, as might be expected, but is gradually molded by external forces. This is the best sentence as it is very brief and does not use a lot of unnecessary words and phrases as in A and B. D is good except that it uses the present tense (explains) and the past tense is called for.

41. A. NO CHANGE. The sentence calls for a word that means "sets forth," "claims," "theorizes," etc. B, C, and D do not do this at all.

42. A. NO CHANGE. This is the best answer because the word **thus** means furthermore, which is the meaning the author is suggesting. Choices B and C both imply a contrast, which is not required. The word **because** makes the sentence a fragment.

43. D. evolve. The context of the sentence tells us that the word the author means is **change,** and **evolve** means just that. The rest of the choices don't make sense.

44. A. NO CHANGE. B, "attitude," is not what they are really bringing to their studies. It is more of a perspective and prism is a very similar word. C, "biases," indicates that they are not being scientific at all. D, "fields," does not hit the mark as we are looking more for a word that indicates a way of looking at things.

ESSAY WRITING GUIDE

* Read the notes on the writing part of the test in the introduction before you start to read this.

Although this is an optional part of the exam, many colleges will use it to exempt you from required writing classes if you do particularly well. If you do very poorly, they may require you to take a writing class for which you receive no credit, but must pay dearly.

It is impossible to make you a much better writer in just a few pages of an SAT book. However, by following the simple guidelines and reading through the sample passages and the critiques carefully, you will have a much clearer idea of how to use the writing ability that you do have to get the most points possible.

You may be a very good writer, but read the essentials below carefully anyway. If your basics are solid, your essay will be solid.

The essay will be given at the end of the multiple choice part of the exam. This allows those who are not taking it to leave.

* You will not be asked to take a stance on any issue and then defend that. In fact, avoid this at all costs as you can be severely penalized for misreading the directions. The support you provide in the essay should not come from your own experience or knowledge. Do not include facts that you know to support the claim of the author, but stick strictly to what is in the text. Your analysis must come completely from the passage on the exam. You will not be given any surprise prompts; the prompt will always be pretty much the same. Instead the passage itself will be changing with each exam. This should give you a sense of confidence going into the exam, as no one likes surprises.

* Scoring: Two graders will independently assign a score from 1-4 and those two scores will be averaged. The writing score will not affect your actual SAT score, but will certainly affect your college entrance with possible exemptions from writing requirements in some colleges.

* Writing Prompt: It is important that you look at the essays from several exams. The sample essays found in this book together with the essays from the online practice tests at www.CollegeBoard.org should be more than enough. Taking a careful look at these will get you comfortable with how the essay question is set up. The essays will require you to know how the author used evidence such as facts, quotes, stats, etc. to support his claims. You must also show how he used specific reasoning techniques to support his thesis. Make note as you read of any stylistic devices he used such as appeal to emotions, level of language, or rhetorical devices.

Instructions for the Essay

Here are the instructions for the essay (they are always the same):

> As you read the passage below, consider how the author uses
>
> - evidence, such as facts or examples, to support claims.
> - reasoning to develop ideas and to connect claims and evidence.
> - stylistic or persuasive elements, such as word choice or appeals to emotion, to add power to the ideas expressed.

You can use any one or more of the elements mentioned in the box, or any of your own, to explain how the author builds his argument to persuade his/her audience.

* Always read the first sentence in the box that immediately follows the passage. This sentence will clearly explain the author's argument. You can then decide as you read whether or not you think he has effectively presented his argument.

How to Read the Passage

If you are a very fast reader, we suggest that you read the passage through rapidly once to establish for yourself what the author's contention is and how he goes about convincing the reader to both understand his contention and agree with it. Then, you can go through again and use the system below to organize your essay.

If you are not a fast reader, then using the system below in a very deliberate manner is the best approach for you. You can just read the passage through slowly and carefully using the notations indicated.

You need to have a definite game plan for this part of the exam. Remember that you are in charge. If you know in advance exactly how you are going to proceed, you will be able to get the job done comfortably. You can use our system or any variation of it that you think might work for you. For instance, you may want to emphasize word choice, imagery, and tone (sarcastic, authoritative, tentative, etc.). Again, our system uses parentheses, brackets, etc. to organize the essay. You might want to use a slightly different notation system, but you need to already have this in place. Make sure you have practiced using your system and that you are very comfortable with it well before the exam date. This is the advice I give to my students, 58 of whom have received perfect scores on the SAT and countless others who received scores of 750 and above.

System: Use ethos, pathos, and logos to organize your essay.

Ethos: This demonstrates the author's credibility. If he uses the first person point of view, then we see him as credible. If he references the American Medical Association or USDA or any such respected resource, that's credibility. If the author is a former President, or an eminent doctor or religious leader, then again he has "cred." Even if he just references allusions that are solidly entrenched in our culture such as the Bible or Shakespeare or some highly reputed authority, then we see him as credible. So, any use of solid stats, quotations, allusions, examples from solid sources, etc. should be organized by *parentheses*.

Pathos: This is an appeal to emotion. This is when the author attempts to invoke sympathy from his readers-when he tugs at your heart strings. He might also appeal to your patriotism, or inspire fear, anger or any other powerful emotion. You might find some of his appeals a bit sensationalist. You can just *circle* any of these as they are usually briefer, sometimes just a loaded word or phrase such as **horror, guilty pleasure, vicious cycle, atrocity.**

Logos: This is an appeal to reason or logic. Here, you can *bracket off* any facts, stats, strongly supported examples, or quotations that you see the author use that help to support his argument. Also, any actual argument he uses can be *bracketed* if you feel it is a reflection of solid logic. Obviously, there will be some crossover between ethos and logos at times. If you feel that the author's logic is not very solid or that he uses sources which are questionable, you should definitely point this out.

Underline any words or phrases the author uses that you find particularly effective or ineffective. Metaphors, alliteration, repetition or any other rhetorical devices that you find pertinent to your case should also be *underlined.*

* Feel free to cite any quotation, stat, etc. that you feel demonstrates the author's attempts to convince the reader that his thesis is sound. Think of yourself as a lawyer arguing a case in front of a jury. The readers of your essay are the jury and you have to use everything you can to demonstrate the effectiveness or futility of the argument the author has put forth.

* If you have been careful about using the above parentheses, brackets, circles and underlinings while you read, your outline should not take more than a few minutes. Any shorthand you can understand is certainly acceptable. Doing all of this, including your outline should take no more than 15-20 minutes, which will leave you 30-35 minutes to write your essay. This should be more than enough time, especially since you will have a strong outline to work from.

How to Write the Essay

The opening paragraph is generally fairly straightforward as you can just go to the paragraph that follows the essay and copy out the thesis presented there. As an example, let's write an opening paragraph for Essay #1 (this is the first essay given after this introductory section). At the end of the passage the paragraph says:

Write an essay in which you explain how the author builds an argument to persuade his audience that "revenge is one of the silliest of emotions and should not therefore be pursued."

We will simply just take the key phrase from this paragraph and use it as the essence of our opening paragraph as follows.

Opening paragraph example: The author is trying to make a case against following through on **revenge, calling it "the silliest of emotions."** He makes his case using quotes and examples from history, literature, cinema and the Bible to convince us that **revenge is truly an empty emotion** that leaves the avenger worse off and even in a dangerous situation when he pursues it. His use of strong, logical connections throughout helps us to follow his argument.

The highlighted words and phrases demonstrate how one can just take the key words from the prompt and use them to write the opening paragraph. One could just memorize the key words from the parts of this paragraph that are **not** underlined to write virtually any opening paragraph. Of course, it is wise to emphasize only the actual things that this particular author has used.

So, if we observe the notations from the sample in Essay #1, we could make an outline fairly easily that looks something like the one below. Of course, it is not necessary to write so many references from the essay as you have it in front of you and if you have used your parentheses, brackets, circles and underlinings effectively, you need only to scan through and pick what you believe are the most effective references.

Here is a complete listing, but again this is not something that you would have time to do in most cases. Notice how after you have done this while reading, it is just a matter of sliding this information into each of your three supporting paragraphs.

Ethos: Homer, Bible, Shakespeare, *The Godfather*, *Inglorious Basterds*, Osama Bin Laden, 9/11, "Cask of Amontillado," Northern Ireland, Israel versus other Mideast countries, Hatfield-McCoys, Francis Bacon, the New Testament.

Pathos: "terrible atrocities," "feel a certain guilt," "architect of the attacks was assassinated," "guilty pleasure," "rejoicing with the execution of hundreds of Nazis," "feel worse," "hurt us doubly," "he has hurt us a third time," "we could begin to put it behind us. Unfortunately, most feel they have not been able to do that." " We lower ourselves." "Would we ever have done such wicked things?" "Just to get back at the other guy?" "We still risk the revenge of this person." "We keep the offense of the first wound fresh." "Keeps his own wounds green." "There's no fun in it and it lowers us to the bestial level." "Revenge is certainly the silliest of emotions."

Logos: We can either list the four paragraphs that demonstrate his strongest logical case (3, 4, 5, 7), or if we write rapidly, we could list the key argument from each paragraph.

Now, it is just a matter of sliding each of these into the three solid supporting paragraphs. We don't have to hunt about for the information as we have already grouped it for ourselves. Where did we get this information? Simply by using the parentheses, brackets, circles and underlinings that we have practiced using on the essays in the book and in the six practice tests available at the College Board's website: www.CollegeBoard.org

It is often tempting to try to fit in all of the material we have placed in our outline. Doing this, however, often results in a boring essay of lists and does not give you the opportunity to demonstrate that you understand how the author has used his material to convince the reader that his thesis is sound. Thus, you must choose carefully the most salient points you think the author has used and delineate his most powerful arguments. This is how you raise your scores from 3's to 4's.

You determine whether the author is effective by carefully considering whether or not you believe the reader will be persuaded by his or her argument.

*It is never enough just to say "the author did a good job on this or that." You must always support such a claim with very specific examples of his doing just that. If you are impressed by the language or logic or any aspect of the original essay, you should mention that, but if you can find anything at all that you think mars the effectiveness of either the writing or the logic, then you must also mention that specifically. If you feel the author has used something other than logic, such as appeal to fear or sensationalism or any such technique, you should certainly mention that and show how he has used this information to convince his reader. More practice for opening paragraphs is available after the essentials. Make sure you take advantage of that practice.

* Read through the essentials below carefully and then start to go through the sample passages to see what average and strong writers have done with some essays. It's best if you actually try to write essays using these prompts before you look at the samples. This way by comparing your essay to the ones in the book and using the rubric to arrive at a score, you will start to get a sense of how you are doing.

Essentials

1. Do not give your opinion. Just use the information contained in the passage and the charts, if there are any, to demonstrate how the author did or did not support his thesis.

2. Use a brief opening paragraph that presents your thesis simply and carefully. If you can write an extra sentence that is stylish and grabs the reader that will certainly enhance your writing. Never write "In this essay I am going to … "

3. Demonstrate by referencing specific information in the passage that you have grasped the central idea and its implications.

4. Give the reader a clear idea of how the essayist has developed his or her thesis. Show how the essayist has used quotations, examples, allusions, statistics, graphs, charts, logical connections, etc. to cogently make his point. Just mentioning examples, etc. is not good enough. You must demonstrate how they were used to support a thesis.

5. Use a strong vocabulary throughout, but don't just use words to impress the reader if you are not sure you are using the word correctly.

6. Use transitional words to guide your reader through your essay. These words, listed below, enable you to make it easier for the reader to grasp your point.

7. Make sure that each sentence builds from the previous one. If you suddenly make a jump to something that has little or nothing to do with your previous sentence, the reader will lose track of the idea you are developing.

8. Vary your sentence structure throughout. A steady flow of simple sentences can be deadening.

9. Avoid redundancy. If you needlessly repeat words, your essay will appear heavy and boring. Certainly remember to use pronouns once you have used a person's name once in a paragraph. Repeating the name of a character or object can make your writing stiff.

10. End strongly. Never use the phrase "In conclusion" or "In summary" or "As you can see I have proven." Don't just repeat what you have already stated previously. Rather, take what you have written and place it in a larger context. Just answer the question "So what?" You have written four or five paragraphs, so use this final one to get your point across in a way that will stay with the reader. Remember that this is the last thing the reader sees before he decides your fate.

11. Use rhetorical devices such as metaphor and repetition to make your point.

12. Avoid colloquial language. These are generally serious essays that require the use of proper language to develop your own thesis. Street language is not acceptable.

13. Use an outline to help you develop a solid structure for your essay.

GO TO Words and Expressions

One way to sharpen your writing skills and to improve your essay scores is to introduce a more varied and sophisticated vocabulary. Just like a hamburger tastes better with cheese, salt, pepper or ketchup, essays benefit from vibrant word choice "condiments." After you have finished writing your practice essay, refer to this list to see whether you can substitute any of these persuasive and potent "go to" words or expressions for any less effective vocabulary of your own. Instead of saying, "The author uses many examples to support his argument," you could write, "The author utilizes concrete evidence to enhance his contention." Doesn't that sound better? Give it a try.

Persuasive adjectives

authentic	multifaceted
cogent	persuasive
cohesive	potent
compelling	powerful
convincing	precise
dynamic	prevalent
effective	relevant
efficacious	reliable
elegant	strong
eloquent	succinct
emphatic	thorough
genuine	thoughtful
impressive	valid
influential	vigorous
insightful	weighty
moving	wonderful

Expressive verbs

accomplishes	explores
attests	focuses
augments	highlights
builds	hones
captures	identifies
clarifies	illustrates
compels	indicates
constructs	insinuates
conveys	pinpoints
delivers	relays
demonstrates	resonates
depicts	reveals
develops	substantiates
emphasizes	suggests
employs	underscores
evokes	utilizes
examines	validates
explains	verifies

Useful expressions

adds to the strength of the argument	properly persuades
alludes to	raise a concern
adjusting his/her diction	rhetorical devices
challenges the audience	seals the deal
citing statistics	solidifies his/her position
concrete evidence	strikingly vivid imagery
crucial data	successfully connects
dramatic statistical evidence	the truth in numbers is undeniable
effectively builds his argument	these claims are well connected
enhances his/her contention	this tightly woven logical approach
further contributing to	tugs at the readers' heartstrings
has developed valid claims	urges the reader
persuasive appeals	his/her vigorous tone
powerful diction	we see the significance

While these lists will most definitely enhance your writing style, they are, however, by no means complete. As you read other student essays, add any words or expressions that you think are useful. A wise man once said, "Imitation is the sincerest form of flattery."

More Help for Writing the Opening Paragraph

Let's look at the contents of those boxes that follow the other two essays below to see if we can write an opening paragraph based on those sentences in just two minutes.

Essay #2: Write an essay in which you demonstrate how President Obama builds his case for our need as a nation to curb the problems of climate control in our world. In your essay analyze how President Obama uses various rhetorical devices and specific arguments to strengthen the logic and persuasiveness of his argument. Focus on the most important parts of the passage.

Your opening paragraph:

_____
_____
_____
_____

Our opening paragraph:

President Obama is trying to convince his audience that the Earth is warming at a rate that is out of hand and that we must take immediate steps to mitigate and reverse this trend. He uses stats, striking examples and appeals to our emotions to convince us to take action now. His image of the astronauts looking at Earth for the first time any human has done so serves as both an inspiration and a call to action to preserve our planet.

Essay #3: Write an essay in which you demonstrate how Susan B. Anthony makes her case to give women the right to vote. In your essay, analyze how the author uses one or more of the features mentioned earlier to strengthen the logic and persuasiveness of his argument. Focus on the most important aspects of the passage.

Your opening paragraph:

_____
_____
_____
_____

Our opening paragraph:

Susan B. Anthony is trying to convince her audience that not only should she not have been arrested for voting, something at her time forbidden to women, but that all women should have the right to vote. She does this by citing the preamble of the constitution, and by using its tenets to demonstrate her right. She also uses appeals to basic family relationships and by simple common sense.

Transition Words

The following words and phrases are important connectors. Always be aware of the role these words play. The words in **bold** are the most important.

Words indicating agreement, addition, or similarity

in the first place	**again**	**moreover**
not only … but also	**and**	**as well as**
by the same token	**also**	**together with**
equally important	then	comparatively
in light of	**equally**	correspondingly
coupled with	identically	**similarly**
in addition	uniquely	**furthermore**
in like manner	**like**	**additionally**
as a matter of fact	as	
to say nothing of	too	
first, second, third	of course	
in the same fashion, way	**likewise**	

Words indicating contrast

but	**however**	**despite**
paradoxically	**yet**	**whereas**
although	**otherwise**	while
on the other hand	even though	unlike
ironically	still	conversely
nevertheless	rather	

Words indicating conclusion, summary, restatement

as can be seen	after all	overall
generally speaking	in fact	ordinarily
in the final analysis	in summary	usually
all things considered	in conclusion	by and large
as shown above	**in short**	to sum up
in the long run	**in brief**	**on the whole**
given these points	**in essence**	in any event
as has been noted	to summarize	in either case
in a word	on balance	**all in all**
for the most part	altogether	**consequently**
accordingly	for example	on the other hand
also	for instance	otherwise
another	furthermore	similarly
as a result	however	such
at last	**in fact**	then

Words indicating emphasis

again	truly	for this reason

Others

this, that, these, those, them   Personal pronouns: he, she, they, its, etc.

ESSAY SAMPLES

The following are three sample essays that you should read over a few times. You should first read the passage and spend some time writing down an outline of what you would write. Then, read the sample and see how it stacks up against what you had in mind. Rate the essay from 1-4 with 4 being the highest score. Then, read the analysis to see how accurately you rated the sample. By carefully reading the analysis of the sample, you will get a sense of how your essay should develop. You will start to understand the criteria by which your own essay will be judged.

Practice Essay 1

> As you read the passage below, consider how the author uses
>
> - evidence, such as facts or examples, to support claims.
> - reasoning to develop ideas and to connect claims and evidence.
> - stylistic or persuasive elements, such as word choice or appeals to emotion, to add power to the ideas expressed.

* Try to use the markings we have discussed: brackets, parentheses, underlinings, and circles. Then, compare your markings to ours in the annotated script below.

The following essay is from a philosopher from the Great Northwest of America.

History and literature amply demonstrate that a thirst for vengeance is timeless. One needs only to study the terrible atrocities of war that resulted from a sense of revenge or to witness it in epics as old as Homer or the great plays of Shakespeare such as *Hamlet* and *The Merchant of Venice*. We see it again in films such as *The Godfather* by Coppola and *Inglorious Basterds* by Quentin Tarantino. In these historical studies and cinematic viewings, virtually all of us feel a certain guilt at the pleasure we feel when viewing such vengeance, but few of us ever take the time to examine why we feel that pleasure or whether or not it is healthy to do so.

Americans have had an excellent opportunity to examine this pleasure in recent years. When the architect of the 9/11 attacks was assassinated, the guilty pleasure that most of us felt was tremendous. Most of us felt that the death of Osama Bin Laden would give us "closure," that we could begin to put it behind us and get on with our lives. Unfortunately, most feel they have not been able to do that.

Tarantino's film ends with the audience rejoicing with the execution of hundreds of Nazis in a theater. Most of us who rejoiced probably did so because we were able to vicariously place ourselves in the position of surviving Jewish people who had suffered such devastating horror. One would think that avengers would feel satisfaction once they have achieved their vengeance, yet studies have demonstrated that in actuality punishers dwell on their deed and feel worse than those who cannot avenge a wrong.

Revenge must be considered one of the lowest of motivations. The Bible and virtually all other religious doctrines warn us of its dangers. Perhaps the main reason is that in "getting back" at someone, we lower ourselves to their level and thus allow that person to hurt us doubly. Would we ever have done such wicked things had someone not hurt us? No. Now we find ourselves lying, cheating, stealing, being physically abusive—things that certainly weaken the solid person we had spent years developing—and for what? Just to get back at the other guy?

Another danger of revenge is that we might break a law and, whereas the cause of our revenge had not been caught, we might be. Now, he has hurt us a third time. Of course, even if we are not caught, we still risk the revenge of this person once he realizes what we have done. Most of us are not content to just take revenge without letting the person know that we had gotten him back. Montresor from Poe's "A Cask of Amontillado" opens his soliloquy on Vengeance with "A wrong is unredressed when retribution overtakes its redresser. It is equally unredressed when the avenger fails to make himself felt as such to him who has done the wrong." Thus, the whole vicious cycle starts again.

We see this on a larger scale with groups fighting each other. The Catholics and Protestants in Northern Ireland have been at war for many years for abuses that started hundreds of years ago. Think of how much destruction has occurred and how many lives have been lost over those years. We see the same thing happening in Israel and other areas of the Mideast over so many years. It's like the old Hatfield-McCoy feud where hardly anyone can remember why they were feuding, but it goes on anyway.

In seeking revenge, we keep the wound of the first offense fresh and then it gets a chance to fester. Perhaps revenge is sweet, or perhaps the words of the philosopher, Francis Bacon, are more accurate: "A man that studieth revenge, keeps his own wounds green, which otherwise would heal, and do well." Yes, it takes a strong person to walk away, but if we develop that habit as a culture, wouldn't we be a stronger people?

Of course, there are some times when we must react to an assault since not doing so would just make the aggressor see us as weak and more attacks would come. Turning the other cheek, one of the central maxims of the New Testament, is a wonderful concept, but it is open to the most horrible abuse. Revenge is like biting a dog because it bit you. There's no fun in it and it lowers you to a bestial level. By not seeking revenge, we are actually forgiving our enemy and perhaps that is the best way to ease the pain all round. It certainly elevates us above our enemy and that's always a good thing. No one wants to be considered silly, and revenge is certainly the silliest of emotions.

> Write an essay in which you demonstrate how the author makes his case that revenge is an emotion of the weak. In your essay, analyze how the author uses one or more of the features mentioned earlier to strengthen the logic and persuasiveness of his argument. Focus on the most important aspects of the passage.
>
> Your essay should not explain whether or not you agree with the author, but rather explain how the author organizes his argument using facts, stats, quotes, examples, and logical connections to persuade his audience.

(ETHOS)   PATHOS   [LOGOS]   *VERBAL EXPRESSION*

The following essay is from a philosopher from the Great NorthWest of America:

History and literature amply demonstrate that a thirst for vengeance is timeless. One needs only to study the terrible atrocities of war that resulted from a sense of revenge or to witness it in epics as old as Homer or the great plays of Shakespeare such as Hamlet and the Merchant of Venice. We see it again in films such as the Godfather by Coppola and Inglorious Basterds by Quentin Tarantino. In these historical studies and cinematic viewings, virtually all of us feel a certain guilt at the pleasure we feel when viewing such vengeance, but few of us ever take the time to examine why we feel that pleasure or whether or not it is healthy to do so.

Americans have had an excellent opportunity to examine this pleasure in recent years. When the architect of the 9/11 attacks was assassinated, the guilty pleasure that most of us felt was tremendous. Most of us felt that the death of Osama Bin Laden would give us "closure," that we could begin to put it behind us and get on with our lives. Unfortunately, most feel they have not been able to do that.

Tarantino's film ends with the audience rejoicing with the execution of hundreds of Nazis in a theater. Most of us who rejoiced probably did so because we were able to vicariously place ourselves in the position of surviving Jewish people who had suffered such devastating horror. One would think that avengers would feel satisfaction once they have achieved their vengeance, yet studies have demonstrated that in actuality punishers dwell on their deed and feel worse than those who cannot avenge a wrong.

Revenge must be considered one of the lowest of motivations. The Bible and virtually all other religious doctrines warn us of its dangers. Perhaps the main reason is that in "getting back" at someone, we lower ourselves to their level and thus allow that person to hurt us doubly. Would we ever have done such wicked things had someone not hurt us? No. Now we find ourselves lying, cheating, stealing, being physically abusive- things that certainly weaken the solid person we had spent years developing- and for what? Just to get back at the other guy?

Another danger of revenge is that we might break a law and, whereas the cause of our revenge had not been caught, we might be. Now, he has hurt us a third time. Of course, even if we are not caught, we still risk the revenge of this person once he realizes what we have done. Most of us are not content to just take revenge without letting the person know that we have gotten him back. Montresor from Poe's A Cask of Amonitillado opens his soliloquy on Vengeance with " A wrong is unredressed when retribution overtakes its redresser. It is equally unredressed when the avenger fails to make himself felt as such to him who has done the wrong." Thus, the whole vicious cycle starts again.

We see this on a larger scale with countries fighting each other. The Protestants and Catholics of Northern Ireland have been at war for many years for abuses that started hundreds of years ago. Think of how much destruction has occurred and how many lives have been lost over those years. We see the same thing happening in Israel and other areas of the Mideast over so many years. It's like the old Hatfield-McCoy feud where no one can remember why they were feuding, but it goes on anyway.

In seeking revenge, we keep the wound of the first offense fresh and then it gets a chance to fester. Perhaps revenge is sweet, or perhaps the words of the philosopher Francis Bacon are more accurate: "A man that studieth revenge, keeps his own wounds green, which otherwise would heal, and do well." Yes, it takes a strong person to walk away, but if we develop that habit as a culture, wouldn't we be a stronger people?

Of course, there are some times when we must react to an assault since not doing so would just make the aggressor see us as weak and more attacks would come. Turning the other cheek, one of the central maxims of the New Testament, is a wonderful concept, but it is open to the most horrible abuse. Revenge is like biting a dog because it bit you. There's no fun in it and it lowers you to a bestial level. By not seeking revenge, we are actually forgiving our enemy and perhaps that is the best way to ease the pain all round. It certainly elevates us above our enemy and that's always a good thing. No one wants to be considered silly and revenge is certainly the silliest of emotions.

Student Essay #1

    The author does not think that people should try to get back at someone when they do something bad to you. He gives a lot of examples of revenge which makes you understand what he is talking about. He discusses why we should not seek revenge and gives examples of what he means. I understand what he means. It does not make us better to get back at people.

    He also talks about big revenge situations like countries fighting each other. I agree with him. Countries should find a way out of fighting by sitting down and talking to each other. That way thousands of people would not have to die and buildings would not have to be destroyed.

    He talks a lot about if we seek revenge we are somehow lowered as a person. He talks about the Hatfields and the McCoys, two families that did not like each other.

    I see what he means, but sometimes it's hard not to want to get back at someone, especially when they do something really bad, like hurting someone or even killing someone.

    So, in summary, I think he feels that if you don't revenge yourself, you somehow make yourself better. He sees revenge as something very silly like biting a dog.

Reading Score: 2. The writer understands that the author thinks revenge is silly, but he does not seem to understand why the author feels this. Try to indicate to the reader that you understand the essay by referencing particular statements, examples, etc. Then, comment on what you learned about the author's thesis based on that example.

Analysis Score: 2. The writer has not demonstrated how the author developed his argument or even what his argument is exactly. State exactly what you think his thesis is in one or two brief sentences. Then, make sure you show how he uses stats, examples, and quotes to support his argument. Further, illustrate the steps he took so that his argument became stronger. **Finally, never give your opinion of whether or not you personally agree or disagree with the author's ideas. The SAT does not care about that, and it should not enter into your essay at all.**

Writing score: 2. This response to the essay is not strongly written. It uses a lot of colloquial expressions such as: "big revenge situations," and "do something really bad." He repeats the phrase "he talks about" three times in one paragraph. Avoid repeating phrases. It shows a lack of variety. He also starts his final paragraph with the phrase: In summary." Avoid phrases like this and "in conclusion" and "as you can see I have proved." The reader can see that it is the final paragraph, so you do not have to inform him that it is. Just write three to four sentences that pull together everything you have said without repeating and then place what you said in a larger perspective. Try to answer the question, "So what?" You have written an essay. What is your point? This writer rarely explains how an example helps to make the writer's thesis clear. His level of language is not strong.

More than the writer's expression, however, he does not demonstrate the techniques that the author uses to get his point across. We get no sense of how the philosopher writes and what is effective or not effective. Make sure you show specific techniques such as repetition, metaphor, sentence variety, stats, allusions, quotations, etc., to make the scorer understand that you are aware of the techniques being used.

Student Essay #2

The author uses all sorts of examples from history and literature to make us understand why we should not allow ourselves to seek revenge on anyone. He cites a number of examples and makes us see the absurdity of seeking revenge.

He starts right out by establishing that revenge has been written about in history and literature for centuries. He brings it home to the reader by alluding to 9/11 and the death of Osama Bin Laden. He lets us know that he thinks we lower ourselves by seeking revenge. This is a good thing to establish right from the start because he can then use plenty of examples to support this idea.

Next he goes into the dangers of revenge by mentioning that it could cause us to break a law and we could get caught and go to jail. Many of us like to let the person we avenge know we did it and this is a cause for another reciprocal round of one guy getting back at the other.

He establishes an historical context by going into the battles and wars of the Irish and Mideast, the Hatfields and the McCoys. This helps the reader to see what happens when this "silly" emotion escalates to a national and international level. I never thought about it in this context but it is actually a good comparison.

He develops his thesis further by discussing how seeking revenge weakens us and by extension any and all in society who pursue it. He does qualify all he has said by bringing up the need at times to confront a vicious aggressor. I liked his allusion to the New Testament.

Finally, he makes us feel the silliness of revenge by his example of the joylessness of biting a dog which has bitten you. I think if more people read this, they would be less inclined to seek revenge.

Reading score: 3. The writer understands the author's thesis, but should have made it clearer by mentioning specific acts of revenge that he finds silly. He does, however, proceed in an orderly fashion and gives us a thorough view of the author's ideas.

Analysis score: 3. This is a good analysis as he breaks down the argument of the author and indicates how he has made his argument with allusions, examples, etc. In the final sentence, he gives his opinion of the thesis, which he should have avoided. He does exhibit a thorough understanding of the process by which the author delineates his argument. He should have explained why he liked the allusion to the New Testament. Ultimately, he does cite specific reasons that the author uses to convince us of his point.

Writing score: 3. Although he uses a relatively strong vocabulary (absurdity, reciprocal, context, escalates) throughout and has some very good sentence structures, he uses some colloquial expressions and deviates from that strong sentence structure a number of times. Expressions like "all sorts of," "starts right out," and the like should be avoided. He consistently uses good transitional words such as "first, next, then, and finally" to help the reader and he establishes a strong structure and sticks to it.

His main failing here is that he does not cite specific rhetorical devices used by the author such as appeals to our better nature, and fear of getting caught. He does not mention the writer's strong use of vocabulary with words such as virtually, vicariously, amply, atrocities, cinematic, doctrines, bestial, maxims nor his many allusions to literature such as Homer and Shakespeare, Bacon, and Poe. He does bring up the writer's allusions to history such as civil war in Northern Ireland or in the Mideast.

Student Essay #3

"An eye for an eye will only make the whole world blind"- Mahatma Ghandi. This quote from one of the world's greatest spiritual leaders seems to sum up this author's thesis. He feels that in the end no one really wins where revenge is concerned. More than anything he develops the idea that if we seek revenge, we lower ourselves as human beings and then our villain has had two victories because we have now lost something very precious - our integrity, our soul. His many allusions to revenge in both history, literature and film enrich his case at every point.

He develops his case by discussing other setbacks we may encounter when we seek revenge—getting arrested for breaking the law and the possible revenge from the original villain. By doing this, he lays out for us a dire list of consequences for taking revenge on someone.

He uses examples from history—the famous Hatfield-McCoy feud. He further develops this idea by mentioning the constant war in the Mid-East and the many years of feuding in Northern Ireland. He even uses the idea of war as a form of revenge and, of course, it can be.

His citing of literary and cinematic allusions truly makes this essay vivid. Two different films, almost fifty years apart makes sure that his reader is likely to know at least one of them. The same is true of his mentioning of Homer and Shakespeare, and his quoting both Francis Bacon and Edgar Allen Poe. His strong use of language throughout makes his writing crisper and more enjoyable.

His essay would not be complete without some mention of the Christian doctrine of "turning the other cheek" when someone strikes you. He does acknowledge the difficulty of doing this and admits that at least when the actions of others might put one in danger, we must consider some action. He does not see this necessarily as revenge but just being practical.

Ultimately, he refers to revenge as the silliest of emotions because little is gained and so much can be lost. He concludes that since it does no one any good, we should try to resist it at all costs. His quote about "biting a dog because it bit you" epitomizes his attitude. He leaves us with a wonderful thought— "What would happen if we as a culture imbued our people with this idea of not seeking revenge?" He suggests we would be so much stronger.

Reading score: 4. This is a thorough essay that leaves no doubt that the reader grasped all of the concepts that the author developed in his essay. He not only mentioned various feuds around the world throughout history, but ties them together in a way that clearly demonstrates his understanding of the author's thesis. At no time does the author seem confused by any point, nor does he intrude with his own take on the subject.

Analysis Score: 4. This is a good breakdown of the process the author uses to make us understand his ideas. This writer not only mentions examples, quotes, etc., but shows us why these are effective means of getting the point across. He does not lump all of the material under one technique, but shows us how the author jumps from examples from literature to history and how he uses the various connections he makes to further our understanding of his ideas. More than anything he shows how these connections concretize our grasp of the theme

Writing score: 4. His strong use of vocabulary (encounter, dire, cinematic, doctrine, epitomizes, imbued) along with the serious tone of the essay makes this a solid 4. He seems to have a very set idea of what he wants each paragraph to say and does not allow himself to stray from that purpose at all. Every element of the original essay gets some consideration and still he does not waste words unnecessarily. He uses apt transitional words throughout to help his reader follow his point. He also varies his sentence structure throughout giving his essay great variety.

Practice Essay 2

> As you read the passage below, consider how the author uses
>
> - evidence, such as facts or examples, to support claims.
> - reasoning to develop ideas and to connect claims and evidence.
> - stylistic or persuasive elements, such as word choice or appeals to emotion, to add power to the ideas expressed.

Transcript of President Barack Obama's speech at Georgetown University announcing his new climate-change policy:

On Christmas Eve, 1968, the astronauts of Apollo 8 did a live broadcast from lunar orbit. So Frank Borman, Jim Lovell, William Anders—the first humans to orbit the moon—described what they saw, and they read Scripture from the Book of Genesis to the rest of us back here. And later that night, they took a photo that would change the way we see and think about our world.

It was an image of Earth—beautiful; breathtaking; a glowing marble of blue oceans, and green forests, and brown mountains brushed with white clouds, rising over the surface of the moon.

And while the sight of our planet from space might seem routine today, imagine what it looked like to those of us seeing our home, our planet, for the first time. Imagine what it looked like to children like me. Even the astronauts were amazed. "It makes you realize," Lovell would say, "just what you have back there on Earth."

And around the same time we began exploring space, scientists were studying changes taking place in the Earth's atmosphere. Now, scientists had known since the 1800s that greenhouse gases like carbon dioxide trap heat, and that burning fossil fuels release those gases into the air. That wasn't news. But in the late 1950s, the National Weather Service began measuring the levels of carbon dioxide in our atmosphere, with the worry that rising levels might someday disrupt the fragile balance that makes our planet so hospitable. And what they've found, year after year, is that the levels of carbon pollution in our atmosphere have increased dramatically.

That science, accumulated and reviewed over decades, tells us that our planet is changing in ways that will have profound impacts on all of humankind.

The 12 warmest years in recorded history have all come in the last 15 years. Last year, temperatures in some areas of the ocean reached record highs, and ice in the Arctic shrank to its smallest size on record—faster than most models had predicted it would. These are facts.

Now, we know that no single weather event is caused solely by climate change. Droughts and fires and floods, they go back to ancient times. But we also know that in a world that's warmer than it used to be, all weather events are affected by a warming planet. The fact that sea level in New York, in New York Harbor, are now a foot higher than a century ago—that didn't cause Hurricane Sandy, but it certainly contributed to the destruction that left large parts of our mightiest city dark and underwater.

The potential impacts go beyond rising sea levels. Here at home, 2012 was the warmest year in our history. Midwest farms were parched by the worst drought since the Dust Bowl, and then drenched by the wettest spring on record. Western wildfires scorched an area larger than the state of Maryland. Just last week, a heat wave in Alaska shot temperatures into the 90s.

And we know that the costs of these events can be measured in lost lives and lost livelihoods, lost homes, lost businesses, hundreds of billions of dollars in emergency services and disaster relief. In fact, those who are already feeling the effects of climate change don't have time to deny it—they're busy dealing with it. Firefighters are braving longer wildfire seasons, and states and federal governments have to figure out how to budget for that. I had to sit on a meeting with the Department of Interior and Agriculture and some of the rest of my team just to figure out how we're going to pay for more and more expensive fire seasons.

Farmers see crops wilted one year, washed away the next; and the higher food prices get passed on to you, the American consumer. Mountain communities worry about what smaller snowpacks will mean for tourism—and then, families at the bottom of the mountains wonder what it will mean for their drinking water. Americans across the country are already paying the price of inaction in insurance premiums, state and local taxes, and the costs of rebuilding and disaster relief.

So the question is not whether we need to act. The overwhelming judgment of science—of chemistry and physics and millions of measurements—has put all that to rest. Ninety-seven percent of scientists, including, by the way, some who originally disputed the data, have now put that to rest. They've acknowledged the planet is warming and human activity is contributing to it.

So the question now is whether we will have the courage to act before it's too late. And how we answer will have a profound impact on the world that we leave behind not just to you, but to your children and to your grandchildren.

As a President, as a father, and as an American, I'm here to say we need to act.

Write an essay in which you demonstrate how President Obama builds his case for our need as a nation to curb the problems of climate control in our world. In your essay, analyze how President Obama uses various rhetorical devices and specific arguments to strengthen the logic and persuasiveness of his argument. Focus on the most important aspects of the passage.

Your essay should not explain whether or not you agree with the author, but rather explain how the author organizes his argument using facts, stats, quotes, examples, and logical connections to persuade his audience.

Student Essay #1

I agree with Obama that our climate is changing. You can see it again and again in melting ice, hotter summers and strange amounts of rain. Obama uses lots of quotes and stats and examples and connections to make his point. He is really good at writing. Lots of hot summers have come our way in the past 12 -15 years and it is drying up our rivers and lakes and reservoirs.

That's why I agree with him, because you can see it all over the place. I see this in the news a number of time and only a few channel seem to disagree with him. He points out that we blow all past times out of the water as far as how much CO2 we have in our air.

Like he said, we owe it to our children and grandchildren and to mankind to stop being so selfish and get out there and do something about it. I really like the way he writes. He's real clear about it. He doesn't pretend to know things. He really does. He gets to the point and really let's you know how he feels. He uses great information to back everything up.

Reading Score: 2. Although he does mention many things that President Obama brings up, it is not clear that this writer has made the connection of how they all fit into the picture of global warming. He does not mention specific quotes or examples or stats that are used in the passage to demonstrate his knowledge of what has been written. He voices his agreement with Obama, which he has been told by the prompt to avoid. At no point are we sure that he has grasped the main point of Obama's speech.

Analysis Score: 1. Although he does mention that the writer uses stats, examples, etc., he never shows exactly how they prove the point or even how they are used. He also gives his opinion of whether Obama is right or wrong and that he writes well when neither of these were part of the prompt.

Also, he does not use specific quotes, stats, etc. to demonstrate how the argument is developed but brings in his own information. He mentions that he saw it on different news shows and mentions that some shows disagreed with him, but does not indicate which ones or in what way they disagreed. It is not sufficient to mention things a writer did. The student must demonstrate in what ways these techniques were or were not effective.

Writing Score: 1. This writer is far too casual in his style, using a lot or repetition and seldom supporting what he says with concrete examples. There is also no apparent structure or game plan for getting his ideas across.

He must avoid expressions like "You can see it all over the place," "Like he said," "blow out of the water," " I really like," and "He's real clear about." These take away from the serious tone of the passage.

He mentions a few times how much he likes Obama's writing without ever being specific about why he likes it so much. There does not seem to be a careful approach to making his point anywhere in the passage and he uses only three paragraphs to develop his point.

Student Essay #2

President Obama makes a very strong case for doing something dramatic about climate change. He not only mentions statistics, but shows how they support his thesis. He alludes to space travel and the wonderful view and then alerts us to how that view might be changing.

What he does particularly well is to use each paragraph for a particular purpose. He discusses the difficulty of raising crops when we have one summer of floods and the next one has almost no rain at all. He mentions the dates for the 12 warmest years in history. He cites the stat that 97% of scientists think that there is global warming and that mankind is contributing.

He also speaks in a style that is very direct. He is not pulling any punches but he is does not come off as an alarmist. He also talks to us about what it will take to halt the terrible climate change that has been causing fires and changing the landscapes of the world.

Finally, he discusses our having the courage to act and why we must - that our children and grandchildren should not have to inherit a world that is crumbling.

Reading Score: 4. This writer gets the point. Every paragraph displays a grasp of this topic and it is not a superficial understanding. He cites examples, statistics and allusions throughout and lets us know in every sentence that he has received Obama's message loud and clear that we must act soon or it may be too late.

Analysis Score: 2. Although the writer mentions many of the techniques that President Obama uses to make his point, he does not consistently show us how he uses them to develop this essay. He also does not show us how the ideas are connected at some points.

Writing Score: 2. The use of language is weak, transitional words are rare and it is not a very thorough treatment of the essay. He begins too many sentences with "He does, he speaks, he talks, he discusses, etc." The subject-verb-predicate pattern adds to the boredom of his writing. He never uses a high level vocabulary word. His grammar, spelling, and punctuation are solid; this raises his score to a 2.

Student Essay #3

So often we students are turned off when reading science essays because they are so technical and just lack any style. Frankly, they are just not written in human terms. President Obama's speech is a welcome exception. He uses the stats, allusions, examples that we might find in a scientific journal, but he speaks directly to us in a style that is folksy, yet serious.

He also has a very definite structure that enables the listener or reader to follow the logic of his arguments as each paragraph progresses. Each one has a point and everything in it revolves around that point.

He alludes first to a photo from space travel that changed our view of the world and then goes on to explain how that view might be changing soon. He then goes on to explain some of those changes from fires, to poor crops to rising insurance premiums, to higher taxes.

He uses striking stats to buttress his thesis and many examples from everyday life so that we can relate to what is happening.

President Obama is able to make us look at these very real problems as adults because that is how he addresses us. This is a no holds barred approach, but not one that hinges on the typical news hour gimmick of scaring us half to death so that we cannot even think straight. If he were my teacher, I think I would learn things more easily.

Reading Score: 4. This writer demonstrates his grasp of the essay in every paragraph. He cites allusions, examples, stats and quotes to show us that he "gets it."

Analysis score: 3. Although he does mention all of the devices used by Obama to get his point across, he does not consistently show us how Obama develops his speech. A more specific back and forth to demonstrate how a particular chart, allusion, stat or example helps us to get his point better might have elevated this essay.

Writing Score: 3. This essay does not have a strong level of vocabulary or a solid amount of transitional words to guide the reader. There is, however, a serious tone that is consistent throughout and it stays focused at every turn. His opening paragraph is excellent in that it establishes the essence of why this is a fine speech, commenting on both the content, use of evidence, and style of the speech.

Practice Essay 3

As you read the passage below, consider how the author uses

- evidence, such as facts or examples, to support claims.
- reasoning to develop ideas and to connect claims and evidence.
- stylistic or persuasive elements, such as word choice or appeals to emotion, to add power to the ideas expressed.

Susan B. Anthony's Speech to Congress:

Friends and fellow citizens: I stand before you tonight under indictment for the alleged crime of having voted at the last presidential election, without having a lawful right to vote. It shall be my work this evening to prove to you that in thus voting, I not only committed no crime, but, instead, simply exercised my citizen's rights, guaranteed to me and all United States citizens by the National Constitution, beyond the power of any state to deny.

The preamble of the Federal Constitution says:

"We, the people of the United States, in order to form a more perfect union, establish justice, insure domestic tranquility, provide for the common defense, promote the general welfare, and secure the blessings of liberty to ourselves and our posterity, do ordain and establish this Constitution for the United States of America."

It was we, the people; not we, the white male citizens; nor yet we, the male citizens; but we, the whole people, who formed the Union. And we formed it, not to give the blessings of liberty, but to secure them; not to the half of ourselves and the half of our posterity, but to the whole people—women as well as men. And it is a downright mockery to talk to women of their enjoyment of the blessings of liberty while they are denied the use of the only means of securing them provided by this democratic-republican government—the ballot.

For any state to make sex a qualification that must ever result in the disfranchisement of one entire half of the people, is to pass a bill of attainder, or, an ex post facto law, and is therefore a violation of the supreme law of the land. By it the blessings of liberty are forever withheld from women and their female posterity.

To them this government has no just powers derived from the consent of the governed. To them this government is not a democracy. It is not a republic. It is an odious aristocracy; a hateful oligarchy of sex; the most hateful aristocracy ever established on the face of the globe; an oligarchy of wealth, where the rich govern the poor. An oligarchy of learning, where the educated govern the ignorant, or even an oligarchy of race, where the Saxon rules the African, might be endured; but this oligarchy of sex, which makes father, brothers, husband, sons, the oligarchs over the mother and sisters, the wife and daughters, of every household—which ordains all men sovereigns, all women subjects, carries dissension, discord, and rebellion into every home of the nation. Webster, Worcester, and Bouvier all define a citizen to be a person in the United States, entitled to vote and hold office.

The only question left to be settled now is: Are women persons? And I hardly believe any of our opponents will have the hardihood to say they are not. Being persons, then, women are citizens; and no state has a right to make any law, or to enforce any old law, that shall abridge their privileges or immunities. Hence, every discrimination against women in the constitutions and laws of the several states is today null and void, precisely as is every one against Negroes. **Susan B. Anthony - 1876**

> Write an essay in which you demonstrate how Susan B. Anthony makes her case to give women the right to vote. In your essay, analyze how the author uses one or more of the features mentioned earlier to strengthen the logic and persuasiveness of his argument. Focus on the most important aspects of the passage.
>
> Your essay should not indicate or stress whether or not you agree with Anthony, but rather explain how she organizes her argument using facts, stats, quotes, examples, and logical connections to persuade her audience.

Student Essay #1

Susan B. Anthony is really angry about not being able to vote so she finds a way of doing it and then gets arrested because she is a woman and they are not allowed to vote. She makes a decision to use this arrest to speak out against the fact that women are not allowed to vote.

She says that the government is using illogical and illegal methods to deny women there right to vote. She tells us that this action separates men and women in the household and thereby makes slaves of women in their own homes.

Anthony makes a lot of comparisons and contrasts throughout, which help us to really get what she's talking about. She never lets up. She just keeps coming at it without ever considering that she might be wrong. She makes some good points at every turn. She won't let it rest.

She even asks at one point if we should ask the question whether or not women are persons. Like I said, she leaves no stone unturned.

I liked this speech a lot because it made sense and historically I think it had a big effect.

Reading Score: 3. This writer seems to understand the thesis fairly well but fails to show exactly how she knows this.

Analysis Score: 2. This writer does not show how the author makes her case. She just mentions a lot of things that Anthony says but seldom puts any of them in perspective. She mentions comparisons and contrasts, but never lists any. She tells us she liked the speech, which is not called for at all. She tells us Anthony is angry, but never tells how specifically she knows this. It is always important to demonstrate to the scorer precisely how the author has laid out her argument and whether or not it is done in an effective way.

Writing Score: 2. Those of you who do not write strongly should look carefully at this as it is a good example of a poorly written essay and why it is not effective. First: the level of language is weak. Second: there is a great deal of redundancy (needless repetition). She says "She won't rest," and "she leaves no stone unturned," and "she never lets up," etc. She uses subject-verb-object throughout, so her sentence structure is really monotonous. She also says she likes it, which is a no-no. **The College Board is not interested in your opinion in these essays, but wants only to observe your ability to analyze an essay accurately, using solid writing technique to do so.** Susan B. Anthony has been arrested for voting, which is illegal for women at her time, and is here defend herself of that charge.

Student Essay #2

Anthony is adamant at every turn and never gives the male dominated government any leeway. She is very particular about every point and uses many examples to support her points. She seems to be well versed in both the law and government and uses both to make her points.

She constantly makes the point that the government is acting illegally and takes pains to show just how that is being done. What I like about her essay is that she is thorough. She develops it through logic at every turn, delving into politics, government, family life and structure. She alludes to statements from famous men.

I also like that she is not above asking shocking questions such as "Are women persons?" I certainly agree with her that not only have women gotten the short end of the stick historically but that they are still getting it. One can truly see how her efforts did eventually bear fruit because at no time does she flinch from her message. Hers is truly a first rate mind and she uses it with a precision that is unmistakable.

Anthony knows what she is talking about and she is not backing down. She has been arrested for voting, but is unwilling to accept this action. She uses it to set forth a series of arguments that are truly compelling. If more women had had her brains and guts, the 19th amendment would have been passed much sooner.

Reading Score: 3. Although this writer appears to understand a fair amount of this essay, we are never really sure how much because seldom is a specific reference given. There are certainly enough statements to indicate that she understood the idea that Anthony was correct and that not giving women the right to vote had been a miscarriage of justice.

Analysis Score: 2. The writer here mentions so many good things that Anthony did but does not demonstrate how they tied together or how the argument is organized. She also mentions that she "agrees with her" and this is something that you should avoid on this exam. Students' opinions are not expected as your job is just to show how the essay was developed, what rhetorical devices were used to organize the thesis and to show what connections the author made to present his or her case.

Writing Score: 3. This essay does have some merit as she uses a solid vocabulary (adamant, leeway, delves, flinch, alludes to), connects ideas well and ends strongly. However, it does jump around a bit and spends too much energy praising Anthony without demonstrating to the reader exactly why this is a solid essay. It also does not comment on the actual writing technique of Anthony; this should certainly be done even if it is only briefly expressed.

Student Essay #3

In a clear, logical essay, Anthony presents her case for women's right to vote. She builds it on a strong foundation, the preamble of the Federal Constitution. She takes a key phrase "we the people" and uses it to develop a simple, straightforward idea - since women are people, they must have the rights of all other people, in this case men, and thus have by definition the right to vote.

The preamble states that we wrote the constitution to "secure the blessings of liberty." Anthony makes the point that those blessings could not have been intended for only half the population. Why should they be given those blessings if they cannot use them while they see any man enjoy them every day? She mentions the vote as the only means of securing those blessings.

She goes on to discuss the absurdity of passing a law for only half the population. She states that women do not live in a democracy but in an aristocracy since a selected group is governing the others. She further develops her point by saying that an oligarchy of race or learning or wealth, heinous though they would be, is far more understandable than one of sex. For her it is as if the government determined that everyone born with red hair should rule all others or that only left handed people could vote. She says that the law creates "the most hateful aristocracy ever established."

She again develops her point by saying that this law "carries dissension, discord and rebellion into every home of the nation." This is just one of her many powerful images throughout this convincing essay. It indicates that women are virtual slaves in every home.

Finally, she asks if women are people and agrees that few would be so foolhardy to say they are not. Since they are people, she says, no state has the right to make a law that should "abridge their privileges or immunities." She adds that this is, of course, also true of Negroes.

Although this speech does not use the traditional stats and examples that a modern one might, it does incorporate a strong quotation and uses many potent examples, coupled with a very strong logical case to bring home her point in a most cogent way. It is clear that Anthony was not only a great leader but an excellent writer.

Reading Score: 4. The reader has an intricate understanding of Anthony's arguments and indicates that in her introduction by showing how Anthony uses the preamble as the basis for her argument. She consistently refers to specific things she has said to validate her arguments and she puts Anthony's comments into a context that shows a clear grasp of the speech.

Analysis Score: 4. With statements like, "Although this speech does not use the traditional stats and examples that a modern one might, it does incorporate a strong quotation and uses many potent examples, coupled with a very strong logical case to bring home her point in a most cogent way," this writer clearly understands how Anthony has made her case. Her step by step breakdown of the speech in paragraphs that specifically show how Anthony has developed her arguments indicates a solid understanding of how Anthony develops her speech. Her use of Anthony's actual quotes to support her analysis is sharp at every turn.

Writing Score: 3-4. The writer states the thesis early on and continues to develop it in each succeeding paragraph. Each of these has a clear goal and achieves it with solid transitional words and excellent quotes from the passage. The style is clear and academic and a solid if not exceptional use of words is incorporated. Sentence structure is varied well and the tone is consistent throughout.

BONUS VERBAL MATERIALS
LEARN THESE AND WIN

The following material is intended to develop your verbal ability so that you will find reading and particularly the words in context more doable. Yes, it does require you to memorize some roots and prefixes, but that will not only help you on this test, but also in many of the fields you might enter. The Words Often Confused section is particularly helpful. Second most important is the Latin Prefix page. Knowing that page and using it as we have directed will definitely give you a weapon you can use to knock off wrong answers.

Taking the etymology quizzes will put you in practical situations where you have to use the techniques to find the right answer. Learn these pages well and you will thank us for many years to come.

A great technique is one that you will find invaluable not only for the SAT but especially if you pursue a career in a health or law. Using **etymology** to figure out words you don't know is effective and even fun. Yes, it does mean that you have to learn some Latin and Greek prefixes and roots, but most of the Greek ones you already know and if you learn just one root a day for two months, you will know enough for this to be a great tool on the test. It's just a matter of learning to play with the root and prefix to see how they have been combined to form a word in English. **First**, look at the examples below to see how combining the roots and prefixes can give you a good sense of the word. You may not glean a perfect definition from doing this, but you will have a good enough feel for the word so that you can use it to break down possible meanings of words. After you do this, we have provided a list of the most important prefixes and roots for you. Check off the ones you already know and then start to work on the rest over the next few months. Any of you interested in a career in medicine (health career) or law will thank us for turning you on to these. **Second,** once you have learned a fair amount of these, try the etymology quiz that follows. It will give you some practical experience in breaking down words you are not sure of. We will provide analysis of some of the words to guide you in this process. Let's get started!

So, you don't know the word CIRCUMSPECT or at least you don't think you do.

However, you do know the root circum from circumference or circumnavigate the globe. You also know the word spect from spectacles, spectator, inspect, spectacle. So if you play a bit you see that someone who is circumspect looks around, or is observant or careful. You would at least know that it is a positive word and could therefore eliminate neutral or negative choices.

CONGENITAL. We will know from our prefix list that **con** means "with or together."

If we play with the sound gen, we will come up with genetics, genealogy, Genesis, etc. and realize that in each case it has something to do with "birth." Therefore, our word must mean "born with." Some diseases are congenital; we are born with them.

OBLOQUY. From our list we will know **ob** = against and **loquy** = speak as in eloquent, one who speaks well. So, this word means speaking against someone, or denouncing them.

CONJECTURE. Again **con** = together, with and **ject** = throw. If you throw two ideas together, you usually come up with a **guess** or a **hypothesis** or even a **theory.**

ENDEMIC. **en** in Greek means in or within; **dem,** which you can easily recognize from democracy is rule by the people. So, something endemic is **within the people** or **native** or **typical.**

INTRACTABLE. **in**, **im**, **il**, and **ir** all mean "not" when the word is an adjective and "in or within" when it is a verb. **Tract** you know because you know what a tractor does and you know what a dentist does when he/she extracts a tooth from you. So, what do we have? Someone who is intractable is "not able to be pulled" or stubborn.

By now you are probably beginning to realize that this is not exactly 2 + 2 = 4. You have to be willing to play with the combinations just a bit to get a sense of the word. However, you are not asked to come up with a perfect definition of the word but just something that will give you a sense of what the word means so that you can eliminate most of the other choices.

Let's try a few more:

MALEDICTION. *try to figure it out on your own first.

You know that **mal** = bad or evil. **Dict** should be somewhat familiar once you start thinking of words that have that root in it and see what they have in common. Dictionary, diction, dictum, edict come to mind. So, it is going to mean a bad or evil word, which is also known as the word **curse.**

Try MALEFACTOR. Here you know **or** is "one who" and if we manufacture something we **make** it. Thus, this is someone who makes or does bad things.

CAP, CEPT means **to hold.** So, what is the meaning of capacious?

Literally, it holds very much or is **roomy.**

A few more and you will have a sense of how you can play with these roots and prefixes to form words you did not think you know. Once you get good at this, you will pretty much be able to figure out most of the words on the test. This will also help you greatly to develop your vocabulary for college and graduate school.

CREDULOUS. Once you play, you will come up with credentials, credit, incredible, credulous, discredit, etc. and see that all of them have something to do with "belief."

So, it must mean one who is "full of belief" or **gullible**, **naïve**, etc.

PROFUSE. **Fus** means "to flow." So, if we know pro-forth, on behalf of or forward, we know that something that is profuse is "flowing forth" or **abundant.**

*Again, it not important for the test that you have a perfect definition of the word. Suppose your choices for profuse were:

(A) binding
(B) connective
(C) abundant
(D) supportive
(E) ignorant

Could you use what you have arrived at, flowing forth, to figure out the answer? Nice, right?

AMORPHOUS. We will learn that **a**, or **an** in Greek means "not, without or lacking" and since most of us know that morph is "shape, form or structure," it is not much of a jump to see this word meaning "shapeless or formless."

Below is a list of Latin and Greek prefixes and roots that will enable you to figure out a tremendous number of words. You already know most of the Greek roots and prefixes, so now you have to spend some time on the Latin roots. One-third of them you know already, so get going on the remaining two-thirds. As soon as you feel you know at least two-thirds of the Latin Roots and all of the rest, take the etymology quiz and you will be amazed at how well you can figure out words that you are unsure of. Check out the pages below so that you begin to get a sense of how the prefixes and roots work together to form words. Words that start with a prefix marked (NEG) are negative at least 85% of the time and with (POS) are positive 85% of the time. If the prefix has one asterisk next to it, then it can be negative or positive at least 95% of the time, and two asterisks 98% of the time.

Latin Prefixes

Prefix	Meaning	Sample Words
a, ab, ab, abs (NEG)	away, off, from	abdicate, averse, abstract, abstain
circu, circum	around	circumvent, circumspect, circuitous, circumference
*co, con, com (POS) col, cor	with, together	coexist, collate, congenital **Exceptions: compunction, contentious, confrontational**
contra (NEG)	against, opposing	contradict, contravene, contrary, contraband
*de (NEG)	down, away, from	demote, decline, demolish, denigrate **Exc: defer**
*dis, dif, di (NEG)	apart, away, opposing not	dissent, digress, diffuse, dispel, discord **Exc: discreet diligent, discriminating, discerning**
ex, e, ef (NEG)	from, out	expulsion, efface, execrate **Exc: exhort, exalt, extol, effervescent, ebullient, exult, elated, exhilarated, exuberant, exonerate, exculpate**
* in, il, im, ir	verb: in, into, within adjective: not	induct, insert, include, inward illogical, innocuous, immaculate, irregular
inter	between, among	intercede, intersperse, intermarriage, interrupt
intra, intro	inward, within	introvert, intravenous, intramural, introspective
** ob, oc, of, op, etc. (NEG)	against, opposing very, completely	obtrude, obstruct, offend, obnoxious, obfuscate
per	through, wrongly completely	permeate, perverted, perfidious, pervasive, perpetual
pre	before, in front of	premeditated, predict, preface
pro (POS)	on behalf of, forward for, forth	proceed, profane, profuse
re	back, again	revoke, recede, remit, rejoin, regain
retro	back, backward	retrospective, retroactive
se (NEG)	apart, away, aside	secede, seclude, secrete, secure
* su, sub, sec suf, sur, sup (NEG)	under, below, sneaky	surreptitious, submerge, suffice, subservient, succumb, suffocate

Greek Prefixes

Prefix	Meaning	Sample words
a, an	not, without, lacking	amorphous, anarchy, amoral, atom, anemia, achromatic
amphi	both, around	amphibian, amphitheater, amphogenic, amphidexterous
arch, archi	chief, first	architect, arch-enemy, archetype
cata	down, away	catalyst, catastrophe, catapult, catacomb
dia	through	diameter, diagnose, diatribe
en, em	in, among, within	endemic, empathy, encircle
epi	on, over, outside	epigram, epidermis, epiglotis, epilogue
eu	good, well	eulogy, euphonious, euphemism, euthanasia
hetero	different	heterosexual, heterogene
homo	same	homosexual, homogenous, homonym, homocentric
hypo	under, beneath	hypodermic, hypothermia, hypo-alergenic
hyper	excessive, over	hypercritical, hyperbole, hyper
meta	change of, over	metamorphosis, metaphor, metastasis, metabolism,
omni	all	omnivore, omnipotent, omnific, omniscient
para	alongside, irregular	parallel, paraphrase, paradox, paradigm
peri	around, near	periscope, perimeter, peristalsis, peritoneum
syn, sym	together, same	synchronize, sympathy
syl, sys	together, with	synergy, synopsis, system

Greek Roots

Root	Meaning	Sample Words
anthropos	man, mankind	misanthrope, anthropology, anthropoid
apo	from, off, away	apogee, aphelion, apologize
arch	ancient, chief	monarch, archeology, arch-enemy
astr, aster	star	astral, astrology, asterisk, aster, astronomy
auto	self	autonomy, autocratic, automaton, autobiography
chrom	color	chromosome, chromatic, monochromatic
cosm	order, world	cosmic, microcosm, cosmos
crac, crat	power, rule	democracy, aristocracy, bureaucrat
dem	people	demagogue, endemic, democracy
derm	skin	pachyderm, dermatitis, epidermis, dermatologist
gam	mate, marriage	gamete, bigamy, polygamy, monogamy
gen	kind, race	genetics, eugenics, genealogy, genesis, generation
geo, gee	earth	geometry, perigee, geothermal, geocentric, geode
gram, graph	write	geography, epigram, biography, cardiograph
hem	blood	hemorrhage, hemophilia, hematoma
iatr	heal	geriatrics, psychiatric, podiatry
iso	same, equal	isotope, isosceles, isometric
log	speech, word, study	theology, monologue, eulogy, epilogue
metr, meter	measure	diameter, trigonometry, metronome, kilometer
micr	small	microbe, microscope, micro-organism
mon	one, single	monotonous, monogamous, monocle, monogram
morph	form, shape	amorphous, metamorphosis, geomorphic, pseudomorph
nom	rule, law, name	autonomy, anomaly, nominal, nominate, synonym

pan	all, entire	pantheist, panacea, Pan American
pathos	feeling, disease	apathy, pathology, sympathy, pathetic, pathological
phil	like, love	philanthropist, bibliophile, Anglophile, philately, philogynist
phon	sound	phonetics, euphonious, symphonic, euphonic, aphonia
pod	foot	tripod, podiatrist, podium
poly	many	polygon, polytheist, polyarchy, polyphonous, polygon
psych	mind	psychology, psychosomatic, psychotic, psyche, psychosis
scop	see, watch	telescope, microscope, spectroscope, periscope
soma	body	chromosome, somatotype
tele	distant	telepathy, telescope, telemetry, telekinesis
tom	cut	atom, appendectomy, anatomy, lobotomy, mastectomy
urg, erg	work, power	metallurgist, ergonomics, urgs
zo	animal	protozoa, zoology, zodiac, zoophobe

Latin Roots

Root	Meaning	Sample Words
ag, act	do, drive, impel	agent, active, transact, enact, react
ac, acr	sharp, bitter	acute, acrid, acrimonious
ali	other	alien, alibi, alias
alter, altr	other, change	alter ego, altruism, alter, alternator
am, amic	love, friend	amity, amicable, amiable
anim	soul, spirit, mind	animate, animosity, animus
annu, enni	year	anniversary, perennial, annual, per annum
aqu	water	aquaduct, aquarium, aquarius (sign)
apt, ept	adjust, fit	adept, inept, aptitude
ben, bene	good, well	benediction, benign, benignant
cap, cept, cip	take, seize, hold	capture, captivate, concept
carn	flesh	incarnate, carnal, carnival, carnation
ced, cede, cess	go, yield	secede, recede, procession, concede
cern, cert	perceive, decide	discern, certify indiscernible
cid, cis	cut, kill	fratricide, homicide, suicide, incision, concise
clin	bend	decline, incline
cogn	know, be acquainted	recognize, cognizant, cognoscente, incognito
corp	body	corpuscle, corpulent, corporeal, corpulent
cred	believe	credible, credulous, credentials, discredit
culp	blame, fault	culpable, exculpate, culprit
cur, curs	run	concur, cursory, current, recurring
dic, dict	say, tell	diction, predict, indict, dictionary, dictum
duc, duct	lead	conduction, aquaduct, abduct

Root	Meaning	Examples
dur	hard, lasting	durable, obdurate, endure
equ	equal	equable, equilibrium, equator, equivocal, equivalent
fac, fect, fic, fy	do, make	manufacture, facsimile, beautify, perfect (verb), pacify
fer	carry, bear	transfer, fertile, defer, refer, confer
fid	trust	fidelity, infidel, confident, fiduciary
flu, fluct	flow	fluent, fluctuate, effusive, profuse, affluent
fort	strong	fortify, forte, fortissimo
frag, fact	break	fragile, fracture, refract, defraction, fractious
fus	pour	transfusion, effusive, profuse, infuse, transfusion
gen	birth, origin, tribe	generate, progeny, genocide, genetics, genesis
grat, grac	please, favor, thanks	gratis, gratitude, gracious, gratis, gratuitous
greg	group, herd	congregate, egregious, gregarious, aggregate
here, hes	cling, stick	adhere, inherent, coherent, adhesion, cohesion
it	go, travel	exit, transit, circuit, transient, itinerary
jac, ject	throw, hurl	eject, projectile, conjecture, dejected
junct	join	juncture, adjunct, conjunction, subjunctive
jud	judge	judicious, prejudice, judicial, adjudicate
leg, lect, lig	law, choose, read	legitimate, legible, election, selective, litigious
loqu, locut	talk, speech	elocution, colloquial, eloquent, loquacious
luc, lus	light	lucid, translucent, elucidate, pellucid
magn	large	magnitude, magnify, magnum opus, magnanimous
mal	bad	malady, malevolent, malicious, maleficent, malign, malignant
mit, miss	send	transmit, remit, emit, commit, mission, remission
mon, monit	warn	admonition, monitor
mob, mov, mot	move	mobile, remote, removable, demotion, commotion
mor, mort	die, death	mortuary, moribund, mortified, riga mortis, mortician, morbid
multi	many	multiplex, multifaceted, multi-talented, multifarious
mut	change	immutable, transmute, commute, mutant

omni	all	omnipotent, omnivorous, omniscient, omnibus
par	equal	disparity, parallel, parity, paradox
ped	foot	pedal, pedestrian, quadruped, pedestal, pedicab
pel, puls	drive	repel, compulsion, propel, propulsion, compel
pend, pens	hang, weigh	suspend, pendant, propensity, pensive, pendulum, pending
pon, pos	put, place	postpone, interpose, deposit, repository, position, depose
port	carry	transport, import, portable, deport, report
prim	first	primary, primitive, primate, prime
rid, ris	laugh	risible, ridiculous, deride
rupt	break	rupture, abrupt, interrupt, disrupt, eruption
scrib, script	write	transcript, manuscript, scripture, conscript, circumscribe
sed, sess, sid	sit, seat	sedentary, residual, sedate, session, assiduous, reside, sedulous
seg, sect	cut	segment, dissect, resect, section, bisect
sent, sens	feel	sensory, sentient, sensuous, sensible, sentimental
sequ, secut	follow	sequel, subsequent, consequence, sequential, consecutive
sol	alone	solitude, solitaire, solo, solitary
spec, spic, spect	look, see	specimen, spectacle, specious, spectral, speculate, aspect
string, strict	bind tightly	stringent, constrict, restrict, astringent, stricture
tang, tact, ting, tig	touch	tangible, contingent, contiguous, contact, tactile
ten, tin	hold, contain	tenure, retention, detention, retinue, attention
tend, tens	stretch	distend, tendency, tension, tensile
tor, tort	twist	distort, contortion, extort, torso, torsion, retort
tract	draw, pull	extraction, distract, intractable, tractor, retract
trud, trus	push	intrusive, protrude, extrude, obtrusion
vac, vap	empty	evacuate, vapid, vacuous, vacate
vers, vert	turn	revert, versatile, divert, adversary, aversion

Suffixes:

Ous, ose   full of, very much   copious, diaphanous, impervious, deleterious, capacious

* There are many suffixes, but they are not as important as the roots and prefixes. The one above is so common and useful that it is good to know it.

Below we have three etymology (study of the derivation of words) quizzes for you to practice your new skills on. If you do this, you will have a much better sense of how words mean what they mean and you will be able to use this skill to help you know some of the words on the exam. Each section gets more difficult. If you do them in the order below, you will gradually learn how to figure out words you do not know. Make sure you go through the explanations after each quiz as we use them to train you how to figure out these words.

Etymology Quiz

Easy	**A**	**B**	**C**	**D**
1 STRICTURE	restriction	certainty	obedience	nuisance
2 LUCID	blessed	failing	cruel	clear
3 CONVIVIAL	manageable	sociable	lively	fanatic
4 SUBVERT	support	undermine	capture	inform
5 DECRY	praise	expose	condemn	lose it
6 CONSPECTUS	summary	viewpoint	deception	allowance
7 IGNOMINY	nobility	horror	disgrace	deception
8 DIAPHANOUS	transparent	blunt	blocked	crossed
9 PROGENY	ancestors	equals	children	contemporaries
10 CONVOCATION	calling	system	meeting	censure
11 ACRIMONIOUS	smart	bitter	sinister	silly
12 ECCENTRIC	clever	odd	special	focused
13 VERBOSE	brief	grammatical	wordy	forceful
14 AVERSION	patience	sincerity	dislike	curse
15 ANTIPATHY	hatred	fear	no feelings	coded message
16 CACOPHONY	loud	melodic	harsh	soft SOUND
17 PRESCIENCE	knowledge	education	foresight	suavity
18 SURREPTITIOU	Sallowable	wicked	careful	sneaky
19 DEBILITATE	break	weaken	stabilize	mature
20 INDEFATIGABLE	lazy	unknown	tireless	camouflaged
21 TORTUOUS	winding	scared	harmful	painted
22 EXACERBATE	void	specify	spoil	worsen
23 CIRCUMSPECT	mediocre	wearied	careful	restricted
24 INCOGNITO	rewarded	mystical	quiet	unknown
25 DEBASE	annoy	degrade	raise up	elevate
26 ELUCIDATE	befuddle	clarify	avert	defend
27 INAPT	slim	unskilled	feverish	unknown
28 EXCISE	destroy	anoint	cut out	bring forth

Answers: 1. A   2. D   3. B   4. B   5. C   6. A   7. C   8. A   9. C   10. C   11. B   12. B   13. C   14. C   15. A   16. C   17. C   18. D   19. B   20. C   21. A   22. D   23. C   24. D   25. B   26. B   27. B   28. C

Explanations

2. Luc, lus, lum = light. If you put light on something, you can see it better. That's why it means clear.

3. Con = together; viv = live. When we live together, we tend to be sociable.

4. sub = under; vert = turn. When you turn something under, you undermine it.

6. When something is seen **(spect)** together **(con)** at the same time, we can easily summarize it.

7. If **nom equals name** and **ig sounds harsh**, we would have a harsh name or would suffer disgrace.

8. dia means across, through in Greek and so does **trans** (Latin). They both mean to see through easily.

9. pro = forth and gen = birth, so when we give forth birth, we get children.

10. con = together and voc = call, so when we call people together, we have a meeting.

12. ec = out and centric = center. When one is outside the center, we look upon him as odd because he is not one of us. So, this word means odd or peculiar.

13. ose = full of. So, if someone is full of verbs, he would tend to be talkative.

14. a- means away and vers = turn. ex. Beauty turned away (disliked) the beast because he was ugly.

15. pathos means feeling and anti means against. So, if we have a feeling against someone we tend to dislike them.

16. We all remember **phon** from grammar school **(sound)** and **cacos does not sound very smooth,** so harsh sounding seems closest here.

17. pre = before and science means knowledge, so if we have knowledge beforehand we have foresight.

19. debil means weak in Spanish, so this must mean to weaken. Not all of you got this because only half of you take Spanish. Try to use the language you study in school to help you figure out words you hear and read. It can really help. Romance languages are the best for the English language.

20. in = not, able, and fatig are all there. You just have to play with them a bit and you end up with not able to be fatigued or "tireless."

21. tort or tors = twist, ous = full of. Put them together and you get full of twists or winding.

24. In = not and cogn = know. Those taking a romance language recognize this from "cognosco" in Spanish, cognoscente in Italian, etc. So, **not and know = unknown.**

These previous problems were labeled "easy' because the jump between putting a prefix and root together and coming up with a fairly accurate word was not too big.

In the next part, you will have to play around with the two parts just a bit more. Let's give it a try.

Medium	A	B	C	D
1 IMPERVIOUS	leaking	silly	common	impenetrable
2 CONCUR	fabricate	ignore	agree	divert
3 ABJURE	swear	renounce	rely on	condone
4 MALEFACTOR	prisoner	evildoer	buddy	philanthropist
5 INTRACTABLE	stubborn	rigid	gullible	obedient
6 RETORT	twist	reply	dislike	resist
7 DELETERIOUS	stupid	forceful	fearsome	harmful
8 ABERRANT	wasteful	annoying	devious	willful
9 LUMINARY	wealthy	fortunate	handsome	enlightened
10 DEPOSE	exalt	elate	dethrone	misplace
11 CREDO	effect	belief	balance	stain
12 INCORRIGIBLE	poor	restrained	inconsistent	uncorrectable
13 DETRIMENTAL	spoiled	soulful	harmful	desirous
14 NEOPHYTE	beginner	laggard	tiny organism	infectious
15 CAPITULATE	surrender	correct	moderate	separate
16 ELUCIDATE	clarify	distill	inform	moderate
17 TENTATIVE	firm	structured	unconfirmed	wiry
18 FLORID	ornate	flowing	basic	aromatic
19 FELICITOUS	fortunate	favoring	fluid	well-known
20 EFFUSIVE	careless	gushy	harmful	pale
21 CORPOREAL	skinny	bodily	organized	deathlike
22 MAGNANIMOUS	friendly	indulgent	allowable	generous
23 SOMATIC	bodily	hairy	thin	constant
24 DISPARAGE	reward	detest	neglect	belittle
25 COSMOPOLITAN	worldly	unrealized	enchanted	confounded
26 EXCULPATE	banish	pretend	acquit	disallow
27 IMPEDE	hasten	stop	corrupt	steal

Answers: 1. D   2. C   3. B   4. B   5. A   6. B   7. D   8. C   9. D   10. C   11. B   12. D   13. C   14. A   15. A   16. A   17. C   18. A   19. A   20. B   21. B   22. D   23. A   24. D   25. A   26. C   27. B

Explanations

1. This is interesting in that there is no root. **Im = not, per = through and ious = very much.** So, very much can't go through is how we would play with this to get "impenetrable."

2. con = with and cur = run. Thus, if I run with you, I probably agree with you.

4. We all know **mal = bad** from our language classes. **Fact = make or do,** so this is just someone who makes or does evil or bad things or an evildoer.

5. in = not; tract = pull as in tractor. So, someone who cannot be pulled is stubborn.

6. re = back; tors, tort = twist. When we twist a word or comment back at someone, we reply.

7. de = down. Deleterious has a 98% negative prefix starting it. Yes, this only allows you to knock off forceful so you will have to pick a really negative meaning word. This leaves you with fearsome and harmful. Not perfect, but a 50/50 shot at it.

8. ab = away. Since deviant behavior is away from the norm, this is our answer.

10 de = down; pos, pon = put or place. When we put someone down, we often dethrone them.

11. cred = belief so this is a gift.

12. in = not; ible = able. So, not able to be corr. Certainly doable.

13. again **de = down,** very negative comes to the rescue.

14. neo = new, so beginner is another gift.

15. caput = head as in capitol, head of the government and decapitate, too many of them in the news of late. So, if we give up the head, we surrender. This took a bit of work, but this is what you have to start doing. Play with these prefixes and roots and they will yield dividends.

18. flor = flower in Spanish, a language many of you have taken. If something is flowery, it tends to be ornate.

19. Again Spanish to the rescue as **felix = happy,** so fortunate is the best choice here.

20. fus = pour; ef = out. If someone's emotions are pouring out, they tend to be gushy.

22. magna = large as in magnify; anim = soul, life; ous = full of. Put it all together and we have someone who has a very big soul or life and would probably be fairly generous.

26. ex = out, from; culpa as in culprit, the person we blame. If we take the blame out of something or from someone, we free them of blame or acquit them.

27. im = in or into since it is a verb here; ped = foot. If we put our foot in someone's way, we stop them. This is a tough jump indeed, but we are getting you ready for the next group.

Difficult	A	B	C	D
1 QUIESCENT	explosive	discerning	inactive	simple
2 COGNIZANT	oblivious	clumsy	informed	specific
3 VACUOUS	empty	friendly	smooth	clean
4 EXECRATE	befriend	claim	spill	hate
5 OBLOQUY	disgrace	defense	denial	misfortune
6 DIFFIDENT	shy	at ease	faithful	careful
7 TENUOUS	firm	weak	angry	sliding
8 DISCURSIVE	upset	suspicious	rambling	picky
9 PROSCRIBE	forbid	invest	sign up for	sketch
10 ANOMALOUS	lost	irregular	adored	famous
11 VERACITY	insight	truth	control	excellence
12 EQUANIMITY	misnomer	calm	certainly	smoothness
13 ABSTRUSE	unclear	absent	wide	understandable
14 FRACTIOUS	divided	favored	unruly	stable
15 VERDANT	fresh	relevant	sweeping	conventional
16 CURSORY	thorough	nasty	insulting	hasty
17 EGREGIOUS	wicked	inaudible	unnatural	partisan
18 ALTRUISTIC	selfless	eager	friendly	self-absorbed
19 INCESSANT	constant	spoiled	careless	unknowing
20 DERIDE	praise	supply	mock	investigate

Answers: 1. C 2. C 3. A 4. D 5. A 6. A 7. B 8. C 9. A 10. B 11. B 12. B 13. A 14. C 15. A 16. D 17. A 18. A 19. A 20. C

Explanations

1. esce = become or grow. We see this in words like adolescent (becoming an adult) and pubescent (being in a time of puberty). If we attach the beginning of the word (qui) to this, it is not too much of a jump to come up with becoming quiet or inactive.

2. cogn- from your Romance languages means to know so informed is a easy jump.

3. vac, vap from our list is empty as in a vacuum, which we all know from science is empty. This is a gift if you use the root. Someone with a vapid personality may be quite nice, but their personality is kind of blah or empty.

4. ex = out and is a strongly negative word, since only spill and hate are negative, we should choose the more negative of the two.

5. Ob = against and has an extremely negative prefix. In 46 years of working with the SAT, we have only come across 5 words that are positive that begin with the letter "o". They are optimistic, opulent, omniscient, omnipotent and opportune. **loqui = speak.** So, if someone speaks against you, it might result in a disgrace.

6. dif = away or not and fid = faith. If I do not have faith in myself, I would probably be shy.

8. dis = apart, away; curs = run. If something is running away, it is probably rambling.

9. pro = in front of; scribe = write. If I write in front of something "danger, do not eat or drink, beware," I am forbidding. This is a difficult jump indeed, but one we hope you can make soon.

10. a = not, lacking in Greek; nom = law or rule. If something does not go along with the rule or law, it tends to be irregular.

11. Again, if we are willing to play with our cognates, words we know from different languages, this is doable. **verdad means truth in Spanish,** so for many of you this is a gift.

12. equ = even as in equilateral or equator. anim is soul. If we have an even soul, we would tend to be calm.

13. ab = away, from and is usually negative. Since only one word is negative, we can get this one.

14. fract = break as in a fraction, which is something broken off from something. **ious = very much.** So, if someone is always breaking things, he tends to be unruly.

15. verde = green in many languages and if something is green it is usually fresh.

16. cur, curs = run. If we do something while running, it is usually done in a hasty manner.

17. This is truly a tough get. **e = out; greg = group** as in your congregation. So, if you are outside the group, we would think you bad, evil or even wicked.

18. altr- = other. If you do things for others, you tend to be selfless or altruistic. A philanthropist is similar as it is someone who does things because he **phil - loves anthropos - mankind.**

20. de = down; rid, ris = laugh. If you laugh down at someone, you tend to mock them.

Words Commonly Confused

We have compiled this list because these words either look alike, sound alike or are spelled the same and therefore are easily confused. Work out ways to help you distinguish them because they can cost you points if you do not.

Adverse- hostile and antagonistic. Think of someone who is your adversary.
Averse- reluctant. ex. He was averse to doing that.

Affect- to influence
Effect- to bring about, to accomplish, to make happen

Anecdote- a brief story. ex. Did you hear the anecdote about the …?
Antidote- remedy for poison or some other serious problem

Ascetic- self-denying. It comes from asceticos, which is the Greek word for monk.
Aesthetic- pertaining to beauty. ex. I loved the aesthetics of the new building.

Capital- the head city in a government
Capitol- The building that houses the government offices

Censor- to exercise the right of deleting or forbidding
Censure- to scold

Childish- refers to the worst behaviors of a child
Childlike- refers to the best behaviors or the innocence of a child

Climatic- refers to weather conditions
Climactic- refers to high or low point of a drama

Complacent- smugly self-satisfied
Complaisant- willing to please

Complimentary- expressing or containing a compliment
Complementary- filling out or completing something

Consummate- adject: showing the highest ability. ex. She is a consummate violinist.
Consummate- verb: to complete. ex. Let's consummate that deal.

- Notice that although these last two words are different parts of speech and are pronounced differently, they are spelled the same. The same is true of the next duo except that they are also pronounced the same.

Countenance- noun: appearance. ex. She had a gloomy countenance.
Countenance- verb: to condone or approve. ex. I cannot countenance that.

Contemptible- deserving contempt or hatred
Contemptuous- bestowing contempt on someone

Credible- believable
Creditable- worthy of praise

Deprecate- disapprove regretfully
Depreciate- undervalue

Discreet- judicious, prudent, wise, careful
Discrete- separate

Disinterested- impartial, fair, unbiased
Uninterested- not caring about

Elicit- extract or draw or bring out
Illicit- not lawful

Eminent- of high reputation. Socrates was an eminent philosopher.
Imminent- about to happen; likely to occur. Those dark clouds indicate an imminent storm.

Equable- even-tempered
Equitable- just, reasonable

Exult- to rejoice
Exalt- to praise

Flaunt- to make a gaudy or imprudent display. ex. An old commercial said " If you've got it, flaunt it."
Flout- to show scorn or contempt for. ex. He was always flouting the rules.

Formally- refers to manners
Formerly- refers to time

Gourmet- lover of fine food and wine, etc.
Gourmand- glutton

Hoard- a secret store of goods
Horde- a large group of animals or people

Imply- To suggest indirectly. The speaker implies; the listener infers.
Infer- to deduce , draw a conclusion

Indigent- poor
Indigenous- native, typical of. ex. Crime is indigenous to that part of the city.

Ingenious- clever
Ingenuous- innocent, frank, naive, credulous, gullible

Incredible- hard to believe
Incredulous- doubting

Laudable- deserving praise
Laudatory- expressing praise

Loath- reluctant, unwilling. ex. I am loath to do that.
Loathe- hate. ex. I truly loathe that person.

Mendicant- beggar
Mendacious- deceitful

Naval- pertaining to the navy and its possessions
Navel- belly- buttons and like shaped objects such as oranges

Penury- poverty
Penurious- cheap, greedy

Perspicacious- shrewd, sharp
Perspicuous- clear

Prescribe- set down as a rule or guide
Proscribe- to forbid or denounce

Prodigal- wasteful as the prodigal son in the New Testament
Prodigious- very large. ex. Barry Bonds is the most prodigious home run hitter.

Regal- royal
Regale- entertain lavishly or tell a great story

Restive- impatient or rebellious under repressive control or an excessively strenuous situation
Restless- describes someone who cannot rest, who must always have something to do

Sanguine- cheerfully confident
Sanguinary- bloodthirsty

Tortuous- winding, twisting
Torturous- causing severe pain

Urban- pertaining to the city
Urbane- polished; suave, sophisticated

Venal- corruptible; someone who is capable of being bought
Venial- excusable. ex. A venial sin is a minor one compared to a mortal sin.

ACTIONS TO COMPLETE AFTER YOU HAVE READ THIS BOOK

1. Take another practice SAT
You should see a substantial improvement in your score.

2. Continue to practice SAT verbal problems for 10 to 20 minutes each day
Keep practicing problems of the appropriate levels until two days before the SAT.

3. Review this book
If this book helped you, please post your positive feedback on the site you purchased it from; e.g. Amazon, Barnes and Noble, etc.

4. Claim your FREE bonuses
If you have not done so already, visit the following webpage and enter your email address to receive additional material for free. In particular you will receive 120 SAT math problems with full explanations.

www.thesatmathprep.com/RevSATVb2016.html

About the Authors

Larry Ronaldson has been teaching SAT for thirty-nine years in high schools, small groups and one-on-one. Fifty- seven of his students have received perfect scores on the reading part and seventy-four on the grammar/writing part in the past fifteen years. He has taught in private and public schools for forty-six years. Mr. Ronaldson has a Master's degree in English Literature from City University of New York and now lives in Seattle.

Tom Speedling a New York native, received his Bachelor of Arts from St. Bonaventure University. After returning from Vietnam, he received a Master's of Science Education from Richmond College. Mr. Speedling taught in the New York city and state school systems for more than forty years. He has also tutored students for the SAT for twenty years and written numerous newspaper articles. This is his first book.

www.SATPrepGet800.com

BOOKS FROM THE GET 800 COLLECTION

Made in the USA
San Bernardino, CA
12 January 2017